A Joyous Service

THE CLEWER SISTERS AND THEIR WORK

Valerie Bonham

NEW EDITION, REVISED AND ENLARGED
2012

BOOKS

Published by CSJB Books
Harriet Monsell House, Ripon College, Cuddesdon, Oxford OX44 9EX

Text © Valerie Bonham 1989, 2012
Line drawings © CSJB
First published 1989
Second edition, revised and enlarged, 2012

Typeset by Books to Treasure
Cover design by Ken Websdale
Printed and bound by CPI Group (UK) Ltd, Croydon, CR0 4YY

ISBN 0 9508710 1 X first edition
ISBN 978-0-9574197-0-4 second edition

Front cover photograph: Convent of St John the Baptist (photograph courtesy of Knight Frank)
Rear cover photographs: Begbroke, Clewer, Cuddesdon, Mendham

Also by Valerie Bonham:
In the Midst of the People (1983)
A Place in Life: The Clewer House of Mercy, 1849–83 (1992)
Sisters of the Raj: The Clewer Sisters in India (1997)
Various articles in the *Oxford Dictionary of National Biography* (Oxford 2004 and later)

By Valerie Bonham & Julie Dexter
A Good Foundation: Holy Trinity Coleford (2009)

Edited by Valerie Bonham:
A Tribute to Maurice Bond (1984)
Windlesora (The Journal of the Windsor Local History Group) Numbers 4–7 (1985–1988)

Harriet Monsell at the time of her marriage, 1839

This book is dedicated
to the Greater Glory of God
and in thanksgiving
for the life and witness
of
The Community of St John Baptist,
its Forerunners,
Founders,
Sisters, Magdalens, Oblates, Associates,
Friends and Benefactors.
"I love that in a life of sacrifice they should give God a joyous service."
(Harriet Monsell, October 1875)

Also in thanksgiving for the life of Canon A M (Donald) Allchin, 1930–2010

CONTENTS

LIST OF ILLUSTRATIONS

ACKNOWLEDGEMENTS
(FIRST EDITION)

First and foremost I am indebted to the Community of St John Baptist for allowing me to write this book. It has been a great joy and privilege to do so, and I have been deeply touched by their love and trust. I know of no other Religious Community which has entrusted its records to a secular person for this purpose, and I have endeavoured to produce something worthy of the Community of St John Baptist and its great work.

Mother Edna Frances has spent a great deal of time with me; a number of Sisters have spoken to me at length about their years in community: Sr Annys, formerly Mother Superior, Sr Eudora, Sr Gladys, Sr Moira, and Sr Charlotte Rand SSJF who has since died. Sr Sheila has allowed me the benefit of her research into Mother Harriet's family, the O'Briens of Dromoland. Sr Olga has provided the designs for the title page (see page xvii) and chapter endings. Sr Pauline CRJBS has helped me with the early history of her own Community. But a special word of thanks must go to Sr Jane Olive, who for four and a half years has cheerfully heaved boxes of books, hunted for archives in countless tin trunks, staggered under piles of photograph albums, and has still found time to keep me supplied with coffee—and all in the knowledge that this book is only the first of three!

Canon Allchin has long been a friend of the CSJB and I am deeply grateful to him not only for providing the foreword to this book, but also for his help and encouragement, and for so generously giving his time.

I acknowledge with gratitude the use of an extract from Queen Victoria's diary in the Royal Library, Windsor Castle, by the gracious permission of Her Majesty the Queen.

Also I am indebted to SPCK for permission to quote from *The Call of the Cloister* by Peter F Anson. I have received help from the staff of the following: St Deiniol's Library, Hawarden; the Bodleian Library; Pusey House; Lambeth Palace Library; the House of St Barnabas-in-Soho (formerly the House of Charity); Windsor Public Library; and the Clwyd Record Office. Also from Dr Mary Donovan, the Revd Dr Paul Rampton, the Revd Denis Shaw and the Revd J N Scott. My colleagues in the Windsor Local History Publications

Group have given their unstinting support and I am especially grateful to Pamela Marson for her photographic expertise and proof-reading skills. The list of people who have enthused over the prospect of this book and have offered to make it known is too long to quote in full but is nonetheless appreciated.

I am very grateful to Roger Cullingham and his team at Thameslink for making my disks into a recognisable book.

Finally, my husband Fred and daughter Louise have helped and encouraged me more than they could possibly know.

ACKNOWLEDGEMENTS
(SECOND EDITION)

In addition to all who made the first edition possible I would like to thank the following people who have helped me in the production of the second.

The Burton Latimer Heritage Society, Margaret Craddock and especially Wynne Malpass, for sharing her memories of the Good Shepherd Home during its wartime evacuation to Burton Latimer Hall.

Martin Graebe and Matthew Edwards for sharing their information and enthusiasm about Sr Emma's folksongs and for allowing me to use it in this book. Also, the staff of the Vaughan Williams Memorial Library at the English Folk Song and Dance Society.

Veronica Colin and the St Stephen's College Old St Stephenites' Society for permission to reproduce the illustration of the main entrance to the College at Clewer from the late Jenny Balston's history of the College; and for information on what has happened to the buildings since the closure of the College in 1991.

Sophie Farrant for help regarding the new buildings at Ripon College, Cuddesdon.

Ruth Smith for information on her forebear, Jane Pedder, and Isobel Syed for putting Ruth in touch with me.

Jacqui Frost for sharing her enthusiasm for the history of the Devon House of Mercy and for bringing to my attention *A Cornish Waif's Story* by Mabel Carvolth (writing as Emma Smith). Also for sharing with me her research into the life of Mabel Carvolth.

Margaret Wright, secretary of the Bovey Heritage Centre, for supplying the photographs of the Devon House of Mercy.

The Victoria & Albert Museum for information on the chalice given to the Clewer Community by Sr Elizabeth CSJB and now in the care of the museum.

The National Trust, custodians of Little Moreton Hall, for providing the Moreton Family Tree (see page 148) and for putting me in touch with their researcher Jill Owen, who generously shared her research into the family history of Sr Elizabeth CSJB (Elizabeth Moreton).

Fr Ainsley Swift, Vicar of Clewer St Stephen, for information about the memorial plaques from the Chapel of St John Baptist at Clewer and now in Clewer St Stephen; and Jane Burr, sacristan at Clewer St Stephen, for supplying the text of Sr Emily's two memorial plaques, and information about the first altar at the Clewer House of Mercy, now at St Stephen's.

John Richardson for permission to reproduce the drawing of Park House, Highgate, the London Diocesan House of Mercy. This drawing appears in his book *Highgate Past*, Historical Publications, New Barnet, Herts 1989.

Sue Hourigan and Lisa Spurrier of the Berkshire Record Office for tracing the 1841 tithe map of Clewer from my very vague recollection of seeing it in an exhibition in Windsor sometime in the 1990s. And for their permission to reproduce that portion of the map depicting Nightingale Lodge (usually known as Nightingale Place), the house formerly on the site of the House of Mercy. Also, my thanks to Caroline McCutcheon and Friends of the Royal Borough Collection who also joined in the search for the elusive map.

I am grateful to Roger Cullingham for scanning the text of the first edition, making the task of revision much easier; and to Pamela Marson for supplying the photograph of Mariquita Tennant's blue plaque.

Emma Cleugh at Knight Frank provided the photographs of Begbroke Priory, which were far better than the ones I took on a cloudy day, and also the images of Clewer used on the cover.

Mrs Annette Jarolin supplied valuable information about St Michael's Home, Leamington.

Rosetta Laybourne of the property developer Westcombe Management for updating my information regarding the chapels at the former convent at Clewer.

Four people deserve particular thanks for preparing this second edition—Ruth Jolly and Alison Neale, who proofread the book, and Ruth again for adding to the index; Adrianne Fitzpatrick, who designed and typeset the book, and Ken Websdale, who designed the cover. I am truly grateful to them for their patient help and expertise.

FOREWORD
(TO THE FIRST EDITION)

It will soon be one hundred and fifty years since the first post-Reformation religious communities were founded in the Church of England. Their story, which in the nineteenth century is in large part the story of sisterhoods, is still far too little known. Valerie Bonham has made a notable contribution to their study in this account of the life of the Community of St John Baptist, Clewer, from its beginnings in 1851–2 until today. As she shows in these carefully researched pages, Clewer came to be the largest of the Victorian communities and in many ways the most influential. It attracted women of great ability, and sometimes of considerable wealth and social status as well. We meet them in these pages, travelling throughout the land, going as far as India and the United States, always seeking to relieve human misery and distress, and to confront the evils of society in their many forms.

From the beginning the Community was blessed with friendly bishops. The first of them was Samuel Wilberforce, and despite the reservations that he felt, in the end he offered the sisters his wholehearted support. It also had friends and advisers of the calibre of Mr Gladstone and his wife Catherine. Its proximity to Windsor Castle even gave it links with the royal family. Queen Victoria's visit to Clewer in 1864 is a rightly renowned event. The Queen was in general a consistent opponent of all that the Oxford Movement stood for. But at Clewer she was charmed, not only by the place, which to her surprise was not at all gloomy, but also by the person who was its life and soul, Mother Harriet, Mrs Monsell.

Perhaps the heart of this book is to be found in Chapter 11, which gives its title to the whole, *A Joyous Service*. There we have a picture of one of the most able and attractive women in the history of the Victorian Church, certainly one of the greatest gifts that the Church of Ireland has ever made to the Church of England. Working together with T T Carter, the founder and first Warden of the community, Mother Harriet came to embody in herself the reality of a life wholly devoted to God in loving prayer and joyful service. The ancient ideal of the religious life took new form in her and around her. She was one of the most hopeful of people. To recall her memory, as this book does, is to renew the hope of all of us, the sisters of her community, their many associates and friends, all who want to serve Christ now in our late twentieth century. Our times may be difficult, but so were hers. She shows us the way in which a life of sacrifice may be a life of joy, a life whose light radiates out into the darkness of the world around.

A M Allchin

PREFACE TO THE FIRST EDITION
by the
REVEREND MOTHER SUPERIOR, CSJB

Many people, looking at the formidable cluster of Victorian buildings in Hatch Lane, Windsor, must wonder how they got there, what goes on there and what they mean—for they do have a history, and the Sisters who live there do have a heritage.

Valerie Bonham has spent several years tirelessly researching our history and teasing out a network of threads, and eventually bringing them together and elucidating how they did get there, and what has gone on and still goes on, and what it all means.

The Community owe a debt of gratitude to Valerie for this work of love and they acknowledge this with their love.

Edna Frances CSJB

AUTHOR'S PREFACE TO THE FIRST EDITION

This book is the first of three devoted to the history of the Community of St John Baptist, Clewer, and is the result of several years' research. In 1983 I published *In the Midst of the People*, a history of St Agnes' Church in the parish of Clewer. My research had brought me to the Clewer Sisters and I soon found the presence of the Community running like a thread through the book. I decided to follow it with a similar history of the church of Clewer St Stephen. Again I found myself doing research at the convent and quickly realised that the Community had in fact started the mission work which grew into St Stephen's Church and parish. It seemed logical to begin at the beginning with the Community itself and to include the many and varied branch works within a much larger history.

Early in 1988 I began the long process of piecing the research together into readable form and I soon encountered a problem. There is a vast amount of hitherto undocumented material, particularly regarding the early years. But it promised to write up into a very long and detailed book with more about the first fifty years than the remainder. After a great deal of thought I was advised by Canon Allchin to write the book in its present form, namely a general history of the Community from the earliest days until the 1980s. This will be followed by a more detailed account of the foundation of the rescue work at the Clewer House of Mercy by Mariquita Tennant, and of the subsequent foundation and development of the CSJB under Harriet Monsell, ending with her death in 1883. A third volume devoted to the work of the Clewer Sisters in India will complete the trilogy.

Valerie Bonham
Lent 1989

AUTHOR'S PREFACE TO THE SECOND EDITION

I was delighted to learn that *A Joyous Service* has sold so well and that the Sisters have decided to reprint it. It has been an enormous privilege to write the Community history and I was really pleased when Sr Anne, on behalf of the Sisters, asked me if I would bring their history up to date.

The work of the CSJB was so vast in its heyday that it is not surprising to find the Sisters mentioned in unexpected places. For instance, whilst visiting the parish church at Down Ampney in the summer of 2011, I came across this notice on one of the altars:

"It is possible that the altar frontals were made by the Sisters of the Order [sic] of St John Baptist at Clewer, near Windsor, from designs by Charles Eamer Kempe (1837–1907), a stained glass designer, between 1895–1908." The collaboration between Kempe and the Clewer Sisters is well known.

There are many Sisters who are mentioned by name in this book, but we should not forget the many others who are not named. This was brought home to me during a holiday in 2010. While on a 'church crawl' in Worcestershire we stopped to look inside the parish church at Bayton, and there on the south wall was a brass memorial plaque to a Clewer Sister (Sr Mary Verena) whom I had never heard of. On returning home I checked all three books in the Clewer trilogy and her name is not mentioned, nor in any of my notes taken from the archives at Clewer. But the work of those un-named Sisters is just as important as those who are well known. Sr Mary Verena stands for all those other Sisters who also served God, as her memorial (see chapter 13) reminds us.

Since the publication of the first edition of *A Joyous Service* the trilogy has been completed and published, but new information is continuing to come to light. This new edition has given me an opportunity not only to bring the Community history up to date but also to include this new information. Therefore I have added three additional chapters, several appendices and more photographs, and I have thoroughly revised the text of the original edition. Thanks to the internet it has been possible to track down most of the buildings in the UK where the Sisters once worked. Information about Sr Emma and her folk song collection has been discovered recently and I am grateful to Matthew Edwards and Martin Graebe for so generously sharing their research with me. New information about an early Sister, who I had mistakenly thought was American, has unfolded a very surprising story. Here for the first time is the story of Sr Jane Pedder. And also for the first time, it has been possible to reproduce almost in full the text of the letter written by Helen Folsom (the American Foundress) to Sr Jane in New York about her visit to Clewer in 1866.

Since 1989, when the first edition of *A Joyous Service* was published, the Community on both sides of the Atlantic has moved on a great deal. And so have I. At that time I lived in the parish of Clewer and the convent was five minutes' walk away from my home. Now no longer at Clewer, the Sisters are doing God's work in a new place; and I am now Priest-in-Charge of two villages in Somerset. So our journeys continue in different surroundings, and at a greater geographical distance, but it is good to still be a fellow traveller with the Sisters.

I hope that you will enjoy reading this revised edition of *A Joyous Service* as much as I have enjoyed preparing it.

Valerie Bonham
Coleford, Somerset 2012

A WORD ABOUT WORDS

All historians have difficulty over words: meanings change even within the short space of a generation. This especially applies to words and phrases associated with religion, racial origins, and sexual equality. But the historian must always bear in mind the meaning and context of the material being used: one has to 'think' with one's mind attuned to the period under review. When the Victorians spoke of 'fallen women' they were not necessarily using it as a term of derision, but in today's climate of political correctness it might be easy to imagine they were. The Clewer Sisters' original work was the rescuing of such women, and after a great deal of thought I am retaining the term because it sums up their plight in the eyes of contemporary society. By no means were all 'fallen women' prostitutes so it would be wrong to call them such. But they had all, for various reasons, fallen out of what was then regarded as respectable society, and stood in need of help. Likewise when quoting from contemporary sources, it would be very wrong to alter words because they are no longer fashionable or because a more liberated generation finds them distasteful. The whole point of using contemporary quotations is to give the flavour of the times. But the use of such words and phrases in this book in no way implies a disparaging or judgmental attitude towards the subject.

INTRODUCTION TO THE SECOND EDITION

"Sr Sheila has recently transcribed Bishop Stuart Blanch's book *Living by Faith* into Braille. Sr Catherine Mary attended several meetings in connection with the Women's World Day of Prayer. Sr Pamela has been elected to the Steering Committee of the Communities' Consultative Council. Sr Eudora, Sr Letitia, Sr Monica and Sr Jane Olive took part in a 'Training the Trainers' weekend in the Convent Retreat Wing. Retreats and Quiet Days have been conducted by Sr Annys, Sr Gina, and other Sisters, both in the Retreat Wing and in various parishes. Sr Doreen and Sr Zoë took part in a mission with Fr Augustine Hoey, CR, and Sr Elizabeth Jane preached at Cookham Dean during their flower festival. Reverend Mother attended the Superiors' conference at Woking. We continue to meet the Bridgeman Court Fellowship Prayer Group, the Hospital Prayer Group, and Day Centre Prayer Group. All this in addition to the regular work of St Anne's House, St John's Convent Home, the Church Workroom, the Convent Retreat Wing and the Sisters' Infirmary."

This quotation does not come from an account of the Community work in the Victorian heyday, but is in fact from the *Associates' Newsletters* of 1987 and 1988. It shows just how broadly based the work of the Community was when the first edition of *A Joyous Service* was published in 1989. Though different from the Victorian work, the Community still shared with its forebears the same ability to recognise a need and to meet it with prayer and action.

The Community of St John Baptist has, from its earliest days, been engaged in all manner of works for those in need. As will be seen throughout this book the wellspring for all the activity has been the life of prayer and worship centred on the chapel. But if ever a Community has fulfilled the command to "Go out into all the World and spread the Gospel," the Community of St John Baptist has done so. It was one of the earliest Anglican Communities, and of them all it probably grew the fastest in terms of numbers of Sisters and multiplicity of works. Like its counterparts it has had to adapt to a changing world, which has included the loss of its original work to the Welfare State. And the changing attitude to the role of women in society has resulted in the opening up of the professions and a fall in religious vocations. Since 1994 women have been admitted to the priesthood in the Church of England and in some cases Sisters have found a second vocation, but in common with the rest of the Church it was a decision that was not taken lightly, but after much prayer and debate.

Sadly, some Communities have not weathered the storms affecting Church and State as the nineteenth century gave way to the twentieth and the twentieth to a new Millennium; those like the Clewer Community which have done so have had to concentrate their work in a main centre and adapt their external work to the needs of modern society. And as the new Millennium dawned, so the Community in England had to think the unthinkable and consider moving to smaller premises. This book attempts to chronicle the development of the Community of St John Baptist from its earliest days, through the flourishing Victorian era, into the twentieth century with all the changes it brought about, and on to the present day as diminishing numbers bring new challenges. Since the beginning of the 21st century the English Sisters of the CSJB have had to face their greatest challenge—how to leave a lasting legacy to the Church after the Community completes its work. As will be seen, that challenge has been met with courage and imagination.

A Joyous Service

✥ 1 ✥

SOMEBODY MUST BEGIN

The Community of St John Baptist has the unique distinction of being founded *after* the work for which it became well known. Like many another great philanthropic endeavour, the rescue work was not planned but began because the need was there and it seemed expedient to answer it. It was a case of the proverbial mighty oak growing from a small acorn, for few could have imagined how greatly the work would grow and prosper.

During the 1840s it had become a point of scandal that, while there were a number of secular Penitentiaries for rescuing so-called 'fallen women', the Established Church was doing nothing. The nearest thing to a specifically *Church* Penitentiary was the Magdalen Hospital in London. This had been founded in 1758 and was governed by a Council and run by a matron and paid servants. It had a tenuous Church affiliation, but in reality fell far short of the ideal of a caring, corrective home. In addition there were a number of other purely secular institutions both in London and in the great industrial cities.

In 1844 Archdeacon Manning highlighted the plight of so-called 'fallen women' in a sermon called *Saints and Penitents*. This inspired a shy, rather retiring clergyman, the Revd John Armstrong, Vicar of Tidenham near Chepstow, and later to become Bishop of Grahamstown, to study the existing Penitentiaries. He found them lacking and felt so strongly that he wrote a number of articles in learned journals during 1848. This culminated in February 1849 in an open letter which was widely circulated, called *An Appeal for the Formation of a Church Penitentiary*.

Armstrong advocated that rescue work should be done by "ladies of a higher class", grouped together as Sisters of Mercy. Those being rescued were to be strictly supervised and trained in laundry work and plain needlework, and at the end of their training would become domestic servants. He realised that some might not wish to return to the pressures and temptations of the outside world and so he envisaged a ward of permanent inmates who would work in and around the house. Here in this appeal is the seed from which the Community of St John Baptist with its choir Sisters, lay Sisters, penitents and permanent Magdalens eventually grew.

Armstrong directed his appeal in two ways. He wanted refined ladies to offer themselves for the actual rescue work, and he needed benefactors to finance and build a House of Mercy. In the latter category he envisaged wealthy gentlemen whose youth had been mis-spent making amends by responding with financial help. And many did so. As a direct result of Armstrong's appeal, the Church Penitentiary Association was founded in 1852 with the express object of assisting in the establishment and maintenance of Church-run Penitentiaries.

The language of Armstrong's appeal seems politically incorrect today with its emphasis on 'ladies' and references to 'higher and lower classes', but Armstrong was addressing himself to a class-conscious audience, and so great was the response that henceforth the Church could no longer turn a blind eye. The gist of his message was that the Church was not doing its duty; that it was a scandal that other categories of the poor and needy were cared for but not 'fallen women'; and that something *must* be done. He concluded by saying, "Somebody must begin and it little matters who that somebody is, though he be only a remote country parson." Unbeknown to him somebody had already begun, though at that time *she* still had no idea of the magnitude of what she was doing.

Twice widowed but still in her thirties, Mariquita Tennant was living temporarily at 'The Limes', a medieval house owned by her sister next to Clewer church near Windsor. Her late second husband, the Revd Robert Tennant, had desired to found a home in Florence (where he was British chaplain) for the 'kept women' taken abroad and subsequently abandoned. He had died in 1842 before embarking on this work, but his widow cherished the hope that one day she might undertake rescue work. During her time at Clewer she became well known as a friend of the poor and needy, and the parish certainly had a vast number in that category.

During the late 1840s the parish of Clewer extended over a vast area, at the eastern extremity of which (ie nearest Windsor) there were some of the most notorious slums outside London. At the time of the 1851 Census the full horror of living conditions was revealed. In Clewer Lane 559 people were crammed into sixty-nine houses; Bier Lane had 259 people in thirty-three houses; and Clewer Fields had 291 people in sixty-nine houses. Most of these dwellings contained several families, and many were not private houses at all but common lodging houses and beer houses, many of which were brothels. These attracted a rough and often itinerant clientele which resulted in frequent drunken brawls and disturbances of the peace. All this was taking place within a few hundred yards of the walls of Windsor Castle.

In addition to these overcrowded, pestilential streets and alleys, which were ill-ventilated and ill-drained, and which suffered badly in the 1849 cholera outbreak, there were within the town two army barracks which housed nearly 1,000 men. And there was also a further, albeit temporary, influx of men in the form of railway 'navvies'. Two railway companies were vying with each other in the race to bring the railway to the royal town.

When all these factors are taken together, and the state of abject poverty in which most of these people lived is also borne in mind, it is understandable that many girls and women stood in grave moral danger. But the full extent was not realised until May 1849 when, in a vain attempt to evangelise the railway navvies by means of a marquee in which services were held, these slum alleys were systematically visited by the clergy. Mariquita Tennant had expressed her willingness to give temporary shelter to any girl who wished to be rescued, until a place could be obtained at the Magdalen Hospital. In doing so she unwittingly founded the Clewer House of Mercy.

In fact Mariquita Tennant had already begun her great work of rescue by giving shelter to a young woman at the end of 1848. A parishioner had alerted her attention to a family of travellers who had moved into Clewer Fields. After sending food she learned that the young woman, Marianne George (aged 24) had recently given birth to a baby. She visited the family and was horrified to learn that Marianne's stepfather was the father, not only of this child, but of several others. There seemed to be only one solution—to remove her as soon as possible to her own home at 'The Limes'. Marianne arrived at Mrs Tennant's home on December 29th 1848 and was employed as a servant. Her name appears as the first entry in the *Roll Book* of the Clewer House of Mercy, although at this stage Mrs Tennant had no intention of starting such a work. It happened by force of circumstance rather than by the execution of a plan.

In May 1849 the Rector of Clewer, the Revd Thomas Thellusson Carter, and his curate the Revd C F Wellington Johnson, began visiting the Clewer Fields and Bier Lane district to spread the news about the railway marquee already mentioned. This brought them into immediate contact with the girls and women who were enmeshed in the ever-downward spiral of poverty which in many cases led to prostitution and drink. It became clear that many of these people genuinely wanted to lead better lives but because of their poverty were unable to help themselves. They needed a place of refuge, together with discipline and training, in order to equip them for a place in respectable society where they could earn a living as servants or laundry women without having to resort to such desperate means.

So it was that on June 14th 1849 Mariquita Tennant gave a home to two women from Clewer Fields: Ruth Player was 24 and Mary Ford, 22. Mary came from Wiltshire and left home after a disagreement with her family following her father's re-marriage. She had thoughts of going to London and headed in that direction on foot: she was not a prostitute, nor had she broken the law in any way, but was merely a naive country girl with no knowledge of the world. Her journey was horrific: frightened by noises in the dark she found herself lost in a bog, her dress froze to her legs, and she finally collapsed from exhaustion by the roadside. A navvy discovered her and took her to Windsor where he found her a lodging, but warned her of the dangers which might befall a young woman alone in such a place. The warning came to naught because the lodging house turned out to be a squalid brothel: the prospect of being turned out onto the street once more was too much, so that Mary unwillingly fell into prostitution.

There were several women in the house and Mary recognised one of them as Ruth Player, from her own part of the world. The two became friends and resolved to seek help, though Ruth had been there much longer and was also in the grip of drink. After several unsuccessful attempts they finally plucked up enough courage to approach the clergy and ask for help. Ruth was the first of the two to be received by Mrs Tennant, Mary following later in the day. The Rector (Mr Carter) accompanied Ruth back to Clewer Fields to fetch Mary. The landlady was so enraged at the loss of both women that she tried to throw Mary out of the window but was restrained from doing so by Harriet Street, who was herself rescued the next day.

Within a few weeks there were a dozen women at 'The Limes' under the care of Mariquita Tennant, and it seems that she was soon persuaded to let them stay rather than go to the Magdalen Hospital. But life was difficult and the strain upon her soon began to show. Marianne George, the very first to be taken in, did not take kindly to this influx. There were wild, unruly scenes between the women whose hitherto unchecked tempers and uncivilised natures were brought under discipline. Such scenes are difficult to understand coming from grown women and were more like the behaviour of small children. Indeed Mrs Tennant frequently had to resort to the methods of punishment at that time meted out to naughty infants—smacks and bed with no supper.

All this time Mrs Tennant was virtually single-handed, except for her Italian servant Maria. But in February 1850 her first and only reliable help came in the person of Charlotte Weale, aged 20, who came for six months. As well as faithfully helping Mrs Tennant, Charlotte Weale kept detailed records of the work. From these records it is clear that Mrs Tennant desired to form a Religious Sisterhood to run the rescue work, and it is equally clear that the lack of helpers prevented her from doing so. But she did her best, and even got as far as writing a Rule which received the approval of Samuel Wilberforce, Bishop of Oxford.

The daily regime at the Clewer House of Mercy, as it was called, was long and strict. Of necessity the women could not be left alone or there would have been a general breakdown in discipline. But Charlotte Weale felt that they did not get enough fresh air and exercise and that there was perhaps a little too much emphasis on hearing sermons and learning lengthy passages from the Bible. Certainly the daily round was much more rigorous under Mrs Tennant than it was under the later Community of St John Baptist. And there was a tendency to constantly remind the women of the awfulness of sin and its dire consequences for the soul, rather than to give thanks for true repentance and to teach about God as a loving and forgiving Father.

By the time of Charlotte Weale's arrival the House of Mercy had left 'The Limes', which was for sale when Mrs Tennant began the work. Two cottages at Clewer Green were taken as temporary accommodation, though these were far from adequate, being ill-drained and generally unhealthy. For some months Mariquita Tennant had been under severe mental and physical strain brought about by the pressure of the work. Numbers were increasing all the time, but helpers were not forthcoming. Those who did come did not stay for long. Letters to and from people who were interested in the work (including Gladstone, with whom she had a lengthy correspondence) reveal something of the pressures and difficulties under which she laboured.

There is evidence to suggest that Mariquita Tennant was a difficult woman to work with and this may well account for the dearth of helpers. The work had been under the spiritual guidance of the Rector, Mr Carter. He knew of Armstrong's writings and doubtless had visions of implementing those ideas in the House of Mercy. But Mrs Tennant wished to run the work her way. All through the summer of 1850 her health was failing; she was refusing new entrants and was threatening to resign the work, but it seemed as though she was reluctant to do so. The answer may well lie in the reply to a letter which Gladstone had written asking who would do the work if she left it. "… It will now be in the hands of those with whom I cannot on all points agree," she wrote on August 1st 1850. There can be little doubt that this is a thinly veiled reference to Carter, who was exerting an increasing influence. In fact Gladstone's enquiry resulted in her staying for another eight months.

February 1851 saw the final move of the House of Mercy to a house in Hatch Lane, Clewer, called Nightingale Place, with an estate of fifteen acres. It was bought for £2,400 and vested in trustees. A few months previously a Council of clergy and laymen had been formed to supervise the House of Mercy, a sign of Carter's increasing control. Mrs Tennant finally withdrew from the work at Easter 1851 and retired to her private house in Windsor, where she continued to do good works until her early death in February 1860, aged 49. Her photograph shows a prematurely aged woman, worn out by caring for others.

Mariquita Tennant has in a sense slipped out of history. Historians of the revival of the Religious Life have ignored her because she did not found a Community, and she has been forgotten by social historians because, after all, there were so many others like her—good, moderately wealthy ladies who wanted to help those in need. And finally she has been submerged under the great work which followed her own, namely the Community of St John Baptist. She cannot be said to have founded the Community, but she did beyond doubt found the work which that Community subsequently undertook. In this sense she was a pioneer at a time when rescue work within the Church was in its infancy. This in itself took great courage, for there were many critics who claimed it was not fitting work for a 'lady'. She was perhaps misunderstood and not given the trust she deserved in her lifetime. It is true she had no real idea of the Religious Life and possibly no real vocation, but it must also be remembered that the first Anglican Communities since the Reformation were still in their infancy: everyone was at the learning stage. Above all, Mariquita Tennant was a woman of such infinite generosity that she gave without reserve for the good of others less fortunate. She could have had no idea of the spiritual, emotional and physical cost when she started: she did not withdraw until she had nothing more to give. In the context of the history of the Community of St John Baptist, she was the Forerunner. But it was for others with different talents to build upon the foundation which she had laid.

Notes

Space does not permit more on Mariquita Tennant but the full story, including detailed case histories and the correspondence with Mr Gladstone, may be read in the second volume of this trilogy, *A Place in Life: the Clewer House of Mercy, 1849–83*.

See also the following articles by Valerie Bonham in the *Oxford Dictionary of National Biography* relating to the history of the CSJB and its forerunners: Canon T T Carter; the Revd John Armstrong; Mariquita Tennant; Charlotte Weale; Harriet Monsell; Angelina Hoare.

There is no known illustration of Nightingale Place but the 1841 tithe map of Clewer shows a house which is listed on the schedule as Nightingale Lodge. This is clearly the house taken for use as the House of Mercy in succession to 'The Limes' and which the Community of St John Baptist would subsequently demolish in order to build their new premises. The name must have been changed to Nightingale Place sometime after 1841 and before 1850. See illustration on page 143.

THE FOUNDERS OF CLEWER

Mariquita Tennant's withdrawal from the Clewer House of Mercy left the Rector, the Revd Thomas Thellusson Carter, with a major pastoral problem, the solution to which had to be found without delay. There were about twenty women in need of care, and it was obvious that if the work should fail for want of someone to supervise it, these women would become social outcasts and their chance of subsequent rescue would be minimal. The short-term answer lay in the help offered by Miss Elizabeth Cozens, who was prepared to run the house along similar lines to that of Mrs Tennant. But Carter was anxious to implement the ideas advocated by the Revd John Armstrong and form a Religious Sisterhood.

Sisterhoods were one of the first-fruits of the Oxford or Tractarian Movement. Since the earliest days of the movement in 1833 a steady flow of tracts and pamphlets (which gave the movement one of its names) had brought a new awareness of the catholicity of the Church of England to its members, both clergy and laity. By 1845 a small group of dedicated women under the spiritual guidance of Dr Edward Bouverie Pusey had formed a Religious Sisterhood near Regent's Park, and within the next five years or so the seeds of the Wantage and Devonport Communities had also been sown.

Thomas Thellusson Carter had become Rector of Clewer in 1844 at the age of 36. He was born and educated at Eton, his father having been Vice-Provost, and in 1826 he went to Christ Church, Oxford, where he became well acquainted with Pusey, John Henry Newman, John Keble and a student who was a year behind him called William Ewart Gladstone. Carter was not a brilliant scholar, his progress being hampered by illness: he passed his exams in 1831 but failed to obtain a Fellowship at Oriel College, Oxford. He was ordained priest in 1833, the year of the start of the Tractarian Movement, and was profoundly influenced by the revival. Carter came to Clewer, which was in the gift of Eton College, after a curacy in Reading, an unhappy incumbency in Dorset and a further curacy in Burnham. He was to reside in the parish of Clewer for the rest of his long life.

The solution to Carter's problem regarding the House of Mercy was found as if by accident. The Revd Charles Amyand Harris had resigned his living at Wilton due to ill health, but by the spring of 1851 was able to undertake light duties. A mutual friend at Eton had put him in touch with Carter, who gladly accepted the extra clerical help. Harris soon found himself involved in the pastoral care of the House of Mercy. His wife, Katherine, was an invalid; her recently widowed sister had come to stay in order to help while away the lonely hours. She immediately became interested in the idea of the House of Mercy and offered her services. Her name was Harriet Monsell.

Harriet Monsell was born in 1811, the seventh of the nine children of Sir Edward O'Brien, Baronet, of Dromoland in County Clare. In 1839 she married Charles Monsell and soon afterwards they came to Oxford, where Charles studied prior to seeking ordination. They then returned to Ireland, where Charles became Prebendary of Aghadoe near Limerick for the next six years until he was taken ill with consumption and ordered to Naples in the hope of recuperating. It was a vain hope, his condition slowly worsening over the next four years until his death on January 29th 1851.

So Harriet had had a long preparation for the widowhood which came to her at the age of forty. During the last weeks of Charles' illness she had been greatly helped by the presence of English friends wintering in Italy, among them the Gladstones and the Hubbards. She kept a journal of those last weeks in which she graphically described his last illness and death. Charles had died in her arms, all her companions in the room having fallen asleep. "I was alone with God," she recalled in the diary. She was persuaded to rest for a while but, "About nine I got up calm … Soon after I went into the room and knelt beside him … And then I felt God's call to work for Him." Next day (January 30th), just before the funeral, Harriet paid a last visit to Charles. "He was laid in his coffin, and kneeling there, the dedication of myself to God was made, which was renewed here [at Clewer] on Ascension Day, the 29th of May, four months after, and has been so often renewed on the 30th of January." Carter was later to call this her "self consecration in sorrow".

Harriet Monsell returned to England in the company of Mr J G Hubbard (later Lord Addington) and upon her arrival on February 21st went to the Harrises'. Charles Harris came to assist Carter sometime in the spring, possibly around Easter when Mariquita Tennant gave up the House of Mercy and Elizabeth Cozens took over. Harriet offered to help and this was readily accepted by Carter and Miss Cozens, but at first it was purely on a daily basis. Gradually it seemed that this was the work to which God had called her and accordingly, on Ascension Day (May 29th) 1851, Harriet Monsell was admitted and clothed by Carter as a Sister of Mercy.

In fact Harriet Monsell had not joined a Religious Community because at this stage there was no Community, no convent, no nuns, no Rule: just Harriet clothed as a Sister of Mercy, alone with a growing conviction that this was the call she had awaited. In parallel there was Carter's growing conviction that *only* if the workers lived as Sisters of Mercy under a Rule would the rescue work grow and prosper, but it seems that Elizabeth Cozens showed no inclination to the Religious Life.

Although she now wore the habit of a Religious, Harriet continued to live with the Harrises until the spring of 1852. During that year, however, three other women came to the House of Mercy to seek admission as Sisters: Sr Aimée, admitted in February, Sr Catherine, admitted in March, and Sr Ellen, admitted in August. (See the note at the end of the next chapter.) Nevertheless it was not until October 1852 that Elizabeth Cozens and her secular helpers withdrew from the work, thus leaving the way clear for the formation of a Sisterhood.

So it was that on St Andrew's Day (November 30th) 1852, Harriet Monsell was professed in the presence of Samuel Wilberforce, Bishop of Oxford, and was installed as first Superior of the Community of St John Baptist. It is this date which the Community has always considered to be their starting date because Mother Harriet, as she now became, had two other companions, thus constituting a Community, whereas at her clothing she was entirely alone.

Harriet Monsell was to be the Mother Superior of her Community until 1875; Carter, who is always reckoned as Co-Founder with her, was to be Warden until his death in 1901. Thus in 1852 there began a long association between two personalities who complemented one another perfectly. This is not to suggest that there were never differences or even difficulties, but they never proved insurmountable.

Carter was at heart a parish priest. He published volume upon volume of sermons, theological treatises, devotional books and tracts. He was a champion of the Tractarian cause in the wider Church and because he was not an extremist (though he was often accused of being so), he did more to promote devotion to the Blessed Sacrament, frequent Holy Communion and the use of Sacramental Confession than many of his more outspoken contemporaries. Throughout his long life Carter won the respect and admiration of all shades of churchmanship and was admired for his depth of spirituality and his personal integrity even by those who disagreed with his theology. He was a deeply humble man and his correspondence with Bishop Wilberforce shows how much he himself learned about the spiritual life from his relationship with the Community of St John Baptist.

But if Carter was the sober, somewhat ponderous pastor, Mother Harriet was the exact opposite. Perhaps the best pen portrait of her was written as her obituary in the Church newspaper called *The Guardian* of April 4th 1883, by Archdeacon Furse (who was none other than Carter's one-time curate, but who had changed his name from Johnson). Looking back to the 1850s, he recalled: "No one who knew her thirty years ago would have described her as especially meditative, retired, profound, far sighted. She was not literary or scholastic or imaginative or critical … Hers was the brightest and gayest of natures, with a quick clear knowledge of men and of manners, the sharpest common sense, great confidence in her power of managing, which was due neither to imperiousness or intrigue, but to that ingenuousness which has been neatly described as the temper which trusts others and expects to be trusted. Her sympathy was a vast power …"

Over the succeeding years Harriet Monsell gained a reputation for her wisdom and understanding which manifested itself in a ministry of counselling to all and sundry, so that people came from far and wide to consult her. Archdeacon Furse tells us in the obituary, "The wheels went smoothly, and the work grew and her [mind] grew with it." All whom she encountered were left with the impression of a dynamic personality, of great spiritual force, yet wholly sensible and down to earth. A fellow Sister described her as "the most living power I have ever come across", and Dr John Mason Neale, founder of the Society of St Margaret (East Grinstead), told a friend that she was "the most sensible woman I ever saw". She was widely consulted by other early Communities and played a conciliatory role in the strained relations between Archbishop Tait, her cousin by marriage, and some of his more extreme Anglo-Catholic clergy. In this capacity she has been described as a latter-day St Catherine of Siena. Such high praise in the higher echelons of the Church could have resulted in a very forbidding personality, but the letters which have survived (most have not) give the lie to such an impression. She could be forceful and sometimes had to be, but she remained an immensely likeable person, full of warmth and with a sense of humour which manifested itself at unlikely times. There can be little doubt that the very special personality of Harriet Monsell attracted women to Clewer, for though by the early 1850s Sisterhoods were springing up like mushrooms, yet none grew so rapidly as the Community of St John Baptist, Clewer.

There was, however, a third personality whose influence on the early Community cannot be discounted: Samuel Wilberforce, Bishop of Oxford. Son of the great evangelical liberator of slavery, Samuel Wilberforce had become Bishop of Oxford in 1845, aged 40. His life had been overshadowed by grief, which gave him a common ground with Mother Harriet. In 1841 his wife Emily died shortly after the birth of their fourth son, Basil. And then several members of his family became Roman Catholics.

The days since the Second Vatican Council have witnessed a remarkable degree of reconciliation between the Roman Catholic Church and the Church of England, and while there are still unresolved differences, yet substantial agreement has been reached on much which has hitherto divided the two Churches. But in the early 1850s there was deep suspicion between the two Communions which had been agitated by the secession of John Henry Newman and friends in 1845, and which in fact had worsened by the end of the century. The re-establishment of the Roman Catholic hierarchy in 1851 was met with anger and rioting. To make matters worse, the outcome of a controversy over the theology of Baptism in 1850–1 resulted in a fresh spate of secessions in which Samuel Wilberforce lost three brothers, a sister-in-law, two brothers-in-law (including Henry Manning, later Cardinal) and his daughter. Secession from Anglicanism at that time meant a complete severing of former ties because it implied that Roman Catholicism was the only true expression of Christianity. Anglicans saw this as a betrayal on the part of those who had formerly professed their Christian faith within the Church of England.

The great personal loss which these secessions inflicted upon Wilberforce blighted his life, not only in the sense of a multiple bereavement (which it undoubtedly was), but also because it instilled within him a mistrust of all things Roman Catholic which at times became quite fanatical. It also made him suspect in the eyes of the Establishment, who thought that where so many of his family had led, he, being a mild Tractarian, would surely follow. He did not. During the twenty-four years of his episcopacy he transformed the diocese of Oxford into a model diocese: he built a theological college at Cuddesdon; a Church of England teachers' training college at Culham; built new churches and parsonages and restored old ones; he visited extensively, confirmed, ordained, instructed and harangued until his clergy and laity were in no doubt that they had a bishop who was a true shepherd of his flock. He was beyond doubt a great bishop, possibly the greatest bishop Oxford has seen.

Only one other bishop would permit the establishment of a Religious Sisterhood in his diocese: Henry Philpotts, Bishop of Exeter. Between them Exeter and Oxford were the host to the earliest Communities, but as will be seen in the next chapter, Wilberforce did not make life particularly easy during the Clewer Sisterhood's infancy.

Note
Carter's curate, the Revd Charles Wellington Johnson, who later changed his surname to Furse, was in fact related through marriage to Harriet Monsell. Her brother-in-law, the Revd J S B Monsell, the hymn writer, had a daughter, Jane, who married Charles Wellington Furse. Also, Elizabeth Moreton who we shall meet in the next chapter, was very indirectly connected to both Harriet Monsell and Charles Wellington Furse. See the Moreton family tree, page 148.

THE MAKING OF A COMMUNITY

One of the attractions of the Nightingale Place estate was that it extended over fifteen acres, and although the house itself was too small there was plenty of room for rebuilding and expansion. This was important for two reasons. The newly formed Church Penitentiary Association was helping to establish Houses of Refuge in London from whence they would send women to Houses of Mercy in the country. So the buildings at Clewer had to expand to help meet the anticipated influx. Secondly, the Community of St John Baptist was itself growing and needed quarters for the Sisters which would be close enough to the rescued women to maintain discipline, but sufficiently removed to follow the Religious Life.

The Community began to grow. The three women who had joined before Mother Harriet's installation were professed in 1853: Sr Aimée on January 25th and Sr Catherine and Sr Ellen on July 29th. The next to join was Augusta Straine, who was admitted on March 28th 1853 and professed on December 12th 1856. She died on August 3rd 1864, the first death within the Community. The next person to join was Elizabeth Moreton, admitted on October 18th 1853 and professed on November 30th 1855. Sr Elizabeth, as she became, lived until 1912. (See note at the end of this chapter.) Her immensely wealthy family owned Little Moreton Hall in Cheshire (now in the care of the National Trust), and she was to be a great benefactress of the Community throughout her long life (see Appendix 6). A year after her profession Sr Elizabeth gave to the Community a silver-gilt chalice set with semi-precious stones, designed by William Butterfield. It bore the inscription on the underside, "Given by E.M. for the use of the Chapel of the House of Mercy, Clewer, June 1856." Other early Sisters included Sr Jane (for further information see Appendix 4), Sr Anne Elizabeth, Sr Frances Elizabeth, Sr Katherine Mary, Sr Harriet and Sr Harriet Mary, all of whom had been professed by 1860. All the 'Harriets' and 'Elizabeths' must have been hopelessly confusing, and after these earliest years names were not duplicated, though sometimes two Sisters of the same name adopted a second one as a variant.

It might be easy to imagine that the great re-building at Clewer came about solely because the Sisterhood had been founded, but as early as October 1851 (over a year before Mother Harriet's installation) the Council Minutes speak of plans for re-building, and Carter had begun writing letters of appeal which were sent to the wealthy and influential. The installation of Mother Harriet in November 1852 gave a fresh impetus to the plans. Carter's friend the architect Henry Woodyer, who had worked for the famous architect William Butterfield, offered his services free and set to work to design an appropriate building.

People responded to Carter's appeals because the purpose of the Community was rescue work. There can be little doubt too that the presence of such a well connected woman as Harriet Monsell as Mother Superior made the idea of such an institution more acceptable. And also the fact that the Church Penitentiary Association had the support of several bishops seemed to give Sisterhoods some sort of sanction.

So it was that on November 29th 1855 Bishop Wilberforce, who was also Visitor, blessed and opened the first stage of the new buildings. By this time there were eight Sisters in the Community. The new buildings consisted of what later formed three sides of the central quadrangle of the convent (see illustration on page 147). There was accommodation for the penitents and Sisters, kitchen, dairy, class rooms and laundry. The dedication service was held in the upper storey of the north wing and 500 people were crammed in there, with another 100 downstairs. Part of this room was to serve as a chapel until funds would permit a purpose-built one. (A cross was built into the exterior brickwork of the gable to distinguish this upper room and is clearly visible in the illustration on page 147.)

It was a good start, but more buildings were needed, though for the time being there was no more money. The number of penitents had been immediately increased to thirty, and by January 1857 there were thirty-eight penitents and eleven Sisters. The greatest requirement was for an adequate chapel, but it seemed a distant ambition until on June 24th 1856 Sr Elizabeth offered the substantial sum of £3,000 for the building of the fourth side of the quadrangle, which would consist of a chapel and the completion of the Sisters' quarters. This sum also provided for the building of an orphanage, of which there will be more in chapter 5.

Throughout 1857 building work was resumed and July 1st 1858 saw the dedication by Bishop Wilberforce of the completed House of Mercy. It was a spectacular day: 1,000 invitations were sent, an estimated 800 people were present including about 200 clergy, and a special train was put on from Paddington to cope with the influx. The list of dignitaries included leading churchmen and gentry together with their ladies. Mr Gladstone was unable to be present but his wife, Catherine, was there. The dedication service started in the chapel at 10.30 am and was followed by Holy Communion celebrated by the Bishop. Then the procession proceeded to the quadrangle and at 1.30 pm the new buildings were blessed. This was followed by a sermon and the lengthy proceedings were concluded by 3.00 pm when lunch was served. Evensong followed at 5.00 pm.

The new buildings which superseded Nightingale Place were of red brick in the Decorated style which was being adopted by the new generation of architects who had been influenced by the Oxford, or Tractarian, Movement. They were looking back to medieval Gothic architecture which was thought to be more devotional than the Classical style. The revival of Sisterhoods gave architects like Henry Woodyer, George Edmund Street and John Loughborough Pearson the opportunity to design whole ranges of conventual buildings in the medieval manner. Within a few years Wantage, Ascot, Clewer, East Grinstead and many more stood like flagships of the Oxford Movement, of which they were the first fruits.

So by the summer of 1858 the Clewer House of Mercy had a splendid new home. By October there were fifty penitents, nineteen Sisters and room for more of both. The new chapel was a great asset. This was not the magnificent edifice built in 1881 which was Henry Woodyer's crowning glory, but the smaller chapel known after 1940 as the Chapel of the Forerunner.

Having looked at bricks and mortar, perhaps it may be well to examine the structure of the Community itself in those early days. The Council of the House of Mercy had been appointed before Mrs Tennant's withdrawal, and after this their influence became paramount, not only regarding the affairs of the rescue work, but also the Community itself. This sometimes made life difficult. For instance, when in 1863 the Community decided to call themselves the Sisters of St John Baptist, the Council agreed to sanction it but disapproved of not being consulted first! The Council consisted of nine clergymen and nine laymen together with the Bishop of Oxford as Visitor, Carter as Warden, the Revd W H Hutchings as Sub-Warden and two treasurers. There were also four Trustees, who in the earliest days were

W E Gladstone (who remained one until his death), W Mount, Esq, the Revd Edward Coleridge, Fellow of Eton College, and Carter.

The first set of *Statutes of the House of Mercy, Clewer* was issued on June 9th 1854. These were the necessary legal regulations for the governing of the Sisterhood. They set out in precise terms the object of the Sisterhood, the way in which it should be governed and by whom, the terms under which the 'officials' were to execute their duties, the terms under which women proposing to become Sisters would join, the financial arrangements and all matters concerning real estate. These first Statutes were revised in 1863, 1870 and 1889 as the Community developed, and have been subject to further revision at different times.

In the very earliest days novices were called 'Sister probationers', and those who decided to remain were known as 'confirmed Sisters'. Bishop Wilberforce, with his fear of all things Roman Catholic, did not approve of vows, and at first Carter was inclined to agree with him. But over the first few years Carter realised that the Sisters themselves wished to make them and was converted. But Wilberforce remained unbending. There was, however a way round it: the Sisters made their promises (still not yet called vows) privately to Carter as Warden immediately before the profession service. The Bishop knew of this but ignored the matter.

Perhaps it was because of Bishop Wilberforce's aversion to vows that the Community *Annals* did not speak of professed Sisters until 1873, and the word novice was not used until 1874. The *Office for the Profession of a Sister* was drawn up in 1873 with the approval of Bishop Mackarness, who had succeeded Wilberforce in 1869, though he too disapproved of vows, so that the rite spoke of 'solemn promises and engagement'. It was not until William Stubbs became Bishop in 1889 that vows were taken, although they were still made before the service until 1920.

But the question of vows was not the only obstacle which the Community had to overcome. Wilberforce's fear of Roman Catholicism made him suspicious of aids to devotion such as crucifixes, and Roman Catholic books of prayers and meditations. During 1853 and 1854 it came to the Bishop's notice that a number of women wishing to join the Clewer Sisterhood used such articles. In the end Carter's persuasiveness together with a certain firmness on Mother Harriet's part secured a partial compromise. The Bishop decided that Sisters could wear a crucifix so long as it was concealed under their habit. But he remained intransigent over devotional books despite Carter's protest that nothing similar existed in the Church of England at that time. There was, however, one more matter of discord: Dr Pusey.

Since Newman's secession to Rome in 1845 Dr Edward Bouverie Pusey, Regius Professor of Hebrew at Christ Church, Oxford, had been acknowledged as the Tractarian leader. He had helped found the first Sisterhood near Regent's Park in 1845 (the Sisterhood of the Holy Cross) and whilst he was not an extremist, he was known to be a strict confessor and spiritual director. During their time in Oxford the Monsells had become friendly with Pusey and he had been Harriet's confessor until she came to Clewer. Now a number of young women who were under Pusey's direction wished to join the Clewer Sisterhood. Wilberforce disapproved of Pusey, and in 1850 had banned him from preaching in the Diocese of Oxford. Upon hearing of Pusey's influence on the life of Mother Harriet and others, Wilberforce made it clear that the Sisters must have no contact with him. Again Carter and Mother Harriet managed to soften the blow slightly. Pusey was never invited to Clewer, a matter which caused him pain, but later the Bishop agreed to Sisters' taking spiritual guidance from other clergy when outside the House on Community business.

But life was not all discord. These were minor teething troubles, and it must be emphasised that Wilberforce generally had a very good relationship with the Clewer Community. He visited the Community at least once a year from 1851–69 and often two or three times. But as he remarked to Carter in 1853, "Sisterhoods are at present an experiment among us; a failure at this moment might deprive us of them permanently …" which is why he endeavoured to prevent any ritualistic excess.

By 1858 when the new chapel was opened, the Community had its own daily office book. Called *The Day Hours of the Church of England*, it went through many editions and revisions and is still in print though now the Community uses a more modern office. Many Communities, including that at Wantage, adopted *The Day Hours*, and its impact on the life and worship of the Church of England was indeed great. There had been nothing like it in the English Church since before the Reformation and yet it was based entirely on the *Book of Common Prayer* and the Authorised Version of the Bible.

The Community *Annals* record that the first Chapter of the Sisters was held on May 30th 1860. The Chapter consisted of the professed choir Sisters and it dealt with all Community matters such as the adoption of branch work, the profession of novices and any internal problems or difficulties. But it would seem that Chapter decisions were subject to the sanction of the Warden. Certainly in Carter's time he, like many of his Victorian contemporaries, remained unconvinced that women could manage their own business affairs, which is also why the Council exercised so much power.

It might seem rather surprising that the Community Rule was not accepted by the Chapter until 1869, but it had taken a good deal of hard work to formulate. This is not to suggest that there was no Rule until this time, but it did not find its way into print until 1869. The earliest Rule of the Community came to light after the publication of the first edition of *A Joyous Service*. It was written in Mother Harriet's handwriting in a small notebook and is headed *Rules: Clewer House of Mercy. Revised by the Visitor October 1854*. The published Rule was founded upon that of St Augustine and was also influenced by the Rule of the Sisterhood of the Holy Cross founded by Dr Pusey in 1845. In the first printed edition of the Clewer Rule, both Rule and Constitutions were closely interwoven, but the two were separated in the 1874 edition.

The 1860s saw the development of the Community along the lines which it would retain until 1946. This involved the adoption of a two-tiered First Order consisting of choir and lay Sisters and a separate Second Order. By the late 1870s the choir Sisters included several daughters of clergymen and a number whose families were titled or landed gentry. It was not uncommon for members of the same family to join: Sr Fidelia and Sr Johanna were sisters, their brother being the well known Fr Maturin of the Society of St John the Evangelist (the Cowley Fathers). Another famous Cowley Father, Fr Congreve, was the brother of Sr Selina. As the century progressed and the influence of Clewer spread far and wide, so an increasing number of well-bred young women were attracted to it, which enabled the Community to embrace even more work.

The choir noviciate was two years, preceded by six months' postulancy. The day started at 6.00 am and finished at 10.00 pm, which made a long, tiring day by any standards. There was a daily Eucharist, and in the early years the Community recited a seven-fold monastic office at intervals throughout the day plus Matins and Evensong from the *Book of Common Prayer*. The fast days as prescribed in the *Book of Common Prayer* were observed and silence was observed at certain times. The Sisters also had specified times for private meditation and spiritual reading, and the opportunity for regular retreats which were given by some of the leading clergy of the day, including Fr R M Benson, founder of the Society of St John the Evangelist, Dr John Mason Neale and Fr A H Mackonochie.

Although the Community of St John Baptist was not the only Sisterhood to have both choir and lay Sisters, it has sometimes been suggested that it reflected the class structure of the outside world. This is partly true, because Victorian society was class orientated, but it is not the whole truth. It is more likely that education played an important part. Women from poorer homes whose families had been unable to afford governesses to teach them would be less able to find their way through complicated office books in chapel; nor would they be suited to administer the many branch works which came under the Community's care. It is true that the duties of lay Sisters consisted largely of the domestic work of the Community; it is equally true that as domestic servants in the outside world their 'lot' might have been far harder.

Lay Sisters are first mentioned in the *Annals* in 1861 when the first two were received on Easter Eve. The earliest separate figures for First Order Sisters date from 1872 when there were fifty-seven confirmed choir Sisters, eight confirmed lay Sisters, and nineteen probationers. By the early 1880s there were over thirty lay Sisters and a dozen or more lay novices; numbers continued to increase and reached a peak in 1928 when there were sixty-three. The lay noviciate was normally four years. The Rule was less demanding than that of the choir Sisters and gave more time for the heavy manual work of the House. Lay Sisters were not required to recite the daily office, nor did they have a vote in Chapter, and though they wore a black habit like that of the choir Sisters, theirs was much simpler in design. But there was a frugality about the Rule which demanded a true vocation in order to live the life. The choir Sisters could not have undertaken the vast amount of external work without the support of the lay Sisters, who provided a strong subsidiary force.

The Second Order never thrived numerically and by the mid-1880s there were eleven members, after which the numbers dwindled. It was founded for women who wished to follow the Religious Life but were prevented from doing so, usually for family reasons. Second Order Sisters lived part of the year at home and part of it at Clewer and had a simple Rule. The noviciate was six months, and the full commitment was for three years at a time. A number of choir Sisters began as Second Order Sisters and transferred when they were able. Among these may be mentioned Sr Emily, who became Sister-in-Charge of the mission work which grew into Clewer St Stephen, and Sr Jane Frances who became Mother Superior 1881–9 and Sr Superior of the Indian work 1889–1918. In 1884 there were eleven Second Order Sisters and this slowly dwindled until the death in 1940 of the last one, Sr Catherine Seal, aged 105. The Second Order Sisters were popularly known as the 'Blue Sisters' from the colour of their habit.

From September 1866 onwards those who wished to have a connection with Clewer could become Associates. This was open to men as well as women and involved financial support as well as prayer.

One of the main objections to Sisterhoods was that they were a means of depriving young women (and the young men who might have married into their families) of their wealth. For this reason Carter exercised the utmost caution. Sisters who could afford to do so contributed £50 annually to the Community Fund but there was no compulsion. Nor was anyone turned away on financial grounds.

In 1875, the year Mother Harriet retired as Superior, there were 138 Sisters in all. The Community had come a long way from November 30th 1852 when Harriet Monsell had been installed as Superior in the presence of the two Sisters who then made up the Community. There had been casualties, of course: such a bulging noviciate (twenty-three choir and sixteen lay in 1875) was bound to see some withdrawals, mostly because of frail health or lack of vocation, though some left to join the Roman Catholic Church.

Having examined the Community structure it is now time to look at the rescue work which was flourishing in the new buildings.

Note

In the first edition of *A Joyous Service* I stated that Elizabeth Moreton was the fourth to join the Community (counting Harriet Monsell as the first). In the early Community Roll Books Elizabeth Moreton's name is listed fourth, before that of Augusta Straine, but in fact Elizabeth joined seven months after Augusta, thus implying that Elizabeth was the fifth. But on page 127 of *A Place in Life* I stated that Elizabeth Moreton was the sixth to join. The basis for this claim lies in the Community *Annals* where the reception of Catherine Brough on March 25th 1852 as a Sister Probationer is mentioned. Sr Catherine, as she became, was professed as a Confirmed Sister, along with Sr Ellen, on July 29th 1853. The *Annals* note that on May 16th 1855, "Sr Catherine, with the consent of the Bishop, left at her own request." It is odd that neither of the Community Roll books that I have seen mention Catherine Brough, whose arrival in March 1852 was shortly after Sr Aimée and before Sr Ellen. Other early Sisters who left are named in the Roll Books, so the omission of Sr Catherine remains a mystery.

TO RESCUE THE FALLEN

Church rescue work had progressed by leaps and bounds in the six years since Mrs Tennant's first endeavours. Not only had the first stage of the new buildings at Clewer been blessed and opened in 1855, but also other Communities, such as the Community of St Mary the Virgin at Wantage, were now doing similar work. Largely influenced by the writings of John Armstrong, the Church Penitentiary Association envisaged Houses of Refuge in towns and cities to provide immediate shelter, from whence the more hopeful cases would be passed on to the Houses of Mercy. These, like Clewer, would be in the country and would provide long-term training, after which the inmates would return to the outside world as laundry-women or domestic servants.

In theory the Houses of Refuge were meant to 'sift off' the worst cases so that the Sisters should have been spared the horrendous scenes which Mrs Tennant had to endure—anger, violence, swearing and general lack of civilised behaviour. Alas, this was not always so, and the Clewer casebooks abound with entries testifying to dismissal for bad conduct or insubordination.

The women and girls were called penitents because they were expected to show a degree of sorrow for the way in which their past lives had been spent and have a genuine desire to lead a better life in the future. (Even so this suggests that a penitent's past lifestyle was always her fault and in many cases it clearly was not.) It has been thought for too long that all the women who came to Clewer were prostitutes. This is certainly not the case; some were, but many of these were driven to it from poverty rather than from choice because they had no other way of earning a living. And that in itself is a terrible indictment on the society in which they lived.

The Clewer casebooks give a very clear picture of the type of women and girls received, and this reflects upon the Victorian social system (and it was not until the coming of the Welfare State that it was finally swept away). It is difficult to generalise, but some patterns may be discerned. Many women and girls were sent by well-meaning ladies who were prepared to pay for their upkeep and perhaps employ them as servants after they left. But not all of them wished to be rescued and some ran away or were so disruptive that they were sent back to their benefactress or on to another institution. Some had been domestic servants who were found to be dishonest: a spell in the House of Mercy was sometimes seen by a compassionate mistress as a better alternative to calling the police.

JM aged 18 was a general servant admitted in December 1866 but was sent away for violent behaviour. EW aged 15 came from Clewer village and was admitted in October 1874. She had lived with an aunt in London and was sent to Clewer instead of going to prison, but her father came and took her away after a year.

Others had been servants and had been deceived or seduced (in many cases this meant raped) either by male servants or by a son of the family: punishment was always bestowed upon the girl, rarely upon the man. She was usually dismissed without a 'character' (ie reference) so that another place as a servant would be practically impossible to obtain. Faced with poverty and homelessness, she might well be forced into prostitution as an alternative to starvation in the same way as Mary Ford (see chapter 1). If she was pregnant the only recourse would be to the Workhouse Infirmary, and perhaps it was a merciful thing that the infant mortality rate was so high (ie from 1866–70 there were 157 infant deaths per 1,000 live births) or there would have been even more poverty and misery. It is easy to see how, as the result of one single fall from virtue (as the Victorians would describe it), a hitherto respectable girl would be dragged into an awful downward spiral. Once in this way of life, the only people who would wish to befriend her would be those in the same situation and so she would be dragged down even further. Drink, which was easily obtainable, would not only drown her sorrows but might also become an addiction. In Victorian England drink was a social problem of a similar magnitude to the drug problem of the mid-20th to 21st centuries.

EG was a typical example of the downward spiral: aged 21 and admitted in October 1882, she came from a good home but had to look after the younger children in the family, so the only schooling she had was at Sunday School. She went into service at 19 as a general servant. Then she became a kitchen maid in the Officers' Mess at Knightsbridge Barracks and 'got into trouble'. She was sent to the Stone House Refuge in London, by this time also run by the Clewer Community, and was duly sent to Clewer. "But," states the casebook, "she would go"—and left after a year.

There was a marked rise in the number of penitents who came from domestic service from the 1870s onwards. These were, as might be expected, lower servants such as kitchen maids, under-housemaids, general servants, and maids-of-all-work. Most were not prostitutes, but like the case mentioned above had only 'fallen' once and had been rescued, hopefully in time to make a fresh start in life. Some upper servants are recorded such as cooks and housekeepers: here the problem was usually drink, to which they would have access. For example, MW aged 29, admitted in 1882, was well brought up. She was a cook and "took to drink from temptation in her situation". Her story had a happy ending, unlike AL aged 35, admitted at the same time and also a cook who was led to drink, "by temptations in unsteady places for about six years". She was obliged to go away and fell to drink again later.

Many of the women who came to Clewer had their childhood blighted by their surroundings: overcrowded dwellings with several families to a house, all ages and both sexes sharing a bed, poor drainage and sanitation, dirt, disease and poverty everywhere frequently formed the background to their lives. The novels of Dickens and Elizabeth Gaskell, the findings of late Victorian social investigators such as Charles Booth and Henry Mayhew, and the campaigns for better conditions led by Lord Shaftesbury and General William Booth form the backdrop to the Clewer casebooks. The conditions which they tried to improve were those which bred these poor unfortunate women. Some had alcoholic parents who brought them up to drink, others were daughters of prostitute mothers, many had violent fathers and some were victims of sexual abuse. But throughout the casebooks it is true to say that drink accounted for quite as many entries as sexual immorality or prostitution.

Some penitents had various types of learning difficulties and would have been incapable of looking after themselves in the outside world. They would have been wrongly placed in the great network of 'lunatic asylums' which were being built from the 1850s onwards. These women were not mentally ill, but as there was little understanding of the difference between mental handicap and mental illness many were sent to an asylum. (Conditions such as autism and Asperger's Syndrome were not identified as distinct from mental illness until the early to mid-20th century.) When such women came to the House of Mercy their presence was sometimes disruptive and they were not always suited to the training, either physically or mentally. For this reason such cases were often passed on elsewhere. Often the only other source of refuge was the Workhouse.

Other penitents were travellers, known then as tramps, and they found the confinement within a building uncongenial, such as EM aged 19, admitted August 1868. She was a tramp who came to the gate but was sent away for misconduct in May 1869. LG was only 15 and was born in Bradford Workhouse before her parents married. They all went about as tramps working in the fields. She "lived a careless life and went astray". Then the parents died and the girl went to live with an aunt with whom she quarrelled and "went off to a wild, bad life". She asked for help and was sent to Stone House Refuge in London and thence to Clewer. "She says of herself that she has always been bad." At the end of her training she was taken in by friends. We do not know the end of her story but her opinion of herself as having "always been bad" reflects the way in which society condemned such girls. Today we would see her as the victim of her surroundings and upbringing (or lack of it), but in the 19th century girls like LG would always be viewed as "bad", thereby implying her guilt or complicity in the bad things that happened to her.

In addition to all this there were many cases which do not fall into any particular category. There were promising cases who refused to stay, and penitents who were dismissed for bad conduct who later wrote to say they were happily married with children of their own, or happily settled in service. There were violent cases and also gentle, sweet-natured women who welcomed a fresh start. Some couldn't wait to leave, others begged to stay longer. Some came from the Workhouse, others from prison, and as the century progressed some were sent from the Police Court Mission, the forerunner of the modern Probation service. Some proved unacceptable from the start, chiefly if found to be pregnant or with venereal disease, or were insane. A few became ill and died, usually of consumption.

In contrast to this motley crowd there were the Sisters who had dedicated themselves to this work: well-bred, cultured, educated by governesses. The whole of the rescue work was done by the Sisters themselves; none of it was delegated to secular helpers, though they did rely upon the financial support of Associates. In his book *The Call of the Cloister* Peter Anson sums up the immense sacrifice which these ladies who joined the early Communities made when they embraced the Religious Life and the social work which accompanied it:

"It is hard for us today to realize what was involved in the case of a mid-Victorian lady who, under the influence of Tractarian teaching, abandoned a sheltered home-life to devote herself to ministering to the poorest of the poor … [They] had been brought up in homes where there were every comfort and luxury, with large staffs of servants to wait on them. These ladies had little or no conception of the meaning of the word poverty, and only a vague knowledge of how the poor lived, still less of sin and vice. One must always remember this; otherwise it is impossible to appreciate what was involved when they dispensed with the services of coachmen, butlers, footmen, parlour-maids, housemaids and ladies' maids and, of their own free will, went to live in the slums, when slums were slums." This equally applies to rescue work, for though the penitents were not allowed to speak to the Sisters about their past life, yet the work was fraught with difficulties and stood as a stark and often sordid contrast to the sort of life the ladies who became Clewer Sisters had previously led.

When first admitted to Clewer a penitent would go to the Probationary Ward for a short time to enable her to settle in and to be assessed. She would then proceed either to the East or the West Class. The East Class comprised penitents of a more delicate nature who would not be suited to the rigours of the laundry, and their principle occupation was needlework. They were trained to be good plain needlewomen and chiefly sewed for the inmates, although they also took orders from outside. But they did not undertake church needlework, which was a far more skilled task. (And there was an underlying, albeit unspoken, suggestion that 'fallen women' were somehow unworthy to undertake this work.)

The West Class did laundry work, and very hard work it was too, toiling over boiling coppers and wash-tubs, turning heavy mangles and learning to iron to perfection. There was no shortage of customers among the gentry for laundry work and the income thus derived helped to finance the House of Mercy, which was always in financial straits because many of the penitents had no one to help pay for their upkeep. As early as 1858 the Clewer laundry won a contract for the Eton College washing, though a disastrous fire in 1883 resulted in no clean collars for the Eton boys that week! In fact the whole House of Mercy stood in grave danger for about two hours and was only saved by the bravery of the local firemen and guardsmen from the barracks who stripped the roof with their bare hands to prevent the blaze from spreading further. At that time the laundry was located in the west wing, near the kitchen and what later became the Sisters' refectory. After the fire the laundry was rebuilt slightly away from the main buildings, and connected to them by what the Sisters called 'Pneumonia Passage' because it was so cold due to the lack of heating. In 1970 the ironing room became Carter Hall.

In addition to needlework and laundry work, the penitents were given basic religious instruction, an annual retreat and daily worship. It was always hoped they would be confirmed before leaving. Many were, but many also lapsed upon leaving; nevertheless the seed had been sown and it held them in good stead when difficulties weighed upon them in the outside world. Even so, all the religious instruction was by no means as oppressive as it had been in Mrs Tennant's day, nor was there quite so much of it. Each penitent was under the special care of a Sister who would correspond with her after she left the House, and many kept in touch for years afterwards. The very nature of the work meant a fairly high failure rate and this was never concealed. Yearly statistics were issued in the annual report, though names were never mentioned.

The penitents' ages varied tremendously. In the early years it was not unusual for girls of 14 to be admitted and this was still the case until well into the 1870s. But the undesirability of mixing young girls with older women was soon understood and gradually Homes grew up specifically for younger cases. By the end of the century hardly anyone under 17 was taken at Clewer. Generally the older the penitent, the more difficult the work of rescue proved. Those over 30 tended to be difficult and often fell back to their former way of life upon leaving, though there were of course always exceptions.

The normal training period was two years and whilst every effort was made to retain the penitents there was no compulsion to stay. Contact with the outside world was very restricted so as to avoid all possible temptation, but the ample grounds at Clewer went some way to compensate for this so that the penitents had space for outdoor exercise. If a penitent stayed the full time and had a good record, she would be found a place in domestic service and would leave Clewer equipped with an outfit. This would have been made in the needlework class and ensured that she had some decent clothing to wear in her new employment.

Life at the House of Mercy was not all work: there were occasional treats too, notably at St John Baptist-tide (June 24th) when there was an outside tea party. From about 1886 it ended with fireworks, or fire balloons as they were called. These were let off by the Warden (Canon Carter) and invariably misfired or refused to light, much to everyone's amusement. From 1889 onwards there was a Christmas treat held on or about January 1st. This consisted of a Christmas tree laden with useful gifts for everyone and an entertainment such as a Penny Reading in which all participated. The Revd Roland Errington (Rector of Clewer 1880–99) was the proud owner of a magic lantern, which he used for parish entertainments, the penitents' treat being no exception.

Following the opening of the new buildings at Clewer in 1855 the number of penitents had steadily increased: at first to thirty, then by 1857 to thirty-eight, and by 1858 to fifty. The building of the chapel in 1858 enabled the top floor of the north wing to be turned into a dormitory (it had been the temporary chapel), which increased the capacity to over eighty by the mid-1860s. Further building in 1873 swelled the accommodation to just over 100, though towards the end of the century the House was not always full.

But some did not want to leave after their training, and a special provision was made for them which harked back to John Armstrong's 1849 Appeal. These were the Magdalens, so named because the Victorians believed that the penitent woman in the Gospel story who wept and anointed the feet of Jesus was Mary Magdalen, although later Biblical scholarship has refuted this. The Magdalens were penitents who had expressed a desire to lead consecrated lives in the House of Mercy, but as it was thought inappropriate to admit them to the Sisterhood a separate Order was formed. A would-be Magdalen had first to complete the ordinary two-year training as a penitent, and then serve a further seven-year probationary period, after which she would be consecrated. They retained their Christian name followed by Magdalen as a corporate surname, wore a distinctive habit and had their own Rule of Life. Probationer Magdalens wore a grey habit and were known as 'grey Magdalens' or 'greys': consecrated Magdalens wore black with a white bonnet and apron, a black cross and black veil for outdoor wear. It was intended that there should be thirty-three of them (for each year of Our Lord's life), but in fact there never were. Carter described the Magdalens as "a dedication in a different way from that of a Sister of Mercy, yet having a beauty of its own, as a rose differs from a lily."

The first Magdalen was Agnes, consecrated in June 1865; she died at St Andrew's Hospital, Clewer, on February 6th 1874, just a few weeks before the new Magdalens' wing was opened on May 1st. This, together with an endowment for the Magdalens' upkeep, was the gift of Sr Elizabeth (who had also paid for the chapel). Associates and other friends visiting the House for the annual Commemoration Day at St John Baptist-tide were able to inspect this new addition, which like the rest was designed by Henry Woodyer. (A year later Henry Woodyer designed a further wing to house the Sisters' refectory, which later became the Community Library.) There was a small oratory in the Magdalens' wing which in 1894 was decorated with murals depicting the life of St Mary Magdalen. This later became the chapel for the Sisters' Infirmary, and later still became St Mary Magdalen's Oratory in the Clewer Spirituality Centre. There were already fifteen Magdalens, some still postulants, when the new wing was opened. Their work was an invaluable support to the regular Sisters, because they had been through the training and knew the difficulties from both sides. There were Magdalens at all the branch Houses of Mercy, and in addition they had their own particular work at St Basil's Home, Oxford (for elderly ladies).

By 1900 there were some penitents who, while not wishing to be Magdalens, wished to stay longer and were allowed to remain for a third year: these were known as 'raised penitents' and were given special privileges. There were also a number of permanent inmates, former penitents who neither wished to become Magdalens nor to return to the outside world. These stayed on more or less as servants and were known as 'the browns' from the colour of their dress.

Not all of the penitents were from poverty-stricken backgrounds. By the 1870s there was a need for provision for 'lady penitents'. The *Annual Report* of the House of Mercy for 1872–3 tells us that "as they belong exclusively to the higher classes, [they] are kept distinct from the rest of the Penitentiary, both for their own sakes and for others, as well as in order that the discipline and occupation may be adapted to their differing circumstances. Such a provision … will meet the needs of those who, from position or regard for others, can only in secret embrace for a time a Penitential Rule, and obtain that seclusion which is necessary for deepening their conversion." These women were the courtesans who were kept in comfort by wealthy (and sometimes famous) gentlemen. Not surprisingly there were never many at Clewer, and their names were not entered in either the House of Mercy Roll Book or the Magdalens' Roll, so their identities will never be known. They were housed in the Magdalens' wing where there was provision for six, "with every convenience for their use and needful comfort and privacy". But perhaps a spell in the laundry would have been more beneficial!

Between 1860 and 1900 a number of other Houses of Mercy were undertaken by the Clewer Sisters. This was made possible for two reasons. Firstly, numbers in the Community continued to grow: seventy-two professed choir Sisters in 1875, 120 in 1885, 168 in 1895, 191 in 1900, although there were by this time many branch works so the large numbers were fully stretched. Secondly, the Community was asked to run these Houses but did not own them, nor did they have to finance them.

The first such House was the Manor House, Oxford, which came under the Community in 1860. Founded in 1852 as a Refuge for five penitents in an Oxford back street, it was removed to Holywell Manor House and became the Oxford Diocesan Penitentiary. A worker from the earliest days later joined the Clewer Sisterhood. A chapel was built and general improvements made to the House so that thirty-six penitents could be accommodated. The training followed the same pattern as at Clewer and need not be reiterated. The lease belonged to Merton College, and upon its expiration in 1929 the institution moved to Littlemore. The House was governed by a Council of Oxford dons and others.

The Devon House of Mercy at Bovey Tracey was almost as impressive a building as Clewer itself and was one of the most important branch Houses of Mercy. It was founded by the vicar of the parish, the Revd the Hon C L Courtney, in 1863 and the Clewer Sisters were invited to run it. At first a farmhouse had to suffice for the three Sisters, led by Sr Bertha, and twenty penitents, but this was totally inadequate. In 1868 the new building of granite and Bath stone was completed and up to 100 penitents could be housed. Sr Bertha was described by a Sister as "a woman full of enthusiasm and a great upholder of the Tractarian movement. She was a Prussian by birth and came to England as a Lutheran. She imbibed her Church principles from her friends, Mr and Mrs Gambier Parry of Highnam Court, Gloucester." Thomas Gambier Parry was to have a close association with the Clewer Sisters through his founding of St Lucy's Hospital, Gloucester. The Devon House of Mercy would always be the special work of Sr Bertha, who was there from the very beginning. She died in January 1907.

As a consequence of taking up mission work in the parish of St Barnabas Pimlico in 1860, the Clewer Sisters were asked in 1869 to run the Stone House Refuge, 15 Commercial Rd, Pimlico. This was founded in 1852 and was one of the first Refuges to be assisted financially by the Church Penitentiary Association. There was accommodation for twelve penitents and many of these were sent to Clewer.

Three other Diocesan Houses of Mercy came under the Clewer Community before the end of the century: at Leamington in 1884, Salisbury in 1889, and Great Maplestead in 1892. The work at Leamington had been started in 1855 by two ladies but was re-organised in 1881 on a Diocesan basis as St Michael's Home, taking girls from the Refuge at Worcester. It was specifically concerned with girls aged between 14 and 17. The work at Salisbury began in 1831 as one of the examples of early rescue work which were not Church inspired. In 1851 Bishop Denison obtained a house near St Martin's church to house twelve penitents and in 1889 two Clewer Sisters went to work there. In 1891 the Home was named St Mary's Home and a year later it was extended so as to accommodate forty. In 1893 a chapel was added in memory of a benefactor, the Hon Christopher Bouverie. St Mary's House of Mercy, Great Maplestead was founded in 1868 by a Mrs Gee and worked by various ladies until it was offered to the Clewer Sisters in 1892 by the Bishop of St Albans, in whose diocese it then was. The Clewer Sisters put it on a firm footing and up to sixty penitents were taken.

Only two other Houses of Mercy were undertaken after the turn of the century: St Mary Magdalen's House of Mercy, Highgate, 1901, and St Mary's Home, Stone, Kent, 1911. The former was begun in 1853 and was at first run by ladies on the same lines as those of Mariquita Tennant. In 1901 the Bishop of London invited the Clewer Community to run it as the London Diocesan Penitentiary. Over sixty penitents were taken at any one time. St Mary's Home, Stone, was founded in 1860 at Tenterden as the Kent Penitentiary by the Rt Hon J E Talbot and was run by ladies. The house at Stone was built in 1866 and went through grave financial troubles. The

Clewer Sisters undertook the work in 1911 a year after Talbot's death but gave it up in 1926.

In order to gain a realistic picture of the magnitude of Church rescue work by the end of the century, one has to imagine all the work done by the Clewer Community and its branch houses and then multiply it by all the other Communities doing similar work. Only then is it possible to even begin to understand the immensity of the task. The methods may seem strange now, and the modern generation might perhaps be forgiven for feeling sorry for those women toiling over the wash tubs. But be that as it may, at least something was being done to improve the lot of 'fallen women'. Had he lived that long, John Armstrong would have been very pleased.

Notes

For a good first-hand account of life in the Devon House of Mercy read *A Cornish Waif's Story* by Emma Smith, the pen-name of Mabel Carvolth. Published in 1954 when she was 56, the author tells the story of her early life from her birth in the Union Workhouse at Redruth, to being abandoned by her mother and living a vagrant life with another family, the father of whom abused her, to being admitted to the Devon House of Mercy c1906 at Bovey Tracey. The House of Mercy is named 'Bramshot' in the book and the Sisters' names unfortunately have been changed although Sr Bertha, 'the German Sister', is easy to recognise. Mabel Carvolth describes watching Sr Bertha's funeral procession in January 1907. Her account of the Devon House is a fair one, not glossing over the hardships, but generally giving the reader a good impression of the place. She also describes St Andrew's Hospital, Clewer, where she was sent to work in the laundry for a short time. She grew to love the Devon House, regarding it as home, and became the laundry matron. She left reluctantly and begged to go back after an unhappy placing in domestic service. Later she left again and married. Emigration to Australia was short-lived and the return to Cornwall brought back memories of childhood abuse leading to a mental breakdown. A short visit to the Devon House as a guest helped her eventual recovery. She died in April 1984, aged 90, of pneumonia and dementia.

For a good, sympathetic account of the Devon House of Mercy see "Society's fallen sisters" by Christina Green in *Family Tree* magazine, May 2007, pp39–41.

ORPHAN GIRLS AND DISGUSTING BOYS

One of the commonest forms of philanthropy in Victorian England was the care of orphans, but perhaps surprisingly the major bodies such as Dr Barnardo's Homes, the National Children's Home and the Waifs and Strays Society (later known as the [Church of England] Children's Society) did not begin their work until the last quarter of the century. Before that there was little provision on an organised basis, though there was the pioneer Foundling Hospital (1739) and Lord Ashley's Ragged School Union of 1844. Other than that, destitute children had nowhere to go except the dreaded Workhouse and many became fugitives on the streets and were easily led into bad company and moral degradation.

There were of course orphanages already in existence, just as there had been Houses of Mercy, but they were founded by private benefactors and usually run by a matron and staff. And cold, heartless places they were too in many cases, as contemporary novels such as *Jane Eyre* will testify, though there must have been exceptions. But with the revival of Religious Communities many such institutions came under their care rather than under secular management as previously. Although there was still a very strict regime at least the Communities introduced the element of compassion: it was a work for Christ's sake.

Although rescue work was the main active work of the Clewer Sisters, the opportunity arose to work with children and this was readily accepted. Mother Harriet was fond of children although her marriage had been childless. Indeed, had Charles Monsell lived they had planned to found an orphanage. Illness and death intervened, but in 1855 the Community was approached by Mrs Rosamira Lancaster to give shelter to an orphanage which she had founded in London but wished to remove to the country. The request was readily acceded to and the orphan girls duly arrived. But there was the problem of accommodation. At first two cottages at Clewer Green were taken and as well as the orphans, some sick women from the parish. Sr Elizabeth was put in charge of the work and she soon realised that orphans do not readily mix with sick people, and also they were situated a very long way from Clewer church.

So it was that Sr Elizabeth made provision for the building of an orphanage within the £3,000 which she gave for the completion of the House of Mercy and chapel in June 1856 (see chapter 3). The orphanage was built a few hundred yards away from the main House of Mercy and was opened by Bishop Wilberforce on May 18th 1858, just a few weeks before he opened the new House of Mercy buildings. It was designed by Henry Woodyer in the same style as the House of Mercy and called St John's Home. Sr Harriet (not to be confused with Mother Harriet) was put in charge.

There is a well-known quotation from a Visitation Charge delivered by Bishop Wilberforce in 1857 where he refers to St John's Home: "The Orphanage is in no way connected with the House of Mercy ... The children are orphans, the children of *respectable* parents ... *illegitimate children are not admissable* [sic]." To modern readers this seems callous and unfair and savours entirely of class-ridden Victorian society. But there is another side to it. It was bad enough being an orphan without people assuming you were from a bad home too. The proximity of the House of Mercy no doubt fostered the idea in some people's minds that the St John's Home children were the offspring of prostitutes and inebriates. This could make life very difficult for them when facing the outside world, so Wilberforce thought it well to emphasise the difference.

There were two grades of orphan: the children aged 6–14, and the industrial girls of over 14 who were trained for domestic service. (The word 'industrial' in this sense means to be busy or occupied.) Some younger children were also taken from time to time and boarded out in the parish. The children received a basic education in the Home, bearing in mind that the concept of education for all did not become statutory until 1870. The industrial girls underwent the same training for domestic service as the House of Mercy inmates but quite separately. The laundry provided a modest income, but the Home had to rely upon the benevolence of Sisters and Associates to keep itself out of dire financial straits, for many of the children came to the Home with no one to guarantee their upkeep. Upon leaving at the age of 17 or 18 they went out as kitchen maids, laundry maids and maids-of-all-work, equipped with their first outfit. Many kept in touch over the years and returned to visit, but alas, some would fall prey to the evils which awaited the innocent and would finish up in the House of Mercy or one similar.

Mrs Lancaster's original London orphanage had consisted of twelve children, but the new building had room for twenty children and sixteen industrial girls. By 1882 there was additional accommodation and forty-six were taken, and by 1888 this had extended to sixty-eight. A new wing was added in 1892–3, which provided rooms for old girls visiting the Home, and also a new refectory and community room. There was a chapel in the Home where a daily service was held at 6.30 am and at 5.30 pm. The altar was the original one from the first chapel of the House of Mercy and later became the nave altar in the Chapel of St John Baptist. (For more about this altar, see Appendix 7.)

Whilst the whole concept of orphanages has now been superseded, there is evidence that St John's Home at least made an attempt to provide a stable family atmosphere, though it has to be said that there is no substitute for a real family, and, alas, there was a social stigma surrounding orphans in general right up until the 1950s. Nevertheless the Clewer Sisters claimed that "St John's Home is essentially a family, not an institution." That many of the girls agreed with this cannot be disputed or surely they would not have kept in touch and paid visits afterwards.

Within a few years, as the influence of the Clewer Sisters spread, other orphanages were undertaken. The first of these was St Barnabas Orphanage, Pimlico, in which parish the Community took up mission work in 1860 (the first work outside Clewer). The orphanage was started in 1855 by some ladies of the parish to care for children whose parents had died in the 1853–4 cholera epidemic. After several moves the orphanage settled in Bloomfield Place near the church and Sisters' mission house, and forty-five girls were taken. Here they were given some basic schooling together with training in needlework and laundry work, and went out as servants when they were old enough. A country branch of the orphanage was founded at Chislehurst in 1879 by the same benefactresses (the Misses Tower, who were Clewer Associates). This would house twenty-five and gave the London children a welcome change of scenery.

A second orphanage in London was also undertaken in 1860. This was at 9 Rose Street, Soho, in the parish of St Mary's, Crown Street, where the Community had been invited by the vicar to do mission work. Mr Charles Randall of Hawley in Surrey enabled the Clewer Sisters to obtain the house in Rose Street. It doubled as their parish mission house and as an orphanage for children and industrial girls. Unlike St John's Home, Clewer, where the children were from respectable backgrounds, Rose Street was specifically for "either the children of bad parents, or [those who are] too unruly to be borne with at home, or who have been refused admission into or sent away from other Homes." It was what came to be known as a 'Preventive' Home: such Homes aimed to take deprived children into care *before* they had fallen victim to their surroundings rather than rescue them afterwards.

The Home in Rose Street could take twenty-two children and twenty-eight industrial girls whose basic routine was the same as at Clewer and elsewhere. The great disadvantage was its position in the worst part of the slums of Soho. For this reason, in 1878 a Clewer Associate gave help to obtain a holiday home at Brighton which was known as St Faith's. This was retained until 1881 when Charles Randall's widow opened an orphanage at Hawley in Surrey in her husband's memory, and asked the Clewer Sisters if they would run it as a country outlet for Rose Street.

The whole property at Hawley was made over to the Community along with the patronage of the church nearby, which was also built by the Randalls and was completed in 1882. This also served as the chapel of the Home, to which it was joined by a cloister. The Home, which could take eighteen children and twelve industrial girls, was situated in spacious grounds set back from the road and bordered by a pine wood. The premises were further enlarged in 1891 by the addition of a new wing, and in 1898, following a disastrous outbreak of typhoid fever which claimed one life, the drains were completely renovated. A contemporary description tells of the pleasant playground: "delightful swings to be rushed for after lessons, and the patient good donkey [who] often gives the children the greatest treats of all by taking them out in a nice little cart to some picnic place or blackberry lane." It was a far cry from Rose Street.

As the Home at Hawley grew in importance it became independent of Rose Street. But by the end of the century there were changes in Rose Street too. In 1865 Miss Agnes Cotton had founded an orphanage at Leytonstone called the Home of the Good Shepherd, next to her house 'The Pastures'. She described the children as 'poor little girls' and indeed they were. Like Rose Street this was a work where the lines are blurred between being an orphanage and a rescue home. The Clewer Community had undertaken to carry on the work in the event of Miss Cotton's death. She died suddenly in May 1899, leaving the property to the Community, and it was decided to close the Rose Street Home and move to Leytonstone, which at that time was still in the country. This was fraught with difficulty, for although the building only dated from 1881 the drainage was found to be in very bad order. Diphtheria broke out as a result and the renovations were costly. However, the work went on there until World War II, when the premises were finally evacuated.

In 1872 the Community of St John Baptist accepted the offer of work in Gloucester at the invitation of Thomas Gambier Parry, father of the well known musician Sir Hubert Parry. In 1866 Gambier Parry had founded St Lucy's Hospital for Children (of which more in chapter 6), together with the Home of Charity at Kingsholme on the outskirts of the city, in memory of his late daughter Lucy. The name of the latter was changed to St Lucy's Home and in 1876 the orphans moved into a large house close to the cathedral, from where the Sisters also conducted parish mission work.

The orphans cared for at Gloucester were from poor, under-privileged homes. Some had one parent living but not in a position to care for them, ie the parent may have been insane, or in prison, in the Workhouse or a perpetual drunkard. Some of these children had been in other Homes and had proved unmanageable. For instance: LD aged 12, admitted 1877, mother dead, father a tramp whose whereabouts were unknown. LM aged 6, admitted 1877, one of ten children, mother dead, father in Workhouse and drinks. CC aged 9, admitted 1877, father in Workhouse Infirmary, mother a tramp. LH aged 12, admitted 1877, orphan, she was sent away from St John's Home, Clewer, for running away. She did the same thing at her own home. She was dismissed for bad conduct in August 1878. ML aged 14, admitted 1878, mother "sometimes off her head", step-father ill-uses her. She was sent by Sr Lucy Anne, CSJB, who is to pay £10 and entrance fee. She went into service as a housemaid September 1881. CH aged 6, admitted 1882, mother died in Workhouse of consumption, father hopelessly ill there of same thing. 1884 sent to grandmother as she was very troublesome. HL aged 8, admitted 1883, father went to Australia—supposed by his friends to have been hung, bad mother took girl away under protest.

There was also another Home near Gloucester. This was Newark House at Hempsted, a Preventive Home which was started by the Clewer

Community in 1883. At first 'fallen' cases were taken too, but it was soon realised that these girls tended to exert a bad influence on the others and so the Home became strictly of a preventive nature. Likewise, girls from Gloucester itself tended to be too near their former companions and so the catchment area was widened.

In 1876 the Clewer Sisterhood undertook parish mission work in Newport, South Wales, an account of which will be found in chapter 8. One of the developments of this work was the Children's Refuge, later known as St John Baptist Home. This was not an orphanage, the children having parents living, but was a rescue home for ill-treated and abused girls between 4–11 years. The *St John Baptist Magazine* of Autumn 1886 cites some typical cases: AB aged 12, "parents drink; several sisters fallen; she plays in the streets all hours of the night; uses dreadful language." CF aged 12, "parents drink; mother a bad character who lives apart from husband and beats children fearfully; they wander the streets and are afraid to come home." IJ aged 10, "father a drunkard; mother was a servant, now fallen; the baby was left with IJ and was burnt to death; IJ has grown old in wickedness; she slept on a pile of rags and did not know how to get into a bed when she came here; has marks on her head and shoulder from being struck by her father with a poker." RS aged 12, "mother dead, father little more than an idiot; seven children in family and they all sleep on the floor together (boys of 8, 10 and 14)."

All these institutions mentioned so far have had one thing in common: they cared for girls only. Orphan boys were far more neglected until the great philanthropists such as Dr Barnardo began their work. Wealthy benefactors for some reason seemed reluctant to build and endow Homes for boys. Whilst the perils which awaited boys were different from those which ensnared girls and young women, they should not be underestimated. Perhaps the greatest champion of destitute boys was Lord Ashley, who later became Lord Shaftesbury, who as early as the 1830s and 1840s was campaigning to stop small boys being used as chimney sweeps and was endeavouring to set up ragged schools in order to get them off the streets, where they could so easily be led into a life of crime.

One of the few women's Religious Communities which worked with boys was the Society of the Most Holy Trinity at Devonport, which by 1850 had a school for twenty-six sailor lads. Not much else was being done by Sisterhoods but the decision to start St Augustine's Home, Clewer, in 1883 was brought about by force of circumstance rather than a definite plan, and the Home was never an official work of the Community, but was very much the brainchild of Sr Emma. The Home which evolved was not strictly an orphanage; many of the boys had both parents living. But it was defined as "a Home where boys could be received, not in spite of their being troublesome, but *because* they are troublesome, or because their surroundings are evil."

By 1883 a new parish had been carved out of Clewer, the parish of Clewer St Stephen, as a direct result of the Sisters' mission work in that district. The St Stephen's National Boys' School had acquired a number of troublesome pupils whose presence was disruptive. It was discovered that they came from bad homes, their parents caring little about them. Sr Emma had joined the Community in 1869 and was professed in February 1872. Early in 1874 she, along with two other Sisters, had been sent to New York to begin the new work in America. On her return she was sent to work in the parish of Clewer St Stephen with particular reference to these poor, troublesome boys from the National School whom she called 'scamps'. She soon realised that these boys would be better placed in a Home if one could be found. The Sisters scoured London and were amazed at the lack of provision for boys, so it was decided to start a Home in Clewer. A temporary abode was found in Grove Road, Windsor, but the eight boys soon outgrew it, and they moved into three new cottages in Bexley Terrace, Clewer. This again proved inadequate and after three years the boys moved into a new purpose-built house in Clarence Road. This was made possible by a Mrs Wren-Hoskyns of Thanet, who built the house and rented it very cheaply to the Community. She had heard about the work from the Sisters themselves who went out on begging trips to raise funds for it. By 1888 there were forty-eight boys and the new house was capable of holding fifty to fifty-five.

Sr Emma was Sister-in-Charge though the actual running of the Home was organised by a Master and Matron. Many of the boys had no hope of paying the £10 per annum for their upkeep, nor had they anyone willing to pay it for them, so as with all the children's Homes run by the Clewer Sisters, there were many free cases. The boys went to Clewer St Stephen on Sundays where many became altar servers, and some also served in the Community chapel and at St Andrew's Clewer and All Saints' Dedworth.

Schooling was had at the Windsor National School and St Stephen's National School, and those under 7 went to St Katherine's Infant School just across the road from the Home. After leaving the Home many of the boys went into service as boot and knife boys, or junior house boys.

In the early days St Augustine's boys were very rough indeed and were locally known as 'the disgusting boys', but as the century turned, so the type of boy admitted became less wild and far more respectable. One of the first boys to be rescued was more or less given to the Sisters by his own mother, a rough woman who lived in a disreputable public house, because he had just had his third reprimand from the police for petty thieving. Shortly afterwards another lad appeared on a cold night near Clewer St Stephen's mission house dressed in a man's tail-coat which swept the ground, with no shoes and an extremely dirty face. There he stood in the snow being jeered at by the other boys. The Sisters took him in and recognised him as a boy whose mother had died after ill treatment by her husband and who had now been turned out by his father. This boy was one of those whom the Sisters had tried to lodge in a Home in London.

Many of these boys were sons of convicts or had suffered extreme cruelty at home. But for the Sisters they might have ended up in the same way of life. These boys were the type described by Dickens in *Oliver Twist*, which was written not merely as an entertaining novel but as a social document. For instance: WH, "father a convict. Boy sent by Society for the Relief of Discharged Prisoners. Language appalling." JK, "dishonest, employed in the Home because of it." RA, "father a burglar and now a convict. Boy very sharp and clever." GS and WS, "brothers sent by Waifs and Strays Society. Father dead, mother lives life of vice. Both will need great care."

Child care has changed dramatically since the 1880s with increased understanding of child psychology and paediatric medicine. Most of the children's charities founded at that time still exist and are constantly updating their image and methods in order to meet what is still a crying need. On the other hand, much of the children's work undertaken by the Religious Communities was given up with the coming of the Welfare State, if not before. But Communities such as the Clewer Sisters must be given credit for addressing a vast social problem. In many ways they laid the foundations of the Welfare State. But it is time now to examine how the Clewer Community tackled another such problem, that of caring for the sick poor.

Note

For further information about St John's Home, Clewer, see: Valerie Bonham, "Poor little Orphans" in *Windlesora* No 11, (the Journal of the Windsor Local History Group), Windsor 1991.

For further information about Sr Emma and her work with destitute boys see: Valerie Bonham, "Scamps reclaimed: St Augustine's Home, Clewer" in *Windlesora* No 12, (the Journal of the Windsor Local History Group), Windsor 1993.

For new information regarding Sr Emma and her role in the collecting of English folk songs, see Appendix 2 in this book.

6

CONSUMPTIVES AND CONVALESCENTS

As early as 1854 the Clewer Sisters had been engaged in visiting the poor in their homes in Clewer parish and had soon encountered cases of sickness which brought real hardship. There was at the time very little in the way of provision for the sick poor: the Windsor Dispensary, founded in 1817 and rebuilt in Victoria Street in 1834, provided very rudimentary care and the situation was little improved by the addition of an Infirmary in 1857. The rules of the latter institution excluded children under 6 years, pregnant women, those suffering from infectious diseases, the insane and the dying, and later consumptives and epileptics were likewise excluded. The only other provision for the sick poor lay in the Workhouse infirmary and this provided little more than a shelter, practically no nursing care being given. It was not until 1868, following an investigation of some of the London Workhouses, that reforms in the care of sick paupers were introduced.

The eighteenth century had seen the growth of voluntary hospitals, many of which became the great teaching hospitals. The revival of the Religious Life indirectly gave a fresh impetus to the voluntary hospital movement because many of the new Communities took the care of the sick and dying as their primary work, eg the Nursing Sisters of St John the Divine, the Society of All Saints and the Society of St Margaret. Also, the whole tone of nursing was raised following the Crimean War, and it is not as widely acknowledged as it should be that Florence Nightingale was accompanied to Scutari by members of Religious Communities—the Sisterhood of the Holy Cross, the Society of the Most Holy Trinity, the Nursing Sisters of St John the Divine, and a number of Roman Catholic Sisters of Mercy.

But the Clewer Sisters' involvement in nursing came about by necessity rather than by a preconceived plan. There were sick women from Clewer parish who needed help, and so in 1855 a few were lodged at Clewer Green with Mrs Lancaster's orphan girls from London, but the two groups were soon separated. Both the sick and orphaned were at this time still temporarily housed in cottages. The early nursing work had several temporary abodes and for a time was known as St Andrew's Cottage. This was opened by Bishop

Wilberforce on November 29th 1861 (but should not be confused with the work of the same name for elderly ladies begun in 1868).

At first the Sisters cared only for women who were mostly bedridden with little hope of recovery, but by 1864 they could no longer ignore the great need to tend sick men. At this time there was very little health care for men and the Sisters found that many were being discharged as incurable from London hospitals such as the Brompton Chest Hospital, and were taking to the roads as tramps because they had nowhere to go. In 1864 a cottage in Bexley Terrace was taken for men both convalescent and incurable, thanks to the help of a Clewer Associate who, assisted by her own maid, nursed many of the worst cases. Two adjoining cottages were added and cases were received from the London hospitals.

The cottage accommodation was vastly inadequate and it was decided that a purpose-built hospital must be provided as soon as possible. A Council was appointed on similar lines to that of the House of Mercy and doubtless the members felt that their opinion was absolute. The project was costly, but there was no time to be lost: Mother Harriet was a woman of faith who saw each new project as an act of faith. Therefore, when no member of the Council would sign the builder's contract because there was still a deficit of £7,000 on the building fund, she was as Carter later recalled, "greatly roused, and, finding no other means available, herself signed the contract …" The Community *Annals* record the event as taking place on May 11th 1865. The hospital was of great interest to Mother Harriet and she personally visited the best London hospitals so that she would know how that at Clewer should be equipped. No doubt it was her indefatigable enthusiasm which inspired the Archbishop of Canterbury (Charles Longley) to convene a meeting in London on July 1st 1865 to raise funds for the hospital. Four days later Bishop Wilberforce came to Clewer for the annual Commemoration Day and laid the foundation stone of the hospital.

St Andrew's Convalescent Hospital was opened by Bishop Wilberforce on St Andrew's Day (November 30th) 1866. It was situated in Hatch Lane opposite St John's Home and was designed by Henry Woodyer in the same style as the Home and the House of Mercy. The ground surrounding it was also acquired and over the next few years this was landscaped into a pleasant, tree-filled garden where the patients could take their exercise.

At first the hospital catered for men and women only but it was soon realised that sick children needed care too. To this end the roof space was converted into a children's ward, but it was inconvenient, being too hot in the summer and freezing cold in the winter. Also, many of the children were severely disabled and had to be carried up and down stairs which proved an arduous business. So it was an occasion of great joy when an anonymous benefactor gave the money for the building of a children's ward which was duly opened and blessed on November 18th 1875 by the new Bishop of Oxford, John Fielder Mackarness.

This new wing, consisting of children's ward and day ward, was a great asset, but the hospital still lacked a refectory and a chapel. The patients had to eat their meals in the dispensary where the odious smell of medicine must have been off-putting. However, there seemed little hope of further building because all funds were needed to keep the precarious finances afloat. But in 1879 a generous donation by the Revd Alfred Gurney, Vicar of St Barnabas Pimlico, and himself a Clewer Associate, in memory of his three sisters who were drowned in the Nile, enabled the work to begin. The completed building was blessed by the Bishop of Oxford on St Andrew's Day 1880. Further smaller additions followed: in 1888 the St Barnabas ward for incurable men; and an observation ward in the garden where suspected cases of infectious diseases such as scarlet fever were kept. Opening out of the St Barnabas ward was the 'Queen's Room' containing a bed endowed by Queen Victoria. In addition to this the Queen made an annual subscription of 20 guineas.

The hospital when completed was an impressive Gothic revival building in red brick with stone dressings, although it must be said that it looked more like a convent than a hospital. The new wing had cost £6,000 and the first floor chapel was more like a full scale parish church, complete with a font for the Baptism of patients. For many, a stay in the hospital was their first taste of religious influence, and whilst some tolerated rather than enjoyed the frequent services, others asked for instruction in the Christian faith. Beneath the chapel was the dining room, which with its vaulted roof gave the impression of being in a church crypt. But it was a vast improvement on the previous arrangement. Judging from contemporary photographs, the wards look rather cluttered with heavy furniture, but the men's ward (Bethany) had bright covers on the beds, and the women's ward (St Cross) had screens to give some privacy. All had characteristic dark paint and high windows, but the overall impression is of basic comfort.

St Andrew's was by definition a convalescent hospital, which is to say that it was not equipped for, nor did it carry out, any surgical operations. But the patients were often far from convalescent, indeed many were terminally ill. The commonest illnesses affecting patients were tuberculosis, especially of the hips and lungs (otherwise called consumption or phthisis), debility (possibly what is known in the 21st century as ME or Chronic Fatigue Syndrome), bronchitis and respiratory disorders, influenza and rheumatism. Many of the illnesses are now known to have been caused by poor nutrition and living conditions, and likewise many cases of consumption may have really been cancer. Very few cancer patients were cared for, chiefly because it was difficult to diagnose (X-rays were not discovered until 1896), and the illness may have been diagnosed as something else. After the implementation of antisepsis in surgery from the 1880s onwards it became easier to treat cancer surgically. Although operations were not performed at Clewer many patients came there to recover from them.

As with most voluntary hospitals St Andrew's catered mainly for the poor, who would be unable to afford private nursing care at home. From the very beginning it relied on philanthropy in order to pay its way. Money came in mostly through subscriptions and donations submitted by the wealthy. The Sisters themselves gave generously and the House of Mercy paid an annual sum for the upkeep of the Good Shepherd ward, a branch of the women's ward set aside especially for the penitents. Admission was by a complicated system. A subscriber would be entitled to a certain number of admission letters annually depending on the generosity of their subscription. A sick person would obtain an admission letter from a subscriber which would admit them to the hospital for three weeks, though this could be extended and many stayed several months. In reality the subscriptions never covered the costs sufficiently so that from the earliest days patients had to make a payment. In 1867 men paid 9/- per week, women 8/-, a nursing mother 10/-, and children under 14 years 5/-. In addition, patients were expected to pay their own travelling expenses and the cost of their laundry. But for cases of real hardship there were a number of 'free' beds. Two local doctors gave their services free.

There were some cases which were inadmissible. In 1867 these were people recovering from smallpox, scarlet fever and whooping cough; those of unsound mind; epileptics; those affected with any contagious disease; women in advanced pregnancy; and so-called 'idiot' children. (Once again, the lack of any distinction between mental illness and other types of learning difficulties comes to the fore.) As time went by fairly stringent rules were applied regarding personal cleanliness upon admission, many of the poorest cases having been found to be verminous. The problem of infectious and contagious diseases was chronic especially in the children's ward. Should measles, whooping cough, scarlet fever or anything similar be introduced then it meant the wholesale closure of the ward, followed by fumigation. Sometimes this happened more than once in a year.

April 1893 saw a severe outbreak of smallpox within the parish of Clewer. A male patient at the hospital developed the illness and subsequently died; the other patients were evacuated and no other cases developed so the hospital was declared out of quarantine by the Sanitary Authority. But no workman would go in to disinfect it. Meanwhile, other cases broke out in the parish including at St Augustine's Home. Cases continued to break out and as there was no isolation hospital the Rector (the Revd Roland Errington) allowed some marquees to be erected on his glebe field. Crockery and medication were sent from the hospital; this was broken up and buried when the epidemic ended at the end of August and was rediscovered in 1978 by Nicholas and Michael Shaw, sons of the then Rector, the Revd Denis Shaw. Crockery bearing the X symbol of St Andrew, and bottles containing coal tar for the relief of the patients' sores were deposited in the Clewer museum and following the museum's closure were placed in the Windsor and Royal Borough Collection.

In 1867–8 the total number of beds was sixty-four, ie twenty-four men, twenty women, twenty children, and altogether 394 patients were cared for during the year, ie 150 men, 129 women and 115 children. By 1878 there was accommodation for ninety-two patients, ie twenty-four men, twenty-eight women, thirty-nine children and one invalid Sister, and the annual turnover had increased to 656. By 1900, 732 patients had been cared for during the year, ie 269 men, 293 women and 170 children. Patients came not only from the local area but also from the large London hospitals who would not admit long-term cases. For many the only alternative would have been the Workhouse.

In 1889 St Joseph's ward was opened at St Andrew's Hospital as an Infirmary for up to nine Sisters because the original Infirmary at the House of Mercy had proved inconvenient. This first Infirmary was typical of Henry Woodyer's 'picturesque' but often impractical style. It may be seen in the illustration on page 147, marked 'M', to the left of the chapel. The only access was by a spiral staircase in a turret and it was soon discovered that it was almost impossible to remove deceased Sisters in a seemly manner! Indeed there was only one staircase where this could be achieved and this became known amongst the Sisters as the 'coffin staircase'! Late 20th century visitors and retreatants would use this wide staircase (which encircled the water tower) to gain access to the 'east wing' where they were accommodated.

It is difficult to assess the standard of nursing care given at St Andrew's Hospital. Standards were improving in nursing throughout the last half of the 19th century so that before 1900 it was becoming a recognised profession even though the Nurses' Registration Act was not passed until 1919. Secular nurses were not employed at St Andrew's, but by the 1890s the Community had acknowledged the requirement for an acceptable standard of training. In October 1894 Sr Blanche Annie went to University College Hospital to be trained in nursing; in May 1899 Sr Laura Jane and Sr Carolina went to London to attend lectures on dispensing, and received certificates. February 1900 saw the return of Sr Edith Emily from Guy's Hospital where she had been for a year's training.

All in all, St Andrew's Hospital provided as high a degree of care as was possible for the sick poor, but the work did not stop there. Other hospitals and convalescent homes at Torquay, Gloucester and Folkestone also came under the Sisterhood as the century progressed. Of these, St Andrew's Convalescent Home, Folkestone, was the more closely related to the work at Clewer. It was founded in May 1875 by an Associate, a Mrs Dawson, in two houses in Guildhall Street and was supervised by the Sisters in connection with St Andrew's Hospital, Clewer. Fifteen women and twelve men were accommodated and very soon larger premises were needed.

The Earl of Radnor granted a site on a long lease on the East Cliff overlooking the harbour, and the new Home was built there. The foundation stone was laid by HRH the Duchess of Edinburgh on April 18th 1882 and the completed buildings were opened and blessed on April 21st 1884. The new buildings cost £16,000 of which £7,000 was given by Mrs Dawson and a friend. The Home was completed by the addition of a large chapel which was made possible by some generous legacies, and it was dedicated by the Archbishop of Canterbury (E W Benson), who was also the Visitor, in January 1890. Also in 1890, a benefactor made it possible to purchase the land on which the Home was built.

St Andrew's Home, Folkestone, was run on exactly the same lines as its sister-home at Clewer. It enjoyed the special Patronage of Their Royal Highnesses the Prince and Princess Christian of Schleswig-Holstein, and the Princess in particular took a special interest in the work. The Home was larger than that at Clewer: in 1876, 290 patients were taken, ie ninety-seven men and 193 women; in 1887, 1,428 were taken, ie 495 men, 706 women and 227 children; and in 1900, 2,182 were taken, ie 799 men, 898 women, 109 boys (in a neighbouring house) and 376 children. Admission methods and rules were the same as at Clewer but by 1899 so many advanced consumptive cases were being sent that it became necessary to refuse admission for fear of spreading the disease.

Three closely related Convalescent Homes at Torquay were undertaken by the Clewer Community, starting with St Raphael's Home in 1866. This had been founded and worked by two ladies for female patients, but after some years they asked the Clewer Sisters to take it over. They accepted the offer and moved to larger premises; within two years they had outgrown the house and finally moved to Higher Lincombe Hill in May 1868. Additions were made, notably the chapel in 1873, and in 1875 the freehold of the property was obtained. This was a small Home with accommodation for twenty-seven in small dormitories and ten single rooms. In addition to the poor, ladies of moderate means were also taken.

In 1883 a gift from an Associate made possible the building of St Luke's Lodge, later known as St Luke's Home, for consumptive men. This was in the same grounds as St Raphael's but quite separate, although the two Homes shared the same chapel. About eighteen men were accommodated in this home overlooking the sea.

It had become increasingly difficult to take consumptive cases as well as general convalescent cases, and so it was decided to take only the latter at St Raphael's and St Luke's. Consequently in 1892, through the generosity of Sr Elizabeth, St Barnabas' Home was opened about ten minutes' walk away from the other two homes. This specialised in advanced cases of consumption and took thirty patients: sixteen men and fourteen women. They were able to remain there until they died. (Thus the Clewer Sisters anticipated the modern hospice movement.)

In 1866 Thomas Gambier Parry, squire of Highnam near Gloucester, founded St Lucy's Hospital at Kingsholme on the outskirts of the city, in memory of his daughter, Lucy. The foundation stone was laid in March 1866 and the building was completed in August 1867. At first the children were cared for by the Sisters of St Lucy, a Religious Community founded by Gambier Parry as a nursing Order in 1864. By 1872 the small Community had failed to flourish, there being only three Sisters, and in that year he invited the Clewer Sisters to run this hospital which was solely for sick children. The Community readily agreed and three Sisters were sent to reside there. (Two of the St Lucy's Sisterhood subsequently joined the Community of St John Baptist and the other one left. It is not clear whether the former St Lucy's Sisters were amongst those CSJB Sisters who worked at St Lucy's.)

Both boys and girls between the ages of 2–10 years were admitted; and 2–12 years in the out-patients' department. It was a small hospital consisting of three wards with eight cots or beds in each. Children were received who were suffering from any disease except the usual infectious ones, and were admitted from any part of England. Children's hospitals were still few and far between especially in country areas (Great Ormond Street hospital had only been founded in 1853). St Lucy's hospital was entirely free and likewise the doctors gave their services free. Nurses were trained at St Lucy's and in addition to helping in the wards were sent out to nurse in patients' homes on request. Ladies wishing to train lived in the hospital and were called 'lady pupils'.

Many of the children's illnesses were directly related to their impoverished backgrounds, such as nutritional deficiencies and bone diseases. In addition to the hospital there was a thriving out-patients' department where medical cases were seen twice a week and surgical cases once a week without charge. In 1882 152 children passed through St Lucy's, forty-eight of whom were from Gloucester itself. Of these, sixty-seven were medical and eighty-five surgical: seventy-one were cured, fifty-three relieved, five died and twenty-three were still on the books at the end of the year. Between 1867 and 1883, 2,202 in-patients were admitted and 11,237 out-patients received treatment.

Before leaving Gloucester, mention must be made of the role played by the Sisters in the smallpox epidemic of 1895–6. In March 1896 Sr Annie Constance and Sr Anna Frances, both from St Lucy's Home, together with two nurses from St Lucy's Hospital, went to take charge of the temporary hospital at Hempsted near Gloucester which had been established for the smallpox victims. Conditions were appalling; the Sisters, arriving at 11.30 am, were informed the first patients would arrive at 3.30 pm! The floors were thick with mud, bedsteads and bedding were piled everywhere and the buildings were little more than wooden shells with tin roofs. There was no drainage of any kind and no water supply except that brought by the water cart which was often too muddy for use.

The first month was an endurance test with the Sisters and nurses working from 6.00 am until 11.00 pm. Fitful sleep was taken in relays and there was barely time for food. The disease was alarming especially when accompanied by delirium; deaths were frequent, and it was difficult to treat the living due to the limited water supply. Towards the end of March things began to improve slightly: a new doctor from Guy's Hospital was appointed who introduced changes including disinfecting the blankets and clothing of the victims.

The Sisters worked in the temporary hospital at Hempsted and in the infectious diseases hospital at Stroud Road, Gloucester for just over six weeks, and the epidemic itself lasted for about five months. The idea of nursing smallpox victims seems horrific, but for members of Victorian Religious Communities it was part and parcel of daily life. Infectious diseases were far more rampant then than now, due to bad drainage, impure water supplies and a general ignorance of the nature and causes of disease. Rich and poor were equally at risk: even Prince Albert had died of typhoid fever due to the bad drainage at Windsor Castle. To be a Sister meant taking all this in one's stride, especially if sent out on parish mission work. With that in mind it is now time to consider aspects of mission work.

7

A CAKE OF SOAP AND THE CATECHISM

The thirty years between 1860 and 1890 saw a rapid increase in the Community, and consequently in the number of its works. At the time of Mother Harriet's resignation as Superior there were 138 Sisters, choir and lay: by 1890 this had increased to 244. As the Community grew, so did its reputation, and this was due in no small way to the magnetism of Harriet Monsell. Even after her death in 1883 the Community still bore her hallmark and women joined in their dozens. But the influence of the Clewer Sisters spread farther afield than those offering themselves for the Religious Life. Many people were drawn to become Associates; there are no accurate figures but they ran into hundreds. There were always well over 500 people present on Commemoration Day in the 1880s. So it is not surprising that the Clewer Sisters should have been inundated with requests from parishes to do mission work. Nor is it surprising that such parishes should become 'Clewer centres' with a wide variety of work being undertaken.

Two of the smaller Community works grew up very close to each other in Clewer, and indeed the second grew out of the first. In 1861 Lady Charlotte Greville opened a house in the parish of St Barnabas Pimlico, for invalid ladies in reduced circumstances. She asked the Clewer Community to run it, but in 1863 the work was removed to a cottage in Clewer. In 1868 St Andrew's Cottage, adjoining the grounds of St Andrew's Convalescent Hospital, was bought by the Ladies Charlotte and Louisa Greville, and given to the Community. Sr Mary Ashpitel of the Second Order presided over this work, and in 1878 it changed from caring for invalid ladies to those in work needing rest and change.

Inspired by this work, Sr Mary Ashpitel then proceeded to build twelve almshouses and a lodge which she very confusingly called St Andrew's Cottages. They were originally intended for both sexes, but were subsequently made into homes for thirteen ladies, rent free. She was assisted in the work by her friend Charlotte Sterky, a Clewer Associate, who took charge after Sr Mary Ashpitel's death in 1892. These almshouses were built immediately in front of St Andrew's Hospital and all funeral cortèges from the hospital had to pass through, hence the wide entrance.

The first invitation to work outside the parish of Clewer came to the Sisterhood in 1859. This was from the vicar of St Paul's Knightsbridge, the Revd the Hon Robert Liddell, for the Sisters to work in the district served by the new daughter church of St Barnabas Pimlico. Although Knightsbridge was wealthy and fashionable, the area around St Barnabas was full of the worst slums and poverty. The new church had, just a few years before, witnessed ugly rioting provoked by fanatics protesting about the elaborate ritual introduced when the church was opened, so that it had acquired a certain notoriety. Notwithstanding this, Mother Harriet did not decline the invitation to work there, and Sr Katherine Mary became Sister-in-Charge.

The Sisters' mission house was in Bloomfield Place, near the church. Here in January 1860 St John's School was opened. Originally intended as a day school for middle-class girls, it had become a boarding school for young ladies by the autumn and was an immediate success. But the premises were inadequate despite expanding into the adjoining houses, and so in the summer of 1877 the school was removed to Hamilton Terrace in St John's Wood, which was a more affluent area. In addition to the general curriculum the girls were taught English and French, and at extra cost, music, drawing, dancing, singing, German and Italian. In 1882 the general fee was 80 guineas a year, or 4 guineas a term for day girls. A further move was made in the summer of 1899 when the school removed to King Henry's Road, South Hampstead. From 1861 until 1875 St John's School was the venue for the Clewer Associates' retreat, after which time it was transferred to St Stephen's College, Clewer. (Retreats were another of the fruits of the Oxford Movement which were pioneered in the wider Church by Carter and others; Clewer Associates were early beneficiaries of this new form of spirituality.)

The work in Pimlico embraced the whole social strata from the young ladies of St John's School, to the waifs and strays of St Barnabas Orphanage and the 'fallen women' of the Stone House Refuge. The orphanage has been referred to in chapter 5 and the Refuge in chapter 4 and need not be reiterated. In addition to all this there was the normal work of a parish mission, which in this case was centred on the Sisters' house in Bloomfield Place. This involved visiting from house to house especially among the sick and poor, instructing and catechising both children and adults, running parish groups known as guilds, and generally taking every opportunity to spread the Gospel and minister to the needy.

In an age when there was no ready-made entertainment such as TV, parish guilds provided a much needed haven away from overcrowded dwellings where the only alternative was the beer house or the streets. The guilds had various names but they all had a strong devotional content, and there was also an important social element. There were 'treats' at Christmas and outings in the summer which were looked forward to all year round at a time when the poor had little at the best of times and not much more at Christmas. All in all, parish guilds helped keep young girls away from vice, and boys and young men away from crime; they helped foster the Temperance Movement, and there was often a savings scheme which helped hard-pressed mothers keep the family reasonably well clothed and shod, or provide a few extras at Christmas. The parish guilds were an integral part of Victorian church life and wherever Sisterhoods worked they were involved in their organisation.

The Clewer Sisterhood undertook work in two other London parishes in the 1860s: St Mary's Soho in 1860 and St Alban's Holborn in 1869. St Mary's Crown Street, Soho, was in one of the worst slum areas behind Oxford Street near the area known as Seven Dials. By the kindness of Charles Randall of Hawley, the Community was able to obtain 9 Rose Street, Soho as their mission house. (This also served as a home for girls as noted in chapter 5.) An important work in its own right began at Rose Street in the form of the Church Workroom. By the 1860s a large-scale transformation in liturgy and worship was taking place, and once drab church interiors now became a blaze of coloured banners and altar frontals. During these years the Church of England rediscovered the use of ceremonial especially in the Eucharist and this was accompanied by the revival of vestments. It was against this background that the Church Workroom earned a worldwide reputation, much of the delicate embroidery being designed by Charles Eamer Kempe, the well known artist and stained glass designer. In March 1869 the Church Workroom was removed to 36 Soho Square and in 1883 it removed to Gower Street where it stayed until 1927 before finally moving to Clewer.

In 1860 the Clewer Sisterhood became responsible for the running of the House of Charity in Greek Street off Soho Square. This had been founded in 1846, its original premises being 9 Rose Street, and it was when it moved to Greek Street that Charles Randall obtained the old premises for the Sisters. The House of Charity catered for respectable people of both sexes who had fallen upon hard times and might otherwise face destitution.

Servants who were between situations, school masters and governesses, self-employed craftsmen and tradesmen in financial straits, out-patients undergoing treatment at the London hospitals, families awaiting emigration were all eligible for help at the House of Charity. 'Fallen cases' were not admissible. There was nowhere else like it, for which reason there was always a great demand for admission. The Gladstones had a special interest in the work and in 1862 Catherine Gladstone laid the foundation stone of the chapel. It was to the Home at 9 Rose Street, not the House of Charity in Greek Street that Gladstone took some of his rescue cases. The casebooks of the House of Charity record many admissions on the recommendation of the Gladstones but none of these were so-called 'fallen cases'. (The chapel of the House of Charity was damaged during World War II, all the stained glass windows being lost. They were replaced with new windows by John Hayward, one of which depicts St John Baptist holding the chapel at Clewer.)

Although the Clewer Sisters had been present in the parish of St Mary's Crown Street, Soho, since 1860, the actual parish mission work had been conducted by another Community (the Society of St Margaret whose mother house was at East Grinstead). After they withdrew, the Revd John Chambers asked the Clewer Sisters to undertake this in addition to the work already being done by them. This was in 1871 and at first all the extra work was conducted from Rose Street. However, this proved too much and a house was taken in Deane Street from which all the guilds, visiting, Mothers' Meetings, Sunday Schools and Bible Classes were conducted. Chambers died in 1874 and the Community withdrew following changes introduced by his successor. But in 1889 the work was resumed. Much had changed for the better in the intervening years, many of the worst slums having been cleared and wide thoroughfares such as Charing Cross Road and Shaftesbury Avenue built in their place, together with new model dwellings. The parishioners now consisted of people largely employed in 'theatreland' or in the numerous restaurants which were springing up to feed hungry theatre-goers. Although these were good, hard-working people, they were largely indifferent to religion and the mission of the Church, so that the work was not without difficulties.

In 1869 the Clewer Sisters were able to respond to the request made by the Revd A H Mackonochie to work permanently in the parish of St Alban's Holborn. (Some temporary work had been undertaken from Soho since

1867.) St Alban's was founded by the Rt Hon J G Hubbard, MP (later Lord Addington) and was consecrated in 1863 with Mackonochie as its first Vicar. Hubbard was an old friend of Mother Harriet and had accompanied her on that sad journey back to England following Charles Monsell's death early in 1851. So perhaps it is not surprising that having decided to seek the help of Sisters in the parish, the Clewer Community should be chosen. A further link with Clewer was forged in 1878 when Hubbard's daughter joined the Community as Sr Lucy Marian. She was professed in November 1880 and died in November 1893. (Sr Margery CSJB was Mary Margaret Hubbard before joining the Community but was not a daughter of J G Hubbard, though she may have been a niece or cousin.)

Whilst the Community never went to ritualistic extremes in the chapel at Clewer, it was associated through mission work with some of the most advanced Anglo-Catholic churches in the country. From the very start, St Alban's Holborn was characterised by the advanced ceremonial which marked the second generation of the Oxford Movement, and which was to provoke angry protests from those who thought this signalled a Romeward direction in the revival. Indeed so vehement were these protesters that they eventually forced Mackonochie's resignation in 1882. The Community took up the work in earnest from the mission house in Greville Street which had been acquired in February 1869, and all the familiar activities of parish mission work—guilds, Mothers' Meetings, Bible Classes, soup kitchens, 'sick dinners', Bands of Hope—were conducted from there. The work soon outgrew the premises so that it became necessary to move, and a new mission house was taken in Baldwin's Gardens, near the church, from 1872–90. In 1880 a school building opposite the mission house was also taken and became known as St John Baptist House. A further move was made in 1896 to 26 Gray's Inn Road, following the demolition of the Baldwin's Gardens premises.

The area around St Alban's was mostly slums, though as the century progressed the worst of these were replaced by model dwellings. A feature of the Sisters' mission work here was that of nursing the sick poor. In 1875 a trained secular nurse came to reside with the Sisters, and when she left others followed so that a system of visiting and nursing the sick in the parish was evolved. Every morning and evening saw the mission house crowded with both adults and children waiting to have their sores, wounds and burns dressed, and to obtain simple medication. This was done in co-operation with the local doctors. There was also a scheme for providing 'sick dinners' for the sick poor, and also 'destitute dinners'. The latter were financed by businessmen who divided the funds between the poorest parishes. By 1884, sixty to seventy 'destitute dinners' were being provided in St Alban's parish twice a week.

On March 9th 1899 a serious fire broke out in a factory near the church and for some time it looked as though all would be lost. Thanks to the efforts of 100 firemen and twenty-nine engines the church escaped destruction though there was damage to the roof and clerestory. St Alban's Holborn was perhaps the most important of the Community's works in London and was not given up until 1955, before which time the Sisters were to see an even more disastrous fire during the Blitz, of which more later.

But London was not the only setting for the Community's missionary endeavours; in 1863 a work was begun much nearer home which was to develop into the new parish of Clewer St Stephen. A number of the Clewer works have become synonymous with a particular Sister, Clewer St Stephen being from the very beginning closely linked with Sr Emily. She was the daughter of an Evangelical clergyman who, while consenting to her joining the Clewer Community, made it a condition that she should not become a professed choir Sister in his lifetime. For this reason she was received as a novice of the Second Order. Following her father's death she was admitted to the First Order in February 1863 and was professed as a choir Sister on St Andrew's Day 1864, aged 29 years. During 1863, while she was still a choir novice, the Rector of Clewer, T T Carter, asked the Community for help evangelising the slum district of Clewer Fields.

This poor district of Clewer parish was the same area from which Mariquita Tennant's first penitents had been rescued in 1849, and Carter, together with his curates, had tried, mostly in vain, to spread the Gospel there. Mother Harriet's brother-in-law, Charles Harris, had held Sunday afternoon services in the open air, standing on a tub to preach, but met with little success. In 1863 Carter obtained the use of a room in a cottage in which he held a weekly evening service, and Sr Emily decided to start a ragged school in the room in the daytime.

This was easier said than done: the room was bare except for a stove, and she had first to encourage some children to join her. She sat in the room until a curious child came in: then she washed the child, whilst its equally curious friend looked on in the doorway. The friend came in too and the process was repeated until she had seven sitting around her on the floor. Her questions brought some shocking replies, for she discovered that these dirty, bedraggled waifs usually slept rough, ate what they could forage and had no one to look after them properly. And of course they had no idea of God or religion, though some had heard of the devil! The *St John Baptist Magazine* of Easter 1884 tells us: "Boys and girls were equally ragged, equally shock headed, equally barefooted and used equally bad language." The story is told of how Carter and Mother Harriet visited the ragged school one day, and while Sr Emily went to the door to receive them, the scholars took fright and ran away through the back door. To Sr Emily's dismay the visitors were confronted by a row of empty seats!

From this small beginning the ragged school grew and flourished. A certain amount of slum clearance had begun at the same time so that the general tone of the area began to be raised and gradually the children became less rough. A room was taken for the school in newly built Bexley Street, and then in 1866 the work took a wholly new turn. Two Associates gave sums of money for the purchase of a site for a mission house with space to build a permanent church later. Work began at once. The foundation stone was laid by Carter on July 3rd 1867 and the Clewer St Stephen mission house was solemnly opened and blessed by him on October 29th 1868.

The ragged school was now transferred to the new mission house, though it was hardly ragged by this time. The classrooms on the upper floor were fitted out as a temporary chapel until the first part of the church was built in 1870. The school was by now catering for a very mixed clientele, and some of the older girls were taken in as 'industrial' girls and taught laundry work and housework, but this proved difficult due to lack of funds to buy equipment. Meanwhile, a number of requests had been received from clergy and professional men for the Sisters to educate their daughters, and from this time onwards the school gradually developed into a fee-paying college for young ladies. It was hoped that the fees would also help to support the poorer scholars. There was a fee of 6d a week for the under 8s and 1/- for over 8s and the girls boarded at the mission house.

The 1870 Education Act brought elementary education for all, and between 1872–7 the parochial National Schools for boys, girls and infants were built. (The National Schools were Church of England schools as opposed to Council run schools.) The Sisters helped fund these by going far and wide on begging trips. In this way it became possible to separate the young ladies' college from the parochial schools. The former became known as St Stephen's College and catered for the daughters of professional men. So successful was it that in 1876 a new wing (the west wing) was added to the mission house, to be followed in 1884 by a large new east wing consisting of schoolrooms and dormitories.

In 1870 a generous benefactor gave £1,000 which enabled work to proceed on the permanent church. Services at the mission chapel had flourished under the new Priest-in-Charge, the Revd George Davenport Nicholas, formerly curate of Clewer. Nicholas was a strict disciplinarian, a man of fixed and firm views, who did not welcome the presence of Sisters. Nevertheless the Sisters were there, and indeed had been there longer than he had (his time as Priest-in-Charge dates from the blessing of the mission in October 1868). Sr Emily was quite as strong-willed and determined as he, so that life was turbulent at times.

On July 25th 1871 the chancel of St Stephen's church was solemnly opened at a High Mass during which the celebrant (G D Nicholas) wore a linen chasuble. From the start advanced ritual, including the wearing of Eucharistic vestments, was a feature of the church, but except for some caustic comments from time to time in the *Windsor and Eton Express* no one objected. The church, like the mission house, was designed by Henry Woodyer, so that there were now two great centres of Woodyer's architecture in Clewer. But the building was incomplete, consisting as it did of the chancel and a temporary nave. It seemed as though it would have to stay that way as there was no money available to complete the building. Also the Rector, T T Carter, had been ordered abroad to recuperate from a serious illness following the death of his wife, and he was away in Italy for almost two years. In his absence responsibility for the parish fell to his curates, of whom Nicholas was the senior. Although Nicholas was Priest-in-Charge of St Stephen's it was still part of Clewer parish at this time.

But then two generous gifts of £3,000 and £1,000 from Mother Harriet and others enabled the work to proceed. The newly completed church was opened on September 24th 1874 and was consecrated on December 22nd by Bishop Mackarness. A year earlier Nicholas had been instituted to the

Perpetual Curacy of the new parish and the Patronage of the church was vested in Carter, Harriet Monsell, Ellen Nixon (Sr Ellen CSJB), the Revd W H Hutchings (Sub-Warden of the Clewer House of Mercy), and Brownlow Edward Layard. The splendid new church must have brought great joy to Carter, who was home in time for the opening. But the greatest debt of all was owed to Sr Emily, whose missionary zeal, while still a novice, had started the whole great work.

The work of parish and schools at St Stephen's went side by side and both flourished. The Sisters began running all the usual guilds—Church of England Working Men's Society, Church of England Temperance Society, guilds for boys, girls and young women, married women, Mothers' Meetings, Bible Classes, Maternity Societies—all of which soon thrived. But beyond doubt their speciality lay in the schools. Because of difficulties with Fr Nicholas they were not greatly involved with the National Schools, which were the parish schools, but instead concentrated on developing St Stephen's College and St Stephen's High School, which grew out of it, and which were the Community's own foundations.

From the beginning St Stephen's College was intended for boarders only and by 1884 there were seventy-five. It was entirely the Community's foundation, though there were some secular masters and mistresses. School life was very closely bound up with the church, attendance at the Eucharist on Sundays, holy days and throughout Holy Week being obligatory. From 1876 an annual retreat was arranged, and in the course of time former pupils also attended it. By 1895 the age-range catered for was 5–20, the top class being educated to Matriculation standard. The College was always very cramped in its premises at Clewer, which soon after World War I led to its removal to Folkestone, of which there will be more in chapter 15.

In the early days of the College there was an increasing demand for provision for day scholars, and so from 1877 the work was divided into two branches. But it was not until 1882 that Sr Emily appointed Miss du Pré as Head Mistress, and from this time the High School flourished. Another who was closely associated with the High School from this time onwards was Sr Miriam. Because it was a day school the fees were lower than at the College, but both schools catered for the same type of girl: the daughters of clergy and professional men. Many girls were local, whereas the College pupils tended to come from farther afield. At first the High School used a room above the National School, but as numbers grew a building of its own became necessary. This was completed opposite the College in 1889. But as the school developed its own separate identity, so the need for a house for boarders was discerned. Consequently St Margaret's was acquired in 1889, and by 1891 there were more than 100 day girls and fifty-four boarders at St Stephen's High School. The rules were similar for both College and High School, but there was great rivalry amongst the pupils of the two establishments.

By the turn of the century, Clewer St Stephen was at the centre of a hive of activity which quite made up for the smallness of the parish. Fr Nicholas was still vicar and Sr Emily was still Sister-in-Charge, and she remained so until 1902. The church attracted an eclectic congregation from far and wide who loved the Anglo-Catholic worship. But more important than that, the church attracted its own parishioners who, though not living in the abject poverty of the Clewer Fields of Mrs Tennant's time, were still poor. The late 1860s and 1870s had seen the worst slums cleared away and terraces of artisans' dwellings put in their place. Those who lived there responded to the ritual of St Stephen's, for there they saw colour and beauty in worship, and heard choral music for perhaps the first time in their lives. By the turn of the century over 1,000 children were being educated under the umbrella of St Stephen's, at the College, High School and National Schools, and all were regular worshippers. The work had come a long way from the ragged school in Clewer Fields.

Notes

For more information about the foundation of Clewer St Stephen, see: Valerie Bonham, "From rags to ritual: the early years of Clewer St Stephen" in *Windlesora* No 11, (the journal of the Windsor Local History Group), Windsor 1992.

For an account of life at St Stephen's College in the 1890s, see Mary MacCarthy, *A Nineteenth Century Childhood*. First published 1924; new edition: Constable 1985 ISBN 0 09 465900 1. Now o/p but copies are available second hand. Mary MacCarthy's father was Vice-Provost of Eton and she attended St Stephen's College, which she called Marsh College, for four terms. Unfortunately she also changed the names of the priest and the Sisters. The priest may be Fr Nicholas, but may also be one of his curates.

But the "old, old Sister Superior, who very rarely appeared before us …"
is beyond doubt Sr Emily who came to wish the girls "A happy Easter, my
children." Mary MacCarthy's account is typical of a homesick child in her
early days at boarding school—not over enthusiastic, but not hating it either!
She refers to the Clewer Sisters as 'Sisters of Mercy', but this should not
be confused with the Irish Roman Catholic order whose proper name was
the Sisters of Mercy.

The definitive history of St Stephen's College is: Jenny Balston, *The Story
of St Stephen's College*, 1994, published by The Old St Stephenites' Society. See
the website www.ststephensbroadstairs.org.uk/ for details of how to obtain
the book. It is also available from the Community of St John Baptist—see
their website for contact details: www.csjb.org.uk

8

THE GOSPEL, GUILDS AND GUARDSMEN

There were several other parishes besides Clewer St Stephen where the Sisters worked prior to a church being built, the first of which was in Folkestone. From 1867 the Sisters had worked for a time in St Peter's Mission, but this does not seem to have lasted long. The work properly dates from 1875 with the commencement not only of St Andrew's Convalescent Home, but also of St Eanswyth's mission.

St Eanswyth's was named after one of the patron saints of the parish church and was opened in August 1875, followed by a larger, more convenient house in April 1877. The work grew and followed the usual pattern: parish visiting, a middle-class school, an infants' school and crèche, and parish guilds. In 1875 Mother Harriet resigned as Superior due to failing health and soon afterwards came to Folkestone together with a Sister companion. A house was taken on the Bale not far from the mission and her remaining years were spent there (see chapter 11). But she still took great interest in the Community work although her active days had passed. It was partly through her that a much greater work grew out of St Eanswyth's mission.

The vicar of the parish had discussed with Mother Harriet the problem of the rapidly developing area around the junction of the Folkestone–Dover railway, where row upon row of artisans' dwellings had grown up to house the railway workers. But there was no church. Mother Harriet suggested planting a mission there. So it was that in October 1880 a mission cottage was opened, called the Mission of the Holy Saviour. Two Sisters were sent to work there and all the usual activities were begun. They were greatly helped by the Misses Jemmett, one of whom later joined the Community as Sr Caroline Esther, and eventually became Sister-in-Charge. An old bakehouse in Sidney Street was made into a temporary chapel and in 1881 the Revd Claud Hankey was appointed mission priest. Mother Harriet followed the early work with interest and kept a collecting card by her side in order to gather donations from her visitors towards a permanent church.

In 1885 the mission district became a separate parish with the patronage vested in the Archbishop of Canterbury. The Earl of Radnor, who had already granted a site for St Andrew's Convalescent Home, now gave a site for a church (St Saviour) on the understanding that a permanent church be built on it within seven years. An iron church was erected temporarily and in the meantime the Revd Hankey worked hard to establish an endowment for the incumbent's stipend.

Mother Harriet had died in 1883 and it was decided to build the church as a memorial to her and to begin it as soon as £2,000 was in hand. But raising enough money was a painfully slow business because the mission was in a poor area. One method has a familiar ring. The Sisters opened what must have been one of the first charity shops. Called St Saviour's Church Shop, it sold religious books and objects together with new and second-hand clothes. The clothes were all donated and provided a much needed service to the poor, the proceeds being used to finance the parish work and to help the building fund.

Slowly but surely the church became a reality. The *St John Baptist Magazine* for Autumn 1891 remarks, "… very beautiful it will be to those who live to see it finished … May that happy day not be so far off as some desponding souls would have us believe who expected it to rise in a night like Aladdin's palace." But all things come to those who wait, and on May 12th 1891 the foundation stone of the permanent church was laid. A little over a year later, on June 27th 1892, the Bishop of Dover opened the chancel as the first stage of the completed church. At least it was a start and it was just within the seven-year time limit. It was to be another nine years before the church was consecrated on July 25th 1901. Even so, the church was still not complete, with several bays of the aisles together with porches and choir vestry still to be built. The church was not completed until November 1913. There was a last-minute hitch before the church was consecrated when it became known that the Church Association was hatching plans to protest about the Anglo-Catholic worship there, but very little came of it.

Further afield, the 1870s saw the Clewer Sisterhood begin its only major work in Wales. The initial mission work at Newport, Monmouthshire, had already begun before the Sisters were invited to work there. In 1875 a group of laymen had formed themselves into a guild called the Guild of St John Baptist (which was not related in any way to the Clewer Community). They met for prayer fortnightly in a house on Stow Hill, Newport. A wealthy gentleman, Mr F J Mitchell of Llanfrechfa, became their Provost and bought a site on Stow Hill in the parish of St Woolos upon which he hoped to build a church. Soon the Guild outgrew the house and sought other accommodation. At this time they were invited to Barnardtown, a poor district two miles away, with no place of worship. Mr Mitchell wanted to build a church there too but, due to opposition, had to be content with two houses internally adapted which became known as St John the Baptist Mission Room. The first Eucharist was celebrated there on Advent Sunday 1875, and at Evensong nearly 200 people had to be sent away for lack of room.

But Mr Mitchell still owned the site for the proposed church on Stow Hill. In February 1876 he was instrumental in inviting the Clewer Community to undertake mission work in Newport, and in May the vicar of St Woolos consented to the work being based in his parish. Later that year a large brick mission room was built on the Stow Hill site and soon afterwards an iron church called St John Baptist mission church was built near it. This was opened in February 1877 as a chapel of ease to St Woolos, and although the two churches were very close to each other they served different congregations. St Woolos operated the pew rent system which made little provision for the poor who could not afford to pay for their seats, whilst at the mission church the seats were all free. This is why so many Victorian churches were built close to older parish churches, and as long as pew rents existed there was a ready clientele for both types of church.

On March 5th 1877, Sr Selina and Sr Lucy Anne took up the work at Newport and were based in a house near the St John Baptist mission church on Stow Hill. Just as Clewer St Stephen was synonymous with Sr Emily, so Newport was with Sr Selina. The sister of the famous Fr Congreve of the Society of St John the Evangelist (the Cowley Fathers), Sr Selina threw herself, and those who worked with her, wholeheartedly into the work. She was Sister-in-Charge from 1877 until 1909 and was famed for her expertise at begging for money to finance the work! During that time the Sisters embraced all aspects of mission work, but because there were some very poor areas in Newport, there was a special ministry to deprived children. The Children's Refuge, later known as St John Baptist Home, which opened in 1881, has been mentioned in chapter 5 along with some of the ill-treated and abused cases. There were also the 'blue boys and girls'. These children were too poor to come to church and Sunday School, having nothing decent to wear, so they were lent a suit of blue clothes every week to enable them to do so.

At the same time the St John Baptist Mission Room in Barnardtown was flourishing and the Sisters were working there two days a week. This consisted mostly of visiting the poor in their homes. The Sisters taught the women the rudiments of sewing which was an enormous help because hitherto many had had no idea how to make even the simplest clothes. The vicar of the parish of Maindee, which included Barnardtown, approved of the mission and did what he could to support it. There was a good attendance at the mission services, which, under the curate-in-charge the Revd N Y Birkmyre, followed Anglo-Catholic lines and even had a surpliced choir.

Then disaster struck. In 1881 the vicar of Maindee resigned through ill health and his successor, who disapproved of advanced ritual, at once proceeded to disband the mission. Appeals were made to the Bishop of Llandaff but he supported the new incumbent. A Communicants' meeting was held on March 20th at which a Memorial was drawn up in support of the mission, but it was to no avail. The last service was held there on March 27th 1882, after which those who could do so transferred to the Stow Hill mission church. During the four years of its life there had been 296 Baptisms, ninety-seven had been confirmed, there were ninety-four Communicants on the roll, and the Sunday Schools had seventy-seven boys, seventy-four girls and 120 infants. The mission church catered for a district of 2,000 souls and held 130, and was the only church in the area where the seats were free. Notwithstanding all this, the whole work in Barnardtown had ceased by Ascension Day 1882.

The work continued in Newport two miles away, but now difficulties began there too. A change of incumbent at St Woolos brought a vicar who was less sympathetic. This, coupled with a curate-in-charge of the mission church who was more advanced in ritual, brought the threat of closure, and from January until September 1884 things were very difficult indeed. Finally, the curate-in-charge resigned and the work was allowed to continue. In 1897 it was proposed that the mission should vacate the parish of St Woolos and form a new parish of its own in a newly developing part of the town on the Risca Road. Lord Tredegar gave the site for the new church, Mr Mitchell gave the endowment and plans went ahead for the new building.

The foundation stone was laid on June 30th 1898, and on Sunday May 6th 1900 the iron mission church was used for the last time. The new church of St John Baptist, Newport was consecrated on May 7th with mixed emotions: joy at the accomplishment of the new building, and sorrow that the original mission area in the centre of the town had been abandoned. A new mission house was built in 1907 and a High School for girls opened in 1901, of which there will be more in chapter 15.

The 1870s brought the Sisters new work in London. Whenever Southwark is mentioned in connection with Sisterhoods, it is not the Clewer Community which automatically springs to mind but the Community of Reparation to Jesus in the Blessed Sacrament, otherwise known as the Mission Sisters of St Alphege. Devotion to the Blessed Sacrament had increased in the Church of England due to the foundation, by T T Carter and others, of the Confraternity of the Blessed Sacrament in 1862. In 1869 the Revd A B Goulden established a group of Tertiaries to honour the Blessed Sacrament and do mission work, but soon they decided they wanted to become regular Religious. (Tertiaries live according to a religious rule but do not live in a Community.) Consequently, in the early 1870s four of them came to Clewer to serve their noviciate. One transferred to the Clewer Sisterhood, and another died six days after her profession in March 1872. Nevertheless the young Community grew and in 1873 took up work in the district of St Alphege, Southwark, where the Revd Goulden had been appointed mission priest. Their house was in Nelson Square until 1883 when they moved to Blackfriars Road.

A wealthy widow, Mrs Hunt of Godstone in Surrey, had helped in the great London Mission of 1874 and had realised for the first time the depths of abject poverty in which many people lived. She placed a sum of money in the hands of one of the priest-missioners and after consulting Samuel Wilberforce, who was by now Bishop of Winchester and in whose Diocese Southwark was, part of the overcrowded parish of St Saviour's Southwark was chosen as a mission district. In 1874 Mrs Hunt appealed to the Clewer Sisters for help but they were unable to take up the work until 1876, when one or two Sisters went daily from St Alban's Holborn to her house in Nelson Square, close to the CRJBS house.

Mrs Hunt had endowed the new parish of All Hallows, Southwark and the Revd G Berkeley was appointed first incumbent. On the Octave of Epiphany 1876 a shed behind the incumbent's house was opened as the first church. This held 100 people and served for two years until the Ecclesiastical Commissioners sold some land as a site for a permanent church. A new temporary church was built there in 1877. Then, alas, in February 1878 Mrs Hunt died after a very short illness. Shortly before her death she had given her house in Nelson Square to the Clewer Sisters and had returned to Godstone. In May 1877 they moved from this house to a new mission house in Union Street.

An important development of the Clewer Sisters' work in Southwark was the Home for Working Girls in Nelson Square. (In the 21st century a different connotation is attached to the phrase 'working girl', but in the 1870s it meant girls who were in poorly paid employment, often living away from home and who therefore were in moral danger.) The Sisters had realised the plight of these girls through running Sunday afternoon teas at the mission, for which the girls paid 1d. Many were as ill-treated and abused as those who found refuge at the Homes in Gloucester and Newport (see chapter 5). The fact that they were working can be misleading: their jobs did not free them from their deprived backgrounds, but were mostly in badly paid sweated industries. The Home in Nelson Square gave them a secure haven and many were able to improve themselves and eventually take better jobs or go into domestic service. Temporary premises were taken in Union Street and then the site was required for the expansion of Waterloo Station. Finally, in December 1884, 49 Nelson Square was opened for fifty girls working in such diverse employments as cocoa-packing, paper bag making, tie making, mantle making, shirt collar ironing, bonnet box making, spice and powder packing. By the end of the century the Home had expanded and could take over seventy girls. In 1899 a holiday home, St Gabriel's at Littlehampton, was taken and gave much pleasure.

The mission work in Southwark proceeded in the usual way under Sr Isabel Mary, who was Sister Superior from 1880–1914, but the unfinished church of All Hallows proved to be a great trial. Not until the church's consecration could the money in the hands of the Ecclesiastical Commissioners be made available, and the consecration could only take place when the church was completed, so it was a vicious circle. Deprived of the benevolence and enthusiasm of Mrs Hunt, it was a great financial struggle. But slowly progress was made: the foundation stone was laid on May 28th 1879 and the chancel was opened on Christmas Day 1880. It took another twelve years to complete the building, which was consecrated on July 9th 1892, just a fortnight before the chancel of St Saviour's Folkestone was opened. The architect was George Gilbert Scott. Matters had not been made any easier by the efforts of the Church Association against the Anglo-Catholic worship.

From London south of the Thames we now turn to the East End. In Advent 1881 Bishop W Walsham How appealed to public schools and colleges to found and financially support missions in the East London slum parishes. In response the students of Christ Church, Oxford, sent the Revd H L Paget to a new mission district in Poplar, carved out of the parishes of St Michael and All Angels Poplar and All Hallows Bromley-by-Bow. In November 1882 the Revd Paget asked the Clewer Community for help and two Sisters were sent. It was very difficult at first, the East Enders being reluctant to accept the Sisters, but gradually they were won over. Soon the Sisters were running a thriving soup kitchen for the workers at the East India Docks, catering for between 100 and 200 men. In addition, 150 children received ha'penny dinners twice a week, which went some way to warding off malnutrition, which was always a real danger.

There was also another equally sinister danger: drink. "It is the great enemy; our deadliest foe and meets us at every turn," wrote a Sister in the *St John Baptist Magazine* of April 1898. One way to combat the foe was to run Bands of Hope as the junior wing of the Temperance Movement, in the expectation of turning children and young people away from drink before it became a habit. Temperance Societies have tended to form the butt of jokes which reflect our modern misunderstanding of their aims. Perhaps we forget that in Victorian times drink was a social problem comparable with drugs today. Be that as it may, the Bands of Hope at Poplar thrived, numbering 250 children and young people.

The work of the mission progressed and on July 6th 1889 the foundation stone of the permanent church was laid by HRH the Duchess of Albany. It was dedicated to St Frideswide, the patron saint of the college and cathedral of Christ Church, Oxford. A year later, on July 15th 1890, the church was opened. On February 11th 1893 a new mission house for the Sisters' work was opened in the presence of a distinguished company. It had been built by Miss Catherine Phillimore, sister of Sir Walter Phillimore the High Court judge and leading churchman, who was present that day. Mrs Gladstone was also there and presented a golden key to the Revd James Adderley, the Priest-in-Charge.

Similar work was undertaken not far away in Hackney Wick, where

Eton College had established a mission in response to Bishop Walsham How's appeal. The Clewer Chapter accepted the invitation to work there and in November 1883 Sr Catherine went single-handed. She was joined soon afterwards by Sr Elizabeth Constance, a newly professed lay Sister. No records of the work have survived in the Clewer archives, but it must have followed the familiar pattern. On June 18th 1892 the new church of St Mary-of-Eton was consecrated and the Sisters withdrew soon afterwards.

Another London work for which very few records remain is that in the parish of St John's Smith Square, Westminster. It was begun in January 1885 at the invitation of the Revd Charles Wellington Furse (formerly Johnson), Canon of Westminster and former curate of Clewer in the days of Mrs Tennant. The work flourished and by 1888 there were six Sisters there. But in February 1894 Canon Basil Wilberforce, younger son of the late Bishop of Oxford, became vicar. The Community found it impossible to work with him and withdrew from the parish. Work had already begun in the neighbouring parish of St Mary's Vincent Square and this was continued.

St Anne's School, Baltonsborough, near Glastonbury, was a rather short-lived work and one which the Community did not found. Two Associates, the Misses Neville, had founded it as a school for the daughters of clergymen and professional men, and it took both day girls and boarders. In 1868 they had asked the Community to run the school when they eventually became incapable of doing so, and when in 1882 one of them died, the Community took over. The school had been largely subsidised by the foundresses, but the Community were unable to do this and after several years' struggle for existence the school closed in July 1894. It had never flourished, due not only to inadequate funds but also to the small number of pupils.

A late work, but one which flourished, was the mission work in the parish of St Mary and St John Cowley, near Oxford. This was a large artisan parish east of Magdalen Bridge, where the presence of both male and female Religious was already familiar. The Society of St John the Evangelist (the Cowley Fathers) had been founded there in 1865, and the Society of All Saints, had a branch house and hospital for incurables. In July 1890 Sr Cordelia and Sr Catherine Esther went to work in Cowley St John at the invitation of the vicar the Revd W Scott. The population in 1890 was 8,000. So fast was the parish developing with new houses that by 1898 there were over 11,000 living there. Much of the Sisters' work was taken up running schools, there being no Board Schools in Oxford at the time. A great deal of time was also given to providing a meeting place for the girls working in the growing number of factories. The Sisters' mission house was replaced in 1904 by a new building near the church and close to the All Saints Sisters' hospital.

Within the parish of St Mary and St John there was another Clewer work: St Basil's Home for Aged Women, which began in 1891. It served a dual purpose in that while it catered for 'respectable poor' women who might otherwise be forced into the Workhouse, it was also intended as a special work for the growing number of Magdalens at the Manor House at Holywell on the other side of Oxford. Originally it was hoped to run it from the Manor House, but premises near the mission house at Cowley were obtained and opened in 1891. Although there was a Choir Sister in charge of the work, St Basil's was always the particular work of the Magdalens.

The last quarter of the century saw a number of great missions to the poor throughout London, with the leading Anglo-Catholic clergy as missioners. They were a huge success and people flocked to them by the hundred. The Clewer Community was particularly involved with the West London Mission in February 1885. A 'shelter' had been opened in Lord Clinton's mews in Bruton Street for rescue work. Sr Constance, Sr Mary Charlotte and Martha Magdalen went to work there along with a number of voluntary ladies, one of whom was Mrs Gladstone. Between seventy and eighty cases passed through, of whom thirty to forty went either to Homes, to relatives or to 'respectable' lodgings.

In 1893 a request came from Lord Methuen for the Clewer Community to visit the families in the married quarters of the Chelsea, Wellington and Tower Barracks. This was later extended to the Windsor Barracks, much to the chagrin of the Revd Arthur Robins, Rector of the Garrison church, who protested (to no avail) at the intrusion into his own territory by what he saw as a 'Romanising' element in the Church of England. The Windsor Barracks were made the responsibility of the Sisters at Clewer St Stephen. The London work was begun by Sr Alexandrina from Westminster, but soon afterwards Sr Georgina Mary was put in charge. She was to make this her particular work and was very popular with the soldiers and their families.

In 1897 Sr Lydia was appointed 'Lady Visitor' to the sixteen female inmates in Gloucester prison. She was allowed to visit them in their cells and several were found places in Homes after leaving. This difficult but rewarding work came to an abrupt end in 1903 when the women's quarters were requisitioned for extra men.

Throughout the century requests poured in for the Sisters to work here and there, and not everything could be undertaken. Work refused included an offer to go to Zanzibar in 1869, penitentiary work in Leeds in 1875, mission work at All Saint's Boyne Hill, Maidenhead, in 1883, and in the Diocese of Brisbane, Australia, in 1891.

Perhaps the mission work of the Clewer Sisterhood can best be summed up by the Revd A H Mackonochie of St Alban's Holborn, who wrote in 1870: "Their presence, bringing the power of the religious life to bear on all the parochial works of mercy and charity, is an unspeakable blessing."

9

STEADY BY JERKS

In the face of so much successful mission work in England and Wales it was perhaps inevitable that the Community of St John Baptist should receive requests from overseas, and while the Chapter felt unable to take up work in Zanzibar, the prospect of work in America seemed a real possibility. Communications had improved greatly since the laying of the Atlantic cable in 1866, masterminded by Brunel's chief engineer Daniel Gooch whose country mansion was at Clewer Park. So although the voyage to America was still long and tedious, and not without danger, at least contact could be made between the old world and the new.

The first American Religious Community was the Sisterhood of the Holy Communion, founded in 1845 (the same year as the first English Sisterhood at Regent's Park). This did not become formally organised until 1852 but it was more of a nursing order than a Religious Community. Out of this work another order grew in 1865 calling itself the Community of St Mary, based at Peekskill, New York. More women's orders sprang up after the American Civil War, due in no small way to the social and economic changes which that upheaval had brought about. In addition to the wholly American foundations, three English Orders established themselves in America: the Society of All Saints in 1872; the Society of St Margaret in 1873; and the Community of St John Baptist, Clewer.

The American work of the Community of St John Baptist got off to a very shaky start. In February 1869 Dr Mahan, with the Bishop's consent, invited the Community to take charge of St Paul's Orphanage, Baltimore. Three Sisters duly sailed from Southampton on May 7th 1870. These were Sr Geraldine, who was to be Sister-in-Charge, together with Sr Anna Maria, who originally came from Baltimore and was professed at Clewer on November 30th 1869, and Sr Augusta (not to be confused with Sr Augusta Straine, who had been professed in 1853 and who died in 1864). At first all seemed well but soon things began to go badly wrong in Baltimore. Dr Mahan had died in September 1870, soon after the Sisters' arrival, and they found themselves in the middle of a wrangle between the new priest and the Diocesan Bishop over their official standing. The three Sisters, by now all Americans (Sisters Geraldine and Augusta having returned to Clewer) felt the work would do better if they separated from Clewer and they wrote back to England accordingly. Carter took the view that they were in breach of obedience and told them so—to no avail. February 1874 had seen the Clewer work planted in New York and with it the Community set on a firm foundation. The Superior of the CSJB in New York tried in vain to pour oil on the troubled waters in Baltimore. In September 1876 the recently elected Mother Ellen sent Sr Lucy, her deputy, to New York to attempt a reconciliation. She was accompanied by Sr Lucy Isabel and a member of the Second Order, Sr Helen Ashdown. Sr Lucy found she had no alternative but to formally resign the charge of St Paul's in November 1876. As to the erring Sisters (Srs Anna Maria, Martha and Lily), they were formally restored into the Community in April 1881, but all rebelled once more and left the CSJB within a few years. (They then formed their own Community and worked in an orphanage at Waverly in Baltimore under the direction of the parish priest. This work continued for over forty years and the Sisters died in the 1920s. They were buried in the parish cemetery of St John's Waverly.)

As mentioned above, the CSJB work in New York had begun in 1874, and we must now return to the day in 1864 when two American women were admitted to the noviciate at Clewer. Frances Paine was a young woman from a well-established Unitarian family in Boston. She visited the Continent and while there felt drawn to the Religious Life. After her reception into the American Episcopal Church she came under the influence of the Revd William Doane, who later became Bishop of Albany. He suggested sending her to Clewer to train in the noviciate there. She came as a visitor first of all and was duly admitted to the Community on Christmas Eve 1864 and took the name Sr Frances Constance. Her profession took place on November 30th 1867. Her friend, Mary Sever, had accompanied her to Clewer and she also was admitted on Christmas Eve 1864 as Sr Mary Virginia. She was professed on July 2nd 1867 and remained in England for the rest of her long life (she died in 1919).

Following the profession of Sr Frances Constance it became clear that there had been a misunderstanding. Bishop Doane had thought she would train at Clewer and then return to America. Instead she was now a fully professed Clewer Sister. He did not wish to have a branch of an *English*

Community within his Diocese, but wished to found his own Order of American Sisters. Mother Harriet saw the Bishop's point of view and offered Sr Frances Constance an 'honourable discharge' so that she might return to do the Bishop's bidding. But the Sister stood firm: she had made her commitment and was a *Clewer* Sister, and would remain so. And so she did for the next six years, working not only at the Clewer House of Mercy but also at St Andrew's Convalescent Hospital, Clewer, and the Devon House of Mercy at Bovey Tracey.

But in 1874 it became possible to take the work to New York. Two years previously, on March 23rd 1872, a young heiress, Helen Stuyvesant Folsom, who owned considerable property in New York, was admitted to the noviciate at Clewer and put the whole of her fortune into the hands of the Community for the establishment of mission work in New York. She was a delicate young woman and had longed to give herself to the Religious Life though she had been considered too frail. She had visited Clewer more than once and a record survives in the form of a long letter to Sr Jane of the Community of St Mary at Peekskill describing one such visit and is dated June 18th 1866. Miss Folsom met Mother Harriet, whom she described as "a person of commanding presence whose dignity however is softened by great motherliness." Sr Ellen, the Assistant Superior, had a "gentle sweet face and [her] kindly reception put us at our ease in a moment." There was a happy meeting between Miss Folsom and the two American novices in Sr Ellen's study. The visit and the warm welcome she received made a lasting impression and no doubt went a long way to influence her decision that she should join the Clewer Sisters. (For the full text of Helen Folsom's letter to Sr Jane, see Appendix 3, 'An American in Clewer'.)

In 1874 Bishop Horatio Potter of New York agreed to the Clewer Community starting work there so long as they worked in downtown New York, well away from the Community of St Mary at Peekskill. Accordingly, Sr Frances Constance was appointed Sister Superior and sailed on January 24th 1874 accompanied by two other Sisters, one of whom was Sr Emma, who stayed for a year before returning to Clewer to work at St Stephen's. They arrived on February 5th and began what was at first called St Margaret's Foundation: this was soon changed to avoid confusion with the Society of St Margaret in Boston, Mass.

The Sisters took up their quarters at 220 Second Avenue, a large house which was formerly the Folsoms' home, and began to organise their work. They were soon befriended by the Revd G H Houghton of the Church of the Transfiguration, who became their Warden for over twenty years. Following her admission to the Clewer Community in March 1872, Sr Helen Margaret (Helen Folsom) had been professed on July 6th 1874. In the spring of 1875 she returned to work in New York under Sr Frances Constance and remained there until her early death from consumption on April 26th 1882. She was described as "of a bright, happy disposition with great love for the poor." Whilst never in charge of the work, she is rightly remembered as the American Foundress.

Sr Frances Constance was Sister Superior of the American work until 1892, and she had just the right mixture of commanding presence, self confidence and warm-hearted humour to steer the work through all its early difficulties. She would describe herself as "half Paddy and half Yankee" and would, especially in the early days, turn her hand to anything. She had an immense personal magnetism which drew people to her, and which brought out the best in them. There was, in short, a great deal of Mother Harriet within her.

There was at this time great misunderstanding about Religious Communities in America, and in 1877 the General Convention of the Episcopal Church attempted to legislate about them. In particular, the presence of English Communities was resented, and an attempt was made to ban them altogether and to empower Bishops to dismiss any Sister from any Diocese. Sr Frances Constance responded characteristically, "Put not your trust in Princes; and I count Bishops as Princes; if God wants us in America, He will take care of us here, if He does not, we can go back to Clewer." But this did not become necessary. "We are going along, steady by jerks, keeping on the upward road," is how the Sister described these difficulties.

Notwithstanding these teething troubles, the work progressed. The Sisters soon outgrew the house at 220 Second Avenue and in December 1877 moved into St John Baptist House, 233 East 17th Street, which was to be their Headquarters for thirty-five years. However, it was difficult being a branch house when the Mother House at Clewer was 3,000 miles away. Accordingly in June 1881 the Clewer Chapter declared the American work to be an Affiliated House of the Community. Sr Helen Margaret, the

American Foundress, had hoped this would be achieved and she lived to see it happen. This meant that the Americans could elect their own Superior, choose their own Visitor and Warden, have their own noviciate and generally run their day-to-day affairs without reference to Clewer, except on major matters. Previously novices had gone to Clewer for their second year but this practice was now discontinued. The Rule and habit remained the same as at Clewer, the Constitutions having been revised for America in 1876. Sr Frances Constance became Mother Superior and the house on East 17th Street became the Mother House.

The American Affiliation grew steadily, though numbers never mushroomed in the same way as they did at Clewer. Perhaps the American membership figures are more typical of an average nineteenth-century Community than those at Clewer, whose growth was nothing short of phenomenal. In 1884 there were twenty-two Sisters in America; by 1890 numbers had grown to twenty-four; and by 1900 the Community had increased to thirty-eight. Numbers continued to increase until 1918 when there were forty-five Sisters. The Community consisted of choir and lay Sisters, although the latter were known as mission Sisters.

Although the Community had met difficulties there was also a great need for their work which gradually became recognised. In the wake of this a number of branch works were undertaken of a very similar nature to the English work. The first branch work was established in 1874: the Holy Cross Mission on Avenue C and 4th Street next to Holy Cross Church. This was aimed at the poor of the east side of New York, especially the large number of German immigrants who lived there.

After the opening of the new Mother House at 233 East 17th Street more work began nearby. St John Baptist School was opened in the Mother House in 1880 as a boarding and day school for young ladies. It moved to an adjoining house on Stuyvesant Square, 231 East 17th Street, and remained there for almost thirty years. Just a short distance away at 237 East 17th Street was St Andrew's Convalescent Hospital, opened in 1886 for women, girls and children. It could accommodate twenty-five patients in the wards and two or three privately in single rooms. A generous gift was made in 1903 by the 'Summer Rest Society' of a rest home at Woodcliffe Lake, New Jersey. This was used in the hot summer months, the New York hospital being closed for the season. In addition to all this there were two other summer houses: St Anna's Cottage, Farmingdale, Long Island, and St Christopher's, also in Farmingdale. St Anna's was a summer home for women, girls and children connected with Holy Cross Mission and was opened in 1881. St Christopher's served as a summer house for the Sisters from the Mother House.

Rescue work was an important aspect of the American work, one of the chief outlets being St Michael's Home, Mamaroneck, New York. This was described in the jargon of the time as a home for sixty 'wayward girls' and was originally a branch of the Midnight Mission which the Sisters took charge of in 1885 at the request of the Board of Trustees. St Michael's was opened in 1887 in the countryside near New York and was a great success, so that in 1896 the city house was given up. In 1880 St Hilda's, Morristown, New Jersey was established as a boarding and day school for girls but in 1897 changed to an 'industrial' school for orphans.

In 1892 Mother Frances Constance resigned her office at the early age of 55. Her Sisters wished her to retain the honorary title of Mother, but she felt this would compromise her successor. And so she returned to being Sr Frances Constance and took charge of the kitchen and the industrial girls. She was Novice Mistress for a time but her health failed rapidly and she had to resign herself to the life of an invalid for the last few years. She died on March 2nd 1901 and was buried in St Michael's Cemetery, Long Island.

Mother Frances Constance had been succeeded by Sr Gertrude Verena. A native of New York, she entered the Community in 1876 and was one of the first novices to come to Clewer after the establishment of the American branch. She served a year at Clewer and was professed in 1878. She worked in several of the branches including Holy Cross Mission and the Midnight Mission. On November 22nd 1880 she was returning from church on the 'East Side' when she was shot at by a man who was later judged as insane. She received five wounds but made a good recovery. Mother Gertrude Verena has been described as "tall, stately, graceful, she looked like a medieval abbess. She was a Religious through and through, one could not imagine her anything else." Certainly she had a profound influence upon the spiritual life of the Community, which by the time she became Superior had overcome the early difficulties and was both well established and well respected. During her time as Mother Superior the Community chapel obtained the Reserved Sacrament, and became a centre of devotion for theological students, for many of whom this was their first introduction to the Religious Life. But she was not a robust woman and in 1902 after ten years of office she resigned.

The new Mother Superior was Sr Mary Angela, a native of Elizabeth in New Jersey who had joined the Community in 1880 and was professed in 1883. She was "a woman of great charm, powerful mind, executive and financial ability as well as of deep spiritual life …" She was installed as Mother Superior in February 1903. It was during her time of leadership that the Community took the momentous step of selling their Mother House in New York and building a brand new convent at Ralston in New Jersey. Much of the New York work was transferred there. Also a few years previously, new work was undertaken beyond the Rocky Mountains in Portland, Oregon. But both these developments lay in the twentieth century and will be looked at in a later chapter.

Note

In her 'fragment of autobiography' called *Search for a Soul* (Faber 1947), the writer Phyllis Bottome describes her experiences as a pupil at St John Baptist School, New York. She was eleven or twelve when her parents moved to America and so she probably entered the school in 1895 or 1896. Her mother had visited Clewer and had been interested to discover that there was a boarding school in New York run by the CSJB.

SISTERS OF THE RAJ

Mother Harriet was to live long enough to see her Community not only established in America as an Affiliated House, but also as a branch work in India. This was to become one of the most important Community works for the next sixty-five years. There were other Communities working in India by the time the Clewer Sisters arrived there in 1881, notably the Society of St John the Evangelist, popularly known as the Cowley Fathers, the Community of St Mary the Virgin (Wantage), and the Society of All Saints. In addition, the missionary societies had been at work for many years, starting with the Church Missionary Society and followed by the Society for the Propagation of the Gospel. A fresh impetus was given by the growth of the University missions: the Cambridge Mission to Delhi in 1877 and the Oxford Mission to Calcutta in 1880.

Calcutta grew up as one of the three principle ports of India established by the British, the others being Bombay and Madras: all three came to be known as the Presidency towns. At first the British were but one of several rival European powers vying for a foothold in an India ruled by a decadent power, the Muslim Moguls, although there were also a large number of princely states ruled by Hindus. But in 1639 the British East India Company acquired governmental rights in Madras and in 1669 gained possession of Bombay. From that moment the East India Company became a ruling power, so that by the 1850s, by fair means or foul, the Company controlled practically all of India. The Company's Governor General ruled from Calcutta, by now the premier city. All other rulers—the Mogul Emperor, and countless Indian princes—were subject to him. Then in 1857 came the Mutiny, now known as the Sepoy uprising, or the first Indian War of Independence, the abiding result of which was the dissolution of the East India Company in 1858. Victoria was declared Queen-Empress in 1877 and was personally represented by the Viceroy in Calcutta; all powers formerly vested in the Company now passed to the Crown in the shape of the Indian Civil Service. The British Raj had been born.

Calcutta has been described variously as the 'city of palaces' and the 'city of dreadful night'. Both were true. The growing wealth and importance of the East India Company had seen Calcutta grow from a small port on the banks of the River Hooghly into a large city. There had been great building development towards the end of the 18th century and the birth of the Raj saw an acceleration in this trend. By the time of the Clewer Sisters' arrival, Calcutta, as the seat of Government, had a vast array of civic buildings (Government House was modelled upon Kedleston Hall in Derbyshire), gentlemen's clubs, gothic churches, and elegant mansions. Most of these looked solid enough but many were built from poor bricks covered in bad stucco. There were large open spaces too, notably the Maidan, a vast area near Fort William, and some pleasant suburbs to the south at Ballyganj, Alipur and Kidderpore. But there was then, as now, another side to Calcutta: poverty. Just a few miles away a ghastly new disease had reared its head for the first time in 1817. This was cholera and it was to spread in wave upon wave throughout the world. Calcutta was the home of abject poverty, dirt, disease, and squalor amidst the splendours of the Raj. Calcutta's poverty was older than the Raj—and it has outlived it.

Sir Ashley Eden, Lieutenant Governor of Bengal, had appealed to the Clewer Community to send Sisters to Calcutta. They had hoped to accompany the newly established Oxford Mission in 1880 but were unable to do so. A further request was made by Miss Milman, sister of a former Bishop of Calcutta, in the autumn of 1880. In July 1881 the Bishop of Oxford (J F Mackarness) formally sanctioned the work and on October 19th he came to Clewer for a service of blessing in the chapel for the three Sisters departing for India. Next day he dedicated the great new Chapel of St John Baptist for the Community in the presence of 104 Sisters and ninety clergy. On November 3rd Sr Lucy, Sr Fanny Gertrude and Sr Anne Frances left Clewer for Liverpool, from whence they sailed next day. On the same day, November 4th, Mother Ellen announced her resignation as Mother Superior. She was succeeded by Sr Jane Frances, who would eventually lay down the office to succeed Sr Lucy as Sister Superior in India.

The journey to India, which was paid for by the Government, took several weeks aboard the SS *Myra* and the Sisters wrote graphic letters describing the voyage and all they saw. At least they were able to take the shorter route which had been made possible by the opening of the Suez Canal just twelve years previously, in 1869. Nevertheless it was still hot and somewhat tedious, the canal being too narrow to allow two ships to pass each other so that there were stations every five miles where ships would wait. "We were most unlucky and had to wait four times. We left Port Said on November 17th at 9.30 and did not get through the Canal until the 19th," wrote Sr Lucy. But there were compensations too: sightseeing in Port Said, the first sight of Arabs and mosques, the Eucharist in sight of Mount Sinai, an early morning view of the Southern Cross and mirages in the desert. It was a different world from Clewer with its red brick Gothic, but one which would become familiar to an increasing number of Sisters. They finally reached Calcutta on December 8th and were met by a welcoming party of English ladies.

Now the work began without delay and very daunting it must have seemed to Sr Lucy, 60 years old and without a word of Bengali. The Clewer Community had been invited to train the nurses for the Presidency General Hospital, although they hoped this would lead to educational or missionary work. The Sisters themselves had their quarters in the Lady Canning Home, near the hospital. The Lady Canning Home had been erected in 1875 as a memorial to Charlotte, Countess Canning, who had done much to organise nursing there. The nurses were mostly Eurasians, ie half English, half Indian. In addition to the hospital nurses there were the 'Canning nurses', who were trained to nurse patients at home.

The Presidency General Hospital consisted of three detached blocks in one compound comprising men's surgical and medical wards, an observation ward, operating theatre, library and private wards; a women's ward of thirty-six beds; a chapel; and a separate cholera ward. Apart from the women's ward the hospital was mainly for sailors of all nationalities and was commonly known as 'Jack's Country House'. It was a large hospital of 200 beds but very different from the average English hospital, consisting as it did of open arcades and verandahs, and not an aspidistra in sight!

It was not very long before the difficulties became apparent. Not only did Sr Lucy and her companions have the task of teaching the basic principles of nursing from scratch, but the peculiarly Indian problems soon became obvious. Firstly there was language, which was literally a case of learning as they went along. "Being here makes one constantly regret the confusion of tongues at Babel! It does so hinder our work! … We make up with kind looks and gestures," wrote Sr Lucy. Then the Eurasian nurses were very sensitive about their racial mixture and were reluctant to do anything which would lower them in the eyes of the Indians. "They will scarcely put a bed tidy without calling for a coolie," commented Sr Lucy in a letter to the Sisters at Clewer. And then there were the patients and their customs: often a whole family spanning three generations would accompany an Indian patient. Food was only given to the patient, the relatives having theirs sent from outside. And it was so easy to break caste both for patients and those looking after them. This could make life very complicated indeed.

As if all this were not enough, there were the perils too—tropical storms, monsoons, extreme heat and cold, together with the alarming noise of jackals, troublesome mosquitoes, and perhaps worst of all, snakes. One Sister almost trod on a cobra one night in the dark: it was just a few inches away swaying backwards and forwards ready to dart at her. When she turned her lamp on it the cobra disappeared into the grass. It was a lucky escape. And there was the ever-present risk of cholera and typhoid fever. Sanitary arrangements were practically non-existent, and all the water was taken from a large pond known as a tank. There was no such thing as clean water in Calcutta. Everyone was at risk and a week rarely passed without a cholera case coming to the hospital, most of whom died. Even so, the letters home to Clewer are so full of enthusiasm that it is easy to forget that the writers were so new to the often uncongenial conditions.

Notwithstanding all these difficulties the work progressed, standards steadily came into line with those of English hospitals and the buildings were improved and extended. So much did things improve that in 1883 the Community was asked to supervise the running of the Medical College Hospital in the north of Calcutta. Whereas most of the patients at the Presidency General Hospital were Europeans, three quarters of the patients at the Medical College Hospital were Indians. It had opened in 1856 as a training hospital with 300 beds and was the largest training college for medical students in Bengal. The senior doctors were European and the junior doctors were Indian. The medical students were divided into the military, who were mostly Eurasian and after training went to military hospitals, and the civil, who were Indians who after training went either to native hospitals or into private practice. When the hospital first opened there were no nurses at all, but in 1859 Lady Canning formed a Committee to raise funds to supply nurses to the men's wards. In 1883 quarters were built for twenty nurses and the Sisters were invited to train them.

Two other hospitals came under Community care at this time. The Eden

Hospital was a sixty-bed gynaecological hospital for Indians, Eurasians and Europeans and was in the same compound as the Medical College Hospital. A year later, in 1883, the similarly named Eden Sanatorium at Darjeeling was taken over by the Community. This sixty-bed hospital was for Eurasians and Europeans of both sexes and had no secular nurses.

The Community had hoped to widen the scope of their work, and this became a reality very soon, for in 1882 the opportunity arose to teach in the Pratt Memorial School, Calcutta. This had been founded in 1878 as a Diocesan school in memory of Archdeacon Pratt of Calcutta. It catered for European, Eurasian and Indian children and was a very small undertaking labouring under great difficulties. All this changed with the coming of the Community, who built it into a good quality girls' school. But it was not without early problems, notably the death of Sr Mary Agatha. She had been sent out from Clewer to take charge of the school and she brought the energy and enthusiasm which was needed to put it on a sound footing. She fell ill with a fever which at first caused no alarm, but it turned out to be typhoid and after twenty-one days' illness she died on September 23rd 1884. Hers was the first death among the Sisters in India. She was buried in the Bhowanipore Cemetery at Alipore, not far from the Presidency General Hospital.

1885 saw the removal of the Pratt Memorial School to larger premises not far from the old school. The move was accomplished in a truly Indian manner with the help of twenty coolies. Sr Christian remarked in a letter, "It is really wonderful to see huge wardrobes, pianos, heavy school desks, dining room tables going along on the coolies' heads." The new buildings gave the school much better facilities and soon fifty to sixty girls were taken. A final move was made in December 1893 to new buildings on the Lower Circular Road which were themselves extended in 1912. By the turn of the century over 100 day girls and about eighty boarders were taken and the school was described as the most important Church of England girls' school in Calcutta.

In 1886 the European Orphanage Asylum in Calcutta came under Community care. This had been founded in 1815, for sixty orphans of British soldiers, by Mrs Mary Martha Sherwood, the Evangelical author of 'improving' stories for children. It had been placed in the hands of Trustees and managed by a Ladies' Committee who now asked the Clewer Sisters to take over the internal running. The house in Lower Circular Road was near the Pratt Memorial School, where after 1893 the children went as day girls. Children under 8 years old were educated in the Home. At the age of 16 the girls left school and worked in the orphanage workroom learning needlework, and at 18 were placed out as children's nurses or nursery governesses.

The death of Sr Lucy in 1889 was not entirely unexpected, her health having been failing for some time. News of her death reached Clewer on Maundy Thursday, the telegram having arrived during Evensong. That same evening, thanks to the Trans-Atlantic Cable, the American Affiliation had been informed, and the Royal Mail carried the tidings to all the English branches. Sr Lucy had been professed since 1869 and was buried next to Sr Mary Agatha in the Bhowanipore Cemetery. She had chosen the plot herself, "for the next Sister who died." At the time of her death there were twelve Sisters working in India: by 1900 this had increased to twenty or more.

In 1888 Mother Jane Frances had visited the Indian work and had fallen in love with it. She had been Mother Superior at Clewer since 1881 and it was well known that she had found the task burdensome. On March 28th, shortly before Sr Lucy's death, the Warden (Canon Carter) announced by letter that Mother intended to resign at the end of the year and take charge of the work in India, Sr Lucy being too ill. "We have for long felt this blow was coming and it is a great sorrow to us all to think of losing Mother," is the comment in the Community *Annals*. Sr Jane Frances, as she now became once more, sailed on November 14th 1889 on the SS *City of Chios* along with Sr Blanche, who was taken seriously ill en route. The voyage was long and difficult and the ship wretched. Letters did not reach Clewer until January 13th telling of their safe arrival. Sr Jane Frances was to find her niche in India, where she was to remain until 1918. Of Scottish birth, she was the grand-daughter of the 2nd Lord Erskine, and her sister had married the second son of the 8th Duke of Argyll. She had been a professed Sister of the Second Order from 1872–4, when she joined the First Order as a choir novice, and was professed in July 1875.

Soon after Sr Jane Frances became the Indian Superior a new development took place. Religious Communities and Missionary Societies were not the only bodies to be working to spread the Gospel in India. Just as wealthy well-connected ladies were doing philanthropic work in England, so similar ladies were doing missionary work in foreign parts. Angelina Hoare was just such a lady. She was the daughter of the banker Henry Hoare and Lady Mary Hoare of London and Staplehurst Manor in Kent. In 1876 she had begun work among the Bengalis in south Calcutta and in the villages of the rice-growing country known as the Sunderbuns. Miss Hoare had bought a large house from the Maharajah of Burdwan in the Lansdowne Road–Elgin Road area of Ballyganj and had named it the Pipalpatti Mission after the leaves of the pipal trees which grew there. These trees are sacred to the Hindu, Buddhist and Jain religions and are a species of fig tree. Within the mission compound there were a number of schools which catered for Indian children both Christian and non-Christian. But in 1891 the work became too much for her and the Bishop asked the Clewer Community to relieve her of the Calcutta work. The Sisters readily acceded to this request as it afforded a real opportunity for mission work. The mission house was large, dry and well drained and as well as being next to St Mary's Bengali church, was also not far from the Pratt Memorial School. The house servants were all Bengali Christians and lived with their families in the compound. Henceforth the Sisters were to make the mission house their headquarters in Calcutta.

The schools in the mission compound eventually consisted of the Milman Memorial School, the Lower or Vernacular School, the Diocesan Mission High School and the Diocesan College. The Milman School had been founded by Robert Milman, sometime Bishop of Calcutta, and was maintained as a memorial to him. It catered for Hindu girls of higher castes and was one of the first efforts to provide education for Indian girls in Bengal. The pupils were mostly the daughters of Indian professional men who had prospered under the British Raj. It was not possible to attain a very high standard of education because all the girls left at 13 and some were married off as early as 10 or 11.

The Lower or Vernacular School was for poor Bengali Christian girls of a lower caste, hence the name. All the work was done in Bengali, English being learned as a second language, and all Bengali customs regarding dress, food, and eating habits were adhered to with no attempt to Anglicise the pupils. Most of the girls came from the Sunderbuns and the object of the school was to train them so that they would return there as native Christian teachers in the village schools. The name of this school was later changed to St Elizabeth's Middle English School.

In 1894 the Diocesan Mission High School was begun for Bengali girls seeking a higher standard of education and in 1900 it gained Government recognition as a High School. The pupils were the daughters of Indian Christians and the fees were kept as low as possible. Lessons were given in Bengali up to the age of 13 and in English thereafter. The lower years, or standards as they were then called, were taught by former pupils; the upper standards had English teachers and took matriculation for Calcutta University. In 1909 the school changed its name to the Diocesan Collegiate School, and later still to St John's Diocesan High School.

In the same compound there was the Diocesan College which began as an offshoot of the Diocesan High School. It was the only Christian College for women in Bengal but was always a difficult work because at the time few people were seriously committed to women's education. In 1909 it became affiliated to Calcutta University.

Angelina Hoare had retained the work in the rice-growing villages of the Sunderbuns south of Calcutta. Following a tour of these villages she fell ill and died of a brain haemorrhage on January 10th 1892 in her 50th year. She was buried in Calcutta and her funeral was attended by many people, both English and Indian. She was a remarkable woman with enormous energy and zeal. "Those who have seen her in her native sari and a pair of topboots plunging through the mud of the ricefields are not likely to forget the sight," wrote a Sister in the *St John Baptist Magazine* of Easter 1892. The immediate consequence of her death was that the Clewer Sisters were invited to take over the Sunderbuns work. Under the circumstances it would have been very difficult to refuse, though it must have stretched the Sisters' resources to the limit.

Sister Jane Frances had visited the Sunderbuns villages with Miss Hoare and had been fascinated by all she saw. The rice country was flat and mostly under water, with isolated villages at intervals where the ground rose slightly. Here in about thirty villages Miss Hoare had planted small schools where the children were given a very basic education and Christian teaching. The work was difficult and could have been disheartening: the children were willing to learn but unless a whole village converted to Christianity it was unlikely that individuals would do so. But she laboured on undeterred. Communication between the villages was by flat-bottomed boats which were punted along with poles. There was room for two passengers under the little thatched sun-roof, while the coolies sat at either end in the blazing sun and slowly made the boat glide through the tall rice plants. The thought of inheriting this side of Miss Hoare's work must have been daunting, but the Sisters took it all in their stride.

In complete contrast to the village schools another school came under Community care in 1895: the Diocesan Girls' High School at Darjeeling, known after 1904 as St Michael's School. Darjeeling was a hill-station where the British servants of the Raj would seek refuge from the Calcutta summer. Built upon a narrow ridge 7,000 feet above sea level in the Himalayan foothills, Darjeeling was 250 miles north of Calcutta. When the Sisters took over, the pupils were both Eurasian and English, but in time it became a predominately English school for girls who would otherwise have returned to England for their education. The fees were higher than at the Pratt Memorial School, which was still a mixed school racially.

Towards the end of the century the Sisters' work suffered a series of disasters. The summer of 1897 saw part of the Pipalpatti mission compound destroyed by fire. It started in the large thatched schoolroom which had been built by Miss Hoare, part of which had been used as a chapel until a new wing was built onto the mission house. The eighty children had broken up for the summer holiday the day before, so that there were only about twenty or thirty of them present and these were brought to safety. No one knew how the fire began, but the wind blew bits of burning thatch towards the main house so that it looked for a time as if all would be lost. Fortunately the fruit trees caught most of the flaming brands and the main house was saved. No time was lost in rebuilding the wreckage in conventional stuccoed brick.

A month after the fire there was a serious earthquake on June 12th followed by cyclonic storms. The Presidency General Hospital was damaged, the Cathedral spire fell down, the Lady Canning Home rocked greatly but was unharmed, and the Pipalpatti Mission was severely damaged. Sr Jane Frances described what happened: "Sr Katherine Maud and I were out on the site of the burnt schoolroom discussing the plan of the new building. We heard a rumbling sound and felt a trembling under our feet … One said to the other, 'What an odd feeling this floor has, as if it were moving under our feet.' Then this curious trembling got stronger … Looking casually towards the house we saw the parapet from the roof falling, the large fruit trees swaying, and all the crows rising in the air cawing loudly." The cool courage which the two Sisters displayed was quite remarkable though it was not until after it was all over that they realised just how serious it had been. But while the buildings were seriously damaged, none of the Sisters nor anyone in their care was injured.

Darjeeling suffered too as the railway, the last stage of which was 18" gauge, was destroyed along with several bridges. But at least the Diocesan Girls' High School survived: two years later it was not so fortunate. There had been an unusually dry season in 1899 and when the rains came on Saturday September 23rd they were torrential. They continued all through Sunday, and during the night there were massive landslips which engulfed the school, tearing away the walls and carrying them downhill. At that time a few small boys were taken at the school and their dormitory was destroyed and the fourteen boys buried in the debris. Sisters, governesses, and Indian servants tore away at the earth and rubble with bare hands to extricate the boys, all of whom were found, with only a few minor injuries. All the other children had been got to safety. But next day the school was a sorry sight: a complete and utter ruin. Lady Woodburn put the Durbar Hall at Government House at the disposal of the Sisters and lessons were held there for a considerable time. The school was rebuilt at great expense and reopened on the eve of St Michael's Day 1904.

The Sisters' work went on 'against all disaster'. Ruins were rebuilt and old works refashioned to meet changing needs until Indian self-government brought about the wholesale withdrawal of the British. But we shall look at the work in the 20th century in chapter 16.

Note

The term 'Eurasian', used above of nurses in the Lady Canning Home, went out of use in later years and was deemed derogatory. The term 'Anglo-Indian' was favoured, although towards the end of the Raj it signified people of English parentage who were born in India.

It is impossible to do justice to the work of the Community in India in the short space of a chapter. The third book in the Clewer trilogy, *Sisters of the Raj: the Clewer Sisters in India* (1997), is a detailed description of the Indian work.

11

A JOYOUS SERVICE

By the early 1870s Mother Harriet's health was beginning to give cause for concern, but nevertheless she was reappointed as Superior at St Andrew's-tide 1873, thereby completing twenty-one years in office. The work was steadily progressing and expanding so that the office of Superior was exhausting, involving as it did extensive travelling to far-flung branch houses, as well as entertaining visiting clergy, members of other Communities and other guests. Whilst Mother Harriet increasingly delegated some duties to her assistant (Sr Ellen), she attended fully to matters of Community policy such as undertaking new work, and was always present on important occasions when her absence would have been keenly felt. But throughout 1875 she was frequently absent from Clewer because of her health, and on September 18th wrote of her intention to resign. The Community *Annals* note, "Though all had known her to be very failing in health this came as a sudden shock to us all." Her intention was confirmed in a letter to the Community from Carter on October 1st.

On October 31st she wrote to Carter expressing her concern for him: "For you dearest Father, as I feel the rest of having laid down my staff, I feel the tenderest sympathy, for I feel as if I have laid an additional burden on you. But I trust all will soon get settled, and that things will go on their quiet course. My own exhortation to the Sisters is not to let the sparkle out of the Community. I love that in a life of sacrifice they should give God a joyous service."

On November 1st Carter nominated Sr Ellen as Mother Superior, a Chapter of Election was held on November 9th and she was installed by Bishop Mackarness on November 18th. Ellen Nixon had been admitted to the Community on August 1st 1852 and professed on July 29th 1853, the third member of the infant Community. She was the obvious successor to Mother Harriet, having been Assistant Superior since the beginning of 1854. This office was now taken by Sr Lucy until she sailed for India in 1881.

At first it was hoped that Mother Harriet would stay at Clewer, either in the House of Mercy itself or at St Andrew's Convalescent Hospital. Gradually, however, it became clear that she needed rest and quiet away from the activity of the Mother House. Also, in her wisdom she realised that her presence could perhaps compromise the position of her successor, not that she would deliberately interfere, but simply because the Sisters would have difficulty in thinking of anyone else as 'Mother' in her presence. So it was that a house on the Bale at Folkestone was taken for Mother Harriet and her Sister companion. Mother Harriet subsequently called this house 'The Hermitage'. As already noted in chapters 6 and 8, the Community had started work in Folkestone and it was to become an important centre of the Clewer Sisters' work. On August 7th 1876 (the Feast of the Holy Name of Jesus) 'The Hermitage' was blessed by the Archbishop of Canterbury, Archibald Campbell Tait, as a house of retreat, for prayer, praise, thanksgiving, intercession and adoration, and was dedicated to the Name of Jesus. Permission was granted for the Eucharist to be offered there, and the Archbishop celebrated and gave Communion to Mother Harriet.

For the first three years Mother Harriet was still able to travel and during this time she visited friends and relations and returned to Clewer for several short visits. The exact nature of her illness was diagnosed as heart disease, although it has also been suggested that she might have suffered from Parkinson's Disease. From 1879 onwards mobility became increasingly difficult so that she was unable to move from a chair without assistance. During the last days she was unable to write but dictated her letters, and though partially bedridden saw the newspapers regularly so that she might pray for those in need. She received visitors until the end of her life and took great pleasure in their company. Happily, one of Mother Harriet's last wishes was carried out: the new Community Chapel of St John Baptist had been dedicated in October 1881 and she wished to see this, the crowning glory of Henry Woodyer's work. On May 31st 1882 she travelled from Folkestone and stayed with Carter until June 27th. Not only was there the Chapel of St John Baptist to see, but also the new Chapel at St Andrew's Convalescent Hospital which had been blessed on St Andrew's Day 1880.

But this was to be Mother Harriet's last visit to Clewer. Holy Week 1883 saw a decline in her condition. She had been aware all week that her time was running short and on Good Friday had said, "I quite know now that this is the beginning of the end. I am going home … I may yet rally, and if I do, I am well content to stay, but if I go, I am more than content to go." On Easter Eve Sr Elizabeth and Sr Mary Virginia came from Clewer: she had greeted them joyously and had said first Vespers of Easter with them. In spite of her serious condition that same morning she had dictated two letters, one to her nephew's fiancée, the other to a friend who had just lost her only child. During the night she lapsed into unconsciousness and very early in the morning as the church bells were ringing to announce the Resurrection, Harriet Monsell died peacefully. Just a few hours previously she had said, "Easter is a lovely time to go home, is it not?" Perhaps it is significant that in 1883 Easter Sunday fell on March 25th, the Feast of the Annunciation, for if ever a woman followed Mary's example of saying "Yes" to God it was Harriet Monsell. The funeral was at Folkestone on March 30th. Mother Ellen, Canon Carter, the Sub-Warden and over fifty Sisters from Clewer, London and other Houses were present.

If Harriet Monsell had founded the Community of St John Baptist and had done nothing else, that fact alone would make her a remarkable woman. Victorian Anglican Communities were full of remarkable women, pioneers in God's name in a male-dominated Church and society, grasping the nettle of social injustice in a multitude of ways which foreshadowed the Welfare State. But in fact Harriet Monsell did so much more. Writing her obituary, Archdeacon Furse (formerly Johnson) recalled her growing intellectual ability as the Community grew, her immense capacity for sympathy and the ministry of counselling which sprang out of it, and her availability to all who sought her. This, coupled with her determination, her strength of character, her wealth of common sense and her sense of humour made her not only a natural leader and guide, but also an immensely likeable person. So many Victorian Mothers Superior present a formidable aspect today, and photographs of Mother Harriet taken late in life look equally formidable. Even so, Harriet Monsell's real personality was quite contrary to that portrayed in the photographer's studio. She was truly a woman for all seasons. Only a few of her letters have survived but they 'speak' to the modern reader as eloquently as they did on the day they were written.

There are several instances of Mother Harriet's ability to get on with people and make them feel at ease. Space will only permit two examples. On July 6th 1864 Queen Victoria paid a 'strictly private' visit to the House of Mercy and has left an account in her journal which is reproduced here by the gracious permission of Her Majesty the Queen. "July 6th … At 6 drove with [Princess Louise] to the Deanery and drove quietly with her and Lady Wellesley in the latter's carriage to the House of Mercy at Clewer where poor 'fallen women' are taken in, of which they have 70. There are similar Houses all over the country. The women are extremely kindly treated and there is nothing gloomy about the whole establishment which is managed by the Clewer Sisters who are dressed like nuns in black with white caps over which hangs a white veil, and they wear a cross suspended round their necks. Mrs Monsell the Mother Superior is an excellent person and manages the whole admirably. Of course it is very like a Convent but very pretty and not gloomy."

The Queen had obviously been favourably impressed by all she saw, not least by the kindness shown to the inmates and by the place itself, having twice remarked that it was not gloomy despite being like a convent! But it is clear too that Mother Harriet had herself made a deep impression. This is borne out by an incident in the oral tradition of the Community: the Queen was interested in all she saw but something displeased her. "I thought you had understood that this was to be a strictly private visit; then why is it that all whom we meet curtsey to me?" "But Your Majesty," replied Mother Harriet, "they are not curtseying to you, they are curtseying to me!" A daring reply indeed, so much so that it must surely be true, for no one would have invented such an incident. And indeed Sisters curtsied to the Superior until well past the centenary of the Community. Whilst maintaining respect for the Sovereign, one can detect that these two widows were at ease with each other.

The second example consists of a letter from Mother Harriet to a young woman who was leaving the noviciate. Though undated it is remarkable for its mixture of genuine love and sound common-sense. "Yes dear you shall have a warm blessing for Easter Day … In the service of God I trust you will find your true test but you must leave here unfettered by the restraint of Rule, I mean such Rule as a Sisterhood binds round one. You have tried it and it did not suit you, do not try it again. Live simply in work for God, attached to some Church and among poor whom you can love and serve." One might have expected an admonition for lack of perseverance, or the suggestion that the novice was opting for an easy way of life, but there is nothing of the kind. Just the Mother's blessing and some sound advice for the future which must have meant a great deal.

Harriet Monsell's wide circle of friends among the influential has already been noted, and this had a marked effect on the development of the Community. The work at St Alban's Holborn, for instance, probably came as a result of her friendship with the founder, the Rt Hon J G Hubbard. Likewise Mr and Mrs Gladstone not only shared a mutual interest in rescue work, but also were old friends of Mother Harriet. But there was another friendship too which had far-reaching effects within the wider Church. Archibald Campbell Tait was married to Harriet Monsell's first cousin, and the two women were close friends. In 1868 Tait was translated from London, where he had been Bishop since 1856, to Canterbury, where he was to remain until his death in 1882. Archbishop Tait had been brought up a Scottish Presbyterian and remained solidly opposed to what he viewed as the ritualist excesses of the second generation of the Oxford Movement: men such as Mackonochie of St Alban's Holborn. As Bishop of London he had to cope not only with ritualistic centres such as St Alban's and St Barnabas Pimlico, but also with the fanatical Church Association, whose members tried all available means to stamp out what they saw as a 'Romeward' tendency in the Church of England. Thus rioting, heckling, and vandalism went hand in hand with legal proceedings to oust the offending clergy. Tait clearly disapproved of ritualism and openly supported and encouraged the passage of the Public Worship Regulation Act of 1874, which Disraeli had described as "a Bill to put down ritualism".

It may therefore come as a surprise to learn that Harriet Monsell was on the closest of friendly terms not only with Mrs Tait, but also with the Archbishop. When he blessed 'The Hermitage' at Folkestone as Mother Harriet's retirement retreat, it was in the capacity of Diocesan Bishop, but there was also the element of welcoming an old friend to his domain. Perhaps strangest of all is the fact that despite his dislike of ritualism, Tait was strangely drawn towards Religious Communities at a time when they were still regarded with deep suspicion by many Low Churchmen. One cannot help but feel that his friendship with Mother Harriet made him understand the Religious Life for what it was, rather than fear it for what it might be.

The terms of Mother Harriet's friendship did not exclude plain speaking.

As Archdeacon Furse pointed out in the obituary, "whoever might be her friend, she held her own." Thus when the Archbishops and Bishops issued a joint Pastoral Letter to the Church before the Public Worship Regulation Act came into operation, Mother Harriet felt moved to plead the cause of the ritualist clergy who would feel they had been abandoned. "I cannot be good and keep silence," she wrote. "Your 'Irish' cousin cannot contain the Celtish spirit within her. What will the English Episcopate gain by sending the Eastern, the Western, the civilised heathen all over the world, such an estimate of their clergy? I … know not how your sons will take it, but your daughter feels very much aggrieved for them … Do please set things a little straight in Convocation, and claim for the English Church her catholic position as a branch of the Primitive [ie the Early] Church. Do not be vexed with me, dear Archbishop. I see life from the foot of the tree, you from the top. If you let the life-blood of the tree flow out where I stand, or get paralysed in dejection, the topmost boughs will soon wither … Your Pastoral comes like an icicle into the hearts of your sons, and they say, 'What would the Army or Navy or Bar say if the Generals and Admirals and Judges sent out to the world such a paper?'"

A year later in 1875 she wrote to the Archbishop in defence of the Revd A H Mackonochie, who had been suspended from duty for alleged ritualism: "My whole soul is roused today by the thought of the silent altar at St Alban's … In the midst of all that sin and misery no longer saying 'Come unto me all ye that travail and are heavy laden and I will refresh you!' You probably will say it is their own fault. Why silence it? All work done in the Church of Christ has been the result of strong convictions and those who have them must be true to them … I grant you they may be mixed up with much imperfection, much impetuosity, much apparent obstinacy … But they are telling convictions, of this I feel sure, and it is just because I am a witness of their power that I venture to plead with you at this present crisis … If the altars are silenced that are now speaking throughout the land through the voices of what are called Ritualists it will be grievous … Dear Archbishop there must be great courage to break through the entanglements that fears and misconceptions and antagonisms have wound around the Church of England … [I know] from practical experience how our teaching does win souls and give a definite faith."

For sixteen years Mackonochie was hounded by the Church Association, until in obedience to a death-bed wish of Archbishop Tait he exchanged his parish for that of St Peter's London Docks. But it was to no avail: the protesters followed him and he was driven to resign. He died, a broken man, wandering in a blizzard on a Scottish hillside in 1887. But perhaps the conciliatory influence of Harriet Monsell had played a part in the olive branch offered on the death-bed of the Archbishop.

This strong determination in the character of Harriet Monsell can be seen in the work of the Community. Her action in signing the contract for St Andrew's Convalescent Hospital, Clewer, in the face of the fainthearted all-male Council, has already been noted. So, too, there are signs that although Bishop Wilberforce had grave misgivings about certain aspects of the early Community (see chapter 3), he did not entirely win the day on all counts. When negotiating the terms under which Sisters would work in a parish or in a particular institution, Mother Harriet had no hesitation in laying her cards on the table: if the terms for work were unacceptable to her the Community would refuse the offer.

Harriet Monsell's capacity for understanding the problems of those both within and outside the cloister has become legendary. "Her sympathy was a vast power," wrote Archdeacon Furse. He continued, "She was the nimble correspondent and quick-witted adviser and generous advocate in 10,000 difficulties, and few 'Belgravian mothers' had a lighter hand in manipulating with tenderness and skill the 'affaires de coeur.' In graver troubles she was the comforter that few could be … No one living in the world was more accessible than the 'Mother of Clewer.'"

None of this intense activity could have been entered into without a corresponding deep spirituality, and this increased over the years. Her period of retirement at Folkestone were years of deep spiritual communion. A note written at the Eucharist in November 1876 shows the way in which her mind was working and her soul reaching forth: "Pray that the active life of our Community may be strengthened and upheld, and the spiritual life deepened, by the prayers of those who in a life of Retreat are withdrawn of God into deeper silence and solitude with Himself, that He may speak with them, as He has ever spoken with His chosen ones face to face as with a friend." Her Sister companion remarked after her death that Mother Harriet's whole life was a life of prayer. This is an eloquent testimony to the total self-giving which had begun by the death bed of Charles Monsell.

She had written or dictated many letters in those last years, not a few of which were to members of the Community and containing exhortations for the fulfilment of the Religious Life. "The one great thing I want to impress on you," she wrote, "is that you must live the life, not [just] do the work. Live a quiet peaceful life alone with God, stayed on Him, and the work will come out of it." Again, "Do not plan out your life. Plans are God's not yours, leave them to him … Look at my life. I made no plans, I never settled what I was going to do, but all was gradually unfolded to me step by step. We must just keep ourselves ready to answer God's call … for we cannot tell what He may do with us." Mother Harriet's last message to the Community was quite simple: "To make the revealing [of] the Mind of Christ Jesus the one aim of their lives, and to remember the Rule is a dead Rule, unless they do—it is all framed on that one idea."

At the time of her retirement Mother Harriet had written what she called the Five Aims of a Sister:

> The one great Aim of her life is the Glory of God.
> The one great Example of her life is the Incarnate God.
> The one great Devotion of her life is the Will of God.
> The one great Longing of her life is Union with God.
> The one great Reward of her life is the Vision of God.

There was about Harriet Monsell a joyousness and hopefulness springing from a life lived in accordance with the Will of God. "We must try to 'serve the Lord with gladness.' Happiness and brightness in God's service is a great gift, and one that wins others to Him. We are told to make melody in our hearts to the Lord, and we cannot do this unless we are bright and cheerful, and serve Him gladly." Such joy in the Lord was sure to attract new members to the Community. Small wonder then that in 1884, a year after her death, there were 201 Sisters at Clewer and twenty-two in America.

Perhaps Archdeacon Furse should have the final word with the closing passage of the obituary: "She was one of the most hopeful women in the world. With a dead pull against the stream of public opinion for twenty-five years of a notorious work, overtaking and overpassing prejudice at every stroke, committed to a venture of great audacity, insisting on the creation and extension of a work absolutely new in the English Church, with no optimistic and sentimental ignoring of hard and ugly facts, she lived by hope … and the facility and gaiety and security of her venturous life was the beautiful product of this hopefulness of her soul. When the history of the revival of Sisterhoods in our Church is written, a golden page will be given to Harriet Monsell."

Note

For more about Mother Harriet, see Valerie Bonham, *A Place in Life: the Clewer House of Mercy 1849–83* (1992).

12

SOLID JOYS AND LASTING TREASURE

The phenomenal growth of the Community of St John Baptist makes it easy to forget that throughout the nineteenth century Religious Communities were still highly unacceptable to a large section of the Church, and that there were still people who genuinely believed that the Religious Life was a cross between perversion and tyranny.

The Clewer Community had never been particularly subject to such misunderstanding, and this must surely be due to the sound reputation which it had gained during Mother Harriet's leadership. Other Communities had not been so fortunate: a Sister from the Society of St Margaret at East Grinstead had the misfortune to die of a fever caught while out nursing. Her father, an Evangelical clergyman, accused her Community of placing her in danger so that they might gain her wealth. Her funeral at Lewes was attended by an unruly mob and there was a riot. Likewise, there was a spate of 'awful revelations' published by disenchanted ex-nuns, which fired the prurient imagination of many who were quite prepared to believe the worst. Again, the Clewer Community never suffered in this way, but if Mother Harriet's compassionate letter to an ex-novice (see chapter 11) is typical of her attitude in this situation, it is easy to understand why. After all, it must have been far easier to leave with a blessing than under a cloud, and while there were some who for various reasons left under a cloud, they kept their counsel.

In May 1870 the House of Commons ordered the formation of a Select Committee *On Conventual and Monastic Institutions* to inquire into the state of the law, mainly as it affected Roman Catholic Communities, but witnesses were also called to give evidence about Anglican institutions including Clewer. This evidence was published in an appendix to the Parliamentary Report. Here for the first time two Anglican women's Communities (the Society of All Saints and the Community of St John Baptist) were subject to intense scrutiny from outside, and what is more important, the findings, including the Rule, were made public. Searching questions concerning money, property and the relationship with the rest of the Church of England were posed and answered satisfactorily. The Report probably allayed a good many fears and certainly gave a much more humane portrait of Community life. In the next few years many young women came to Clewer from the upper echelons of society, their families perhaps feeling reassured that the findings of a Parliamentary Select Committee were more authoritative than the hysterical accusations of the Church Association and its ilk.

Nevertheless the Church Association did not desist from discrediting the Anglo-Catholic movement whenever it could do so. In 1897 Walter Walsh published a highly successful book called *The Secret History of the Oxford Movement* in which he had collected together documents and rules relating to Anglo-Catholic societies, the intention of the book being to unmask the supposedly 'Romeward' movement in the Church of England. In fact all the so-called revelations had already been aired many times and were no longer controversial. Religious Communities, including that at Clewer, also came under fire, Walsh having used the Report of the Select Committee as the basis for his information. Doubtless the Clewer Sisters would have been surprised to find themselves counted as a 'Ritualistic Sisterhood'. In the event the book served little purpose though it went through several editions and may still be easily found in second hand bookshops. It was in fact merely scurrilous nonsense, but today makes highly entertaining reading.

Although the Community was involved in so many activities, the life revolved around the chapel, with the daily celebration of the Eucharist, the recitation of the Divine Office and periods of private prayer and meditation. The active work radiated out from the chapel like the ripples when a pebble is thrown into a pond. This of course was wholly in line with Mother Harriet's injunction to live the Religious Life and the active work would come out of it, and it is exactly what happened. But the devotional life of the Community was, and is, in a sense the 'hidden' aspect: the staple diet which nurtured all the other work, in a quiet unobtrusive way. The prayer life of a Religious Community is the most important work of all, but it is not the stuff of headlines or history books. Nevertheless it is the 'lasting treasure' of this chapter heading and without it there would be no Community. It is implicit in all the active work which the Clewer Community has ever undertaken: every time a Sister was sent to work at a branch house her departure was preceded by a service of blessing in the chapel, and the most important part of every branch house was its chapel.

The Community chapel had been dedicated in 1855 but as numbers both of Sisters and penitents increased it became extremely cramped. By June 1875 the Community had decided that something must be done: the chapel must either be extended or demolished altogether to make way for a new one. After consulting Henry Woodyer, it was decided to abandon the idea of demolition and build a new chapel alongside the old one—when the money could be found.

In fact the work was soon embarked upon: in August 1878 the great elm was felled to make way for the new foundations adjacent to the existing chapel. On October 20th 1881 the new chapel of St John Baptist was dedicated by Bishop Mackarness. It must have been an impressive sight, with ninety clergy and 104 Sisters in procession together with the choir from St Andrew's Clewer and members of the Council of the House of Mercy. The next day the Eucharist was celebrated for the first time in the new chapel—Low Mass at 7.00 am and High Mass at 8.30 am—in the presence of many Associates. On the Sunday a special Evensong was said for all the workmen employed on the building and all the local tradesmen, the text for the sermon being, "Ye are the salt of the earth."

The new chapel was beyond doubt the crowning glory of the whole range of buildings: it was indeed a 'solid joy'. In his book *Abbeys of Europe* Ian Richards has described the Chapel of St John Baptist Clewer as "a superb expression of Victorian confidence and must be one of the greatest feats of virtuoso brick-laying in England." It was certainly Henry Woodyer's masterpiece.

The main materials consisted of red brick with stone dressings, but Henry Woodyer made use of other materials too such as coloured marble, terracotta panels, inlaid floor tiles and contrasting black brick. Woodyer had worked briefly with William Butterfield and at Clewer the latter's influence was apparent in the use of black and red polychrome brickwork. This was particularly striking above the chancel arch. In the choir the banded brickwork was interspersed with diamond-shaped terracotta panels bearing sacred monograms. The nave was wider than the choir (although the choir itself was deceptively long), the choir being reserved for the Sisters whilst the other residents and visitors used the nave. The nave roof was of a hammerbeam construction whilst the roof of the choir was vaulted. The stone corbels from which the choir vault springs were carved with the birds, plants and animals, including a camel! There was a good deal of woodwork, not only in the choir stalls but also in the rood screen and west gallery. But the best workmanship was in brick, stone and terracotta. The exterior was just as rich in its meticulous use of brickwork and patterned terracotta friezes, particularly at the west end of the choir.

Although the chapel was ready for use by October 1881, this was not the end of the story by any means. The fittings were still incomplete and the next few years saw the gradual embellishment of the interior. This often involved evacuation from the chapel altogether so that recourse was made to the old chapel. In November 1884 a large brass was placed in the floor of the choir as a memorial to Mother Harriet. Lent 1885 saw the erection of the Stations of the Cross around the nave, followed by the stone Calvary at the east end of the north aisle in July. The crucifix and figure of St Mary Magdalen were installed first of all followed by St Mary and St John in September 1888. The stained glass windows were a gradual process, some of which were given as gifts by Sisters. Two of the best known firms in the country were responsible for them: Hardman of Birmingham in the choir and Clayton and Bell in the nave. The Community seems to have been at a loss to know what to do with the old chapel, and it was used at times for Chapter meetings though acoustically it proved inadequate. Generally it stood empty and unused, except for times when the new chapel was occupied by workmen, but it came back into its own towards the end of the 20th century when Community numbers dwindled.

The sanctuary of the new chapel was spacious, and much more so at close quarters than the view from the nave would suggest. In June 1886 seven hanging lamps were put up, involving the erection of scaffolding and a week-long exile into the old chapel. They were the gift of a Sister and comprised a 13th-century silver Italian lamp in the centre flanked by three on each side specially made to match it. In the same year work was begun on facing the brickwork around the sanctuary with alabaster, and the work was completed early in 1888 by highlighting the details in gold. 1887 saw the beginning of the embellishment of the trefoil niches within the sanctuary with portraits of the Saints. The reredos behind the high altar was the focal point of the whole sanctuary. This depicted Christ in glory surrounded by angels holding thuribles with incense rising upwards within the pinnacled framework of the whole. It was a splendid example of the stonemason's craft and must have looked magnificent in 1887 when the details were first picked out in gold. It certainly contradicted the argument of those who claimed Victorian craftsmanship to be stereotyped.

All in all, the Chapel of St John Baptist at Clewer was to Victorian architecture what St George's Chapel, Windsor Castle, was to the late medieval period, and while the Clewer chapel seemed dark upon one's first entrance, there was in fact much colour in the decoration and warm tones in the building materials. The crowds of Associates and others who flocked to Clewer for Commemoration Day during the 1880s must have looked forward to the event in anticipation of new things to see each year. By 1890 most of the work was done, and in the autumn of that year the old chapel was restored. The new chapel completed the House of Mercy buildings (until an infirmary was added in the 1920s), which had gradually been extended by the addition of the Magdalens' wing in 1874, the Sisters' refectory in 1875, the new laundry in 1887 following the fire of 1883, and the new kitchen wing and penitents' dining hall on the site of the old laundry in 1888.

In August 1896 Henry Woodyer died and was buried at Grafham in Surrey near the church he had built there. He was a 'loner' in his profession and had always disdained publicity; perhaps he would have been gratified that no architectural journal mentioned his death. But it did not go unacknowledged at Clewer, a memorial plaque being placed in a recess in the exterior of the south wall of the chapel.

Despite Walter Walsh's accusation of ritualism, the Clewer Community was not a 'Ritualistic Sisterhood', especially in the early years. It had always been mindful of Bishop Wilberforce's wish that it should be "Church of England and no more", a sentiment shared by his successors. The Community was very restrained in the degree of ceremonial used in the Clewer chapels, although many of the Sisters worked in some of the most famous Anglo-Catholic parishes. (Having made that statement, it must also be noted that the funerary ritual for Sisters was elaborate. For an example see Appendix 4 for an account from the Community *Annals* of the funeral of Sr Jane in 1885.) It is true to say that the amount of ritual increased over the years, especially after Bishop Wilberforce's time. As Sisterhoods became more acceptable so the early caution was relaxed and more ritual was introduced, especially in the 20th century between the two World Wars.

As noted in chapter 3, the Community had been using *The Day Hours of the Church of England* since at least 1858 and this office book came to be widely used by other Communities. In 1874 the Community had been endeavouring to improve the method of reciting the office and it was decided to monotone [ie sing on one note] all offices except Vespers, which was to be chanted. On Saturdays, Sundays and festivals Vespers would be fully choral with organ accompaniment. It is not absolutely clear when the Eucharistic vestments were first used, but on Whit Sunday 1887 a new red set was used for the first time, and new white ones on Commemoration Day that year. There was always a High Celebration on Commemoration Day, often with a well known preacher; Solemn Vespers or Evensong usually brought the day to an end.

Incense was introduced at the Midnight Mass of 1884 but its regular use is not mentioned apart from the Dedication festival of 1885. The next we hear is that the choir and congregation were censed for the first time at the Midnight Mass of 1895. This was not well received: "many of the Sisters did not understand beforehand what would be done and did not wish for a more elaborate ritual to be introduced," note the *Annals*. Even so, the Sisters were censed at Solemn Vespers on December 31st and at the Solemn Celebration next day. But at the Solemn Celebration on Easter Day the censing was discontinued, "many of the Sisters having wished it."

The Community numbered 138 when Mother Harriet resigned in 1875, 201 in 1884 and 244 in 1890. By 1900 there were 276 in the Community, choir and lay. This includes the Sisters in India, but in addition there were thirty-eight in the American Affiliation. The number of vocations was therefore still increasing and those who joined came from varied backgrounds. By no means all came from wealthy families, but from about 1870 onwards an increasing number of women joined from genteel backgrounds, whose families were perhaps confident that a Community led by Mrs Monsell would be a safe haven for their daughters. One of the hallmarks of Mother Harriet's Superiorship was that she believed Sisters should exercise their talents, which doubtless accounts for the wide variety of work undertaken. This is in distinct contrast to some Communities where the exercising of individual talents was not encouraged.

Among those who joined as choir Sisters may be mentioned Sr Alice Mary, professed in 1882, formerly Lady Alice Howard; she left the Community in 1891. Sr Katherine Elizabeth, professed in 1889, was the Hon Katherine Onslow; Sr Amabel, professed in 1895, was the Hon Alicia Amabel O'Brien,

Mother Harriet's niece; Sr Mary Louise was another niece of Mother Harriet's, but she left the Community in 1897 and joined the Roman Catholic Church. Other famous surnames include Spencer-Churchill (Sr Ethel, professed 1865 and died 1881); Rollo (Sr Constance Agnes, daughter of Lord Rollo, professed 1890); Hyde Parker (Sr Amy Grace, professed 1897); and Cave Brown Cave (Sr Mary Evelyn, professed 1907).

Another Sister with a famous surname was Frances Henrietta Kilvert, sister of the famous diarist. She was 43 years old when she came to Clewer on February 1st 1892 to test her vocation. She gave the name of her brother Edward Kilvert of Streatham Hill, London, as her next of kin, her diarist brother the Revd Francis Kilvert having died in 1879. She was professed on April 23rd 1894 and took the name of Sr Frances Harriet. After her profession she worked at Clewer but in 1898 she was sent to work at All Hallows' Mission, Southwark. From there she went to work at the Devon House of Mercy, Bovey Tracey, until c1920. From 1924–6 she worked at St Andrew's Convalescent Hospital, Clewer, until she was admitted to the Sisters' Infirmary in September 1926. She died there on October 4th 1929 aged about 80 years and was buried in the Garth, the Sisters' burial ground, at Clewer. Sr Frances Harriet was a member of the Guild of All Souls, an Anglo-Catholic society founded in 1873 to promote prayer for the departed. This would indicate that she and her brother the Revd Francis Kilvert, though both members of the Church of England, held vastly different views on 'churchmanship'. In his diary he recorded a visit to St Barnabas Oxford and described the censing of the altar during the Magnificat as 'pure Mariolatry'. No doubt had he lived long enough he would have objected in the strongest terms to her joining a Sisterhood. (Of the 535 names of departed CSJB Sisters recorded on plaques formerly in the Chapel of St John Baptist at Clewer and now in Clewer St Stephen, 141 are on the roll of departed members of the Guild of All Souls.)

Harriet Monsell was not the only widow to become a Religious Sister at Clewer. While it is no longer possible to know just how many others there were, the Hon Caroline Amelia Saumarez may stand to represent them all. She was born on September 9th 1839 and on July 20th 1861 married, as his second wife, George Ives Irby, 4th Baron Boston, and was styled Baroness Boston. She was widowed in 1869 and her two children (both girls) died in 1865 and 1873. As an Anglo-Catholic, Amelia, Lady Boston, as she was now known, came under the influence of Father John Bourdieu Wilkinson, who had decided to build a church at Lavender Hill. She was also beginning to feel called to the Religious Life and with Fr Wilkinson's encouragement she came to Clewer. She was received as a choir novice, taking the name of Sr Mary Caroline, on January 21st 1874 and was professed as a choir Sister on March 31st 1876. At some point soon afterwards she left Clewer in order to devote herself and her wealth to the people of Lavender Hill, where she established a mission house and a Community called the Community of the Compassion of Jesus. Mother Mary Caroline, as she was now styled, was one of the three principle benefactors of the church of the Ascension, Lavender Hill. She died at Tankerton in Kent on December 20th 1927 and is commemorated at the church of the Ascension, Lavender Hill, in a stained glass window depicting St Francis of Assisi.

Several Sisters had links with the Windsor area. Sr Constance, professed in 1876, was a Vansittart Neale, whose brother Sir Henry resided at Bisham Abbey; Sr Elvira, professed in 1884, was the sister and niece of the Misses Macbean of Clewer, two staunch supporters of Clewer parish church; Sr Blanche Annie, professed in 1893, was the daughter of the Revd John Kitcat, sometime curate of Clewer St Stephen; Sr Agatha, professed 1906, was the sister of the Revd Henry Tower, Rector of Holy Trinity Windsor.

In addition, a number of Sisters had transferred from the Second Order: Sr Emma Augusta was formerly a member of the Third Order of the Society of the Most Holy Trinity, Devonport, who transferred to the Second Order at Clewer 1866–87 and became a professed choir Sister in 1888 until her death in 1918. Several others also transferred from Second Order to choir. Sr Clara was professed as a lay Sister in 1875, and was received as a choir Sister in 1885, but left in 1888. It was still very unusual to transfer from lay to choir at this time, but even more unusual was the case of Sr Madelena, formerly Isabel Magdalen, who was professed as a choir Sister in October 1898.

A large Community such as that at Clewer was bound to have a fairly high number of departures from the noviciate, most of them being for lack of vocation or because the way of life was too rigorous. A few, both novices and professed Sisters, also left, some of them deciding that their path lay in the Roman Catholic Church. This was perhaps inevitable at a time when Anglo-Catholicism was undergoing difficulties and particularly in the wake of the Papal Bull *Apostolicae Curae* of 1896, which pronounced the Anglican orders of bishop, priest and deacon to be "absolutely null and utterly void".

By the turn of the century the Community had been in existence for almost fifty years. Mother Harriet had been dead since 1883, Bishop Wilberforce since 1873, and many of the early Sisters had gone to their rest. Of those professed before 1860 only Sr Elizabeth, Sr Anne Elizabeth and Sr Katherine Mary were to outlive the century, though many who were professed in the 1870s did so. By 1900 there had been four Mothers of the Community: Mother Harriet 1852–75, Mother Ellen 1875–81 (died 1892), Mother Jane Frances 1881–89 and Mother Betha 1889–1907. There had been three Episcopal Visitors: Bishop Wilberforce 1852–69, Bishop Mackarness 1870–89 and Bishop Stubbs 1889–1901. But by 1900 there had only been one Warden: the Revd Canon T T Carter, the last link with the founding days.

Canon Carter had resigned as Rector of Clewer in 1880 following a ritualist controversy. Space does not permit a detailed account of what came to be known as the 'Clewer Case', except to say that Bishop Mackarness defended Carter right through to the House of Lords and won the case on appeal. But the Bishop was no ritualist and had defended Carter in the name of justice rather than in defence of ritualism. Therefore Carter felt honour bound to resign his benefice rather than remain in office and incur Episcopal disapproval for the mild ceremonial practised at Clewer church. Just a few years previously, in 1877, the Revd Arthur Tooth had been sent to jail for contempt of court for refusing to accept a legal ruling on similar ceremonial practices such as wearing vestments at the Eucharist. Other jail sentences followed in the next few years. It is against this climate of opinion that Bishop Mackarness' courage in defending Carter must be appreciated; and Carter's humility in accepting that canonical obedience to his Bishop must result in his resignation of office.

In fact only a minority of Carter's parishioners disapproved of his churchmanship; unfortunately they were the most influential. But his resignation provoked strong feelings, so much so that a public meeting was held to dissuade him from leaving and two petitions, with 316 and 568 signatures respectively, were presented to him. But in spite of all this support, which moved him deeply, Carter resigned. His resignation meant that he had to vacate Clewer Rectory and would therefore be homeless. However, some land opposite the House of Mercy was granted by its Council and work soon began on a house, called St John's Lodge, which was paid for by public subscription. This was completed and blessed in July 1881 and Carter resided there until his death in 1901. For the remaining years of his life he continued as Warden of the Clewer Community, and as a highly respected 'elder Statesman' of the Church.

Increasing age and infirmity did not lessen Carter's considerable influence on the life and work of the Community, especially as his duties elsewhere diminished. Perhaps inevitably, older members of the Community who remembered the early partnership with Mother Harriet could not envisage a day when the Community would be without him too. To the very end of his days Carter kept a firm grip on the Community Chapter, refusing to sign the Minutes if he disagreed with a decision! There is evidence too that even when the opinions of all the Sisters were sought on important matters, the general feeling was to defer to the opinion of the Warden.

Even though it may seem as if undue deference was made to the Warden, towards the end of the century important forward steps were taken. The *Statutes* which had been revised in 1870 were again revised in 1889, and at the same time the Consultative Council was extended from four members to six. This purely advisory body had first been elected in the Chapter of November 1874. The Community Chapter had also seen some changes: it had always been policy to allow Sisters absent at branches to express their opinion by letter. In 1874 it was decided that if the number of letters were sufficient to turn a decision, a second Chapter must be held. Until 1886 all professed choir Sisters had a vote in Chapter, but after this date only choir Sisters professed five years or more had a vote. The finance regulations were also brought up to date along with alterations in the Rule during the 1890s. In 1889 the property of the Community was brought under a single General Trust Fund, of which seven Sisters were Trustees. In 1893 a Business Committee was established to deal with legal and property matters, including oversight of the various Community works and of the Community Fund for the maintenance of the Sisters. The Land Trust was established in 1899 to hold the Community's real estate, and the Money Trust had been established in 1898 to hold personal property, including real estate let to tenants. In 1906 these two Trusts were jointly incorporated as a limited company called the Land and Money Trust. (Many years later, in 1953, it would be replaced by Clewer Trustee Ltd.)

In 1891 it was finally acknowledged that the Sisters did in fact take vows, even though they were made before the profession service rather than within it. At the Chapter in November 1891 Mother Betha read a letter from the Warden in which "he desires to inform the Sisters that he thinks it advisable to insert into the Constitutions a notice of *what has long been in general use and has been taught from the beginning, i.e. that vows of Religion are taken* and the relation they bear to the promises made in the Profession service."

Carter had never enjoyed robust health, but he made a good recovery from illness in the early 1870s despite the strain of harassment by the Church Association throughout that decade. But in May 1891 he was taken seriously ill and the Community feared the worst. All branch houses were notified and special intercessions offered. Even so he continued to send messages to the Community until his full recovery. In September he was present at the reception of novices, though the Sub-Warden, the Revd G S Cuthbert, officiated. After this time Carter became increasingly frail, but he lived for another ten years.

1901 saw the end of an era for Empire and Community. Queen Victoria died on January 21st after a reign of almost sixty-four years. Just four years previously the Community and penitents had rejoiced at the Diamond Jubilee, and the penitents had enjoyed a sausage-and-mash supper illuminated by Chinese lanterns and culminating in fireworks and 'God save the Queen'. Now Community and penitents mourned her passing: the chapel bell was solemnly tolled after Compline, the whole household said the Litany for the Departed, which the Sisters followed with Nocturnes and Lauds for the Dead. On February 1st there were two Celebrations of the Eucharist for the late Queen. The funeral was next day and many of the Sisters watched the solemn procession from houses in Windsor. A few Sisters were still alive who would have recalled that memorable visit to the convent by the Queen in 1864.

The same year was to see the death of Canon Carter. From August his health failed rapidly, but on October 26th Carter was present at the Chapter which re-elected Mother Betha as Superior. Next day, October 27th, he was poorly and retired to bed and died peacefully on the 28th. Carter's body, clad in full vestments and holding chalice and paten, was laid at St John's Lodge for two days, and many came to pay their last respects including boys from St Augustine's Home. At 8.00 pm on the eve of the funeral the body was brought into the Community chapel and an all-night vigil was kept (as was also the case with departed Sisters). The funeral was on October 31st, the Solemn Requiem being celebrated by Carter's nephew, the Rt Revd William Carter, Bishop of Zululand. The procession to St Andrew's churchyard was a quarter of a mile long and it was estimated that there were 100 clergy and 150 Sisters present. Even so a critic described it as "Popish mummery", but the last word should go to the *Daily Telegraph*, who described Carter as "the last Tractarian". Perhaps that sums up this great man best of all.

Notes

It is difficult to unravel the history of the Community of the Compassion of Jesus. In his book *The Call of the Cloister*, second revised edition, 1964, Peter Anson notes three different Communities with the same dedication. For further information about Mother Mary Caroline and the history of the Ascension, Lavender Hill, see the website www.ascensionlavenderhill.org.uk

For more about Carter and the accusations of ritualism made against him, see: Valerie Bonham, "A Complication of Circumstances: Canon Carter and the 'Clewer Case'" in *Windlesora* No. 8, 1989.

13

FROM VICTORIA TO VERSAILLES

The death of Queen Victoria brought a new Sovereign for Country and Empire; the turn of the century also heralded a new era for the Community of St John Baptist with a new Warden, new Visitor and within a few years, the death of many of the older Sisters.

The new Warden, the Revd George Seignelay Cuthbert, was blessed in his office by Francis Paget, Bishop of Oxford, on January 30th 1902. (Bishop Paget had become Visitor in September 1901 following the death of his predecessor Bishop William Stubbs, and was to hold the office until 1911.) Cuthbert had been Carter's curate in Clewer parish from 1873–5 and Sub-Warden of the Community from 1884–1902. He was to hold office as Warden until his retirement in 1912, so there was for the time being a strong link with the past.

The summer of 1902 saw plans set afoot by the Council of the House of Mercy for a memorial to Canon Carter in the Chapel of St John Baptist. The cost was estimated at about £1,500, and G F Bodley, the eminent architect and designer, was asked to execute it. The work took longer than anticipated, Bodley favouring a position directly in front of the high altar, which was not favoured by the Community. Eventually it was erected on the north side of the apsidal sanctuary and was unveiled on St Thomas' Day (December 21st) 1903. The recumbent alabaster effigy of Carter was exquisitely portrayed in dignified old age, robed in the Eucharistic vestments, the wearing of which had brought him so much persecution in his lifetime. The actual set of green vestments, decorated with Tudor rose orphreys, is still in the care of the Community, a much treasured link with Canon Carter.

A number of well known, and by now aged, Sisters passed to their eternal rest in the years preceding the Great War, among them Sr Emily, Sr Georgina Mary, Sr Emma, Sr Elizabeth and Sr Katherine Mary. First there was Sister Emily, pioneer of the work in Clewer Fields which grew into the parish of Clewer St Stephen. She died on September 23rd 1905 after five years' failing health, and was buried at Clewer churchyard on September 28th. Although she died at Torquay she was brought back to Clewer where her life's work had been. In addition to her work at Clewer St Stephen's, Sr Emily was also for many years the organist at the House of Mercy and undertook all the musical arrangements of the choir, and also taught the penitents how to sing in chapel. Her death brought a lengthy obituary in the *Church Times* which described her quite rightly as "the moving spirit" of the work at St Stephen's. She was also compared with a 'sleuth-hound' in her dedication to the work in hand! There are two commemorative plaques to Sr Emily at Clewer St Stephen. The inscription on the first one is in Latin:

In piam memoriam sororis
Emilia CSJB
Que abdormuit in Christa XXIII Sept MCMV
(In pious memory of Sister
Emily CSJB
Who fell asleep in Christ 23 Sept 1905)

The second plaque bears the following inscription:

Emily daughter of the Rev C E Hutchinson
Canon Residentiary of Chichester Cathedral
Born June 29th 1835
Sister Community of St John Baptist Nov 29th 1868
Sister Superior of St Stephen's 1868
Died Sept 23rd 1905
Not I but Christ
RIP
This window is placed to her memory by her sister's children.

Sr Emily's window portrays St Ethelburga, one of a series of English saints depicted all the way along the south aisle of Clewer St Stephen's. (St Ethelburga was an Anglo-Saxon nun, possibly of royal blood, who became Abbess of Barking and who died in 675. She is commemorated in the *Common Worship* Calendar on October 11th and is therefore possibly better known in the 21st century than she was in Sr Emily's lifetime.) There is a discrepancy in the dates on the second plaque: her profession as a choir Sister was in November 1864, not 1868.

A month later, on October 23rd 1905, Sr Georgina Mary died. Born Georgina Sophia Hoare, she was the sister of Sir Henry Hoare, 5th Baronet, of Stourhead. (On page 127 of *A Place in Life* it was erroneously stated that Sr Georgina Mary was the daughter of Sir Henry Hoare.) As a young woman she and two friends (who later became the Mother Foundresses of the Society of All Saints and the Sisters of Bethany) took great interest in the early Tractarian Movement. Sr Georgina Mary spent most of her professed life in London, at St Barnabas Pimlico, St Alban's Holborn, St John's Westminster and St Mary's Westminster, with a brief twelve-month period from December 1881–2 when she returned to Clewer as Assistant Superior. She was greatly loved by all who knew her and at Holborn was known as "Sister Georgy" in an age not given to over-familiarity. But most of all she was held in deep affection by the men and their families of the Brigade of Guards and the Household Cavalry over whom she had assumed pastoral care in 1893, so much so that her funeral took on a distinctly military air.

Both *The Times* and the *Church Times* gave Sr Georgina Mary lengthy obituaries, and we learn that following the funeral service in the Community chapel, the funeral cortège was conveyed to Clewer churchyard under the escort of a bearer party consisting of six sergeants from the 2nd Battalion Coldstream Guards, and that the men themselves had requested this duty. Among the mourners were Lord Methuen and other senior officers, and there were a number of wreaths from the officers and men of the Brigade of Guards, and from their families. A memorial plaque was placed in the Guards' Chapel, Wellington Barracks, but this was destroyed in 1944 when the chapel suffered a direct hit by a flying bomb.

On March 22nd 1909 Sr Emma died in London after a short illness. Her chief work had been at St Augustine's Home, Clewer, where she had a special rapport with the boys. She was buried at Clewer churchyard on March 26th and a number of her old boys were present. She was at least spared the horror of the forthcoming war in which many of her old boys served and a number died. Since the first edition of this book was published new information has come to light about Sr Emma. It seems she was a collector of English folk songs at a time when many were being irretrievably lost. For the full story see Appendix 2, 'Sister Emma and her songs'.

January 20th 1912 saw the death at Torquay of Sr Elizabeth and her burial there four days later. She was one of the earliest and most generous benefactors of the Community, having contributed financially to the building of the first chapel, St John's Home and the Magdalens' wing. She served as Novice Mistress from 1853–89, after which she retired to Torquay and took charge of St Luke's Home for invalid men. In 1892 she bought the nearby property that became St Barnabas' Home for advanced consumptive cases. She was the youngest of the four children of the Revd William Moreton Moreton of Westerham, Kent and Moreton Hall, Cheshire. Her two elder brothers died young, leaving Elizabeth and her sister, Frances Annabella, who married Mr John Craigie and was listed in the Community records as Sr Elizabeth's next of kin, residing at Pau in France. It seems as if this was a childless marriage and when Frances died in 1892 Sr Elizabeth became the sole heiress. Thus a Clewer Sister inherited Little Moreton Hall in Cheshire, a house now owned by the National Trust and one of the most famous timber-framed houses in England. The silver-gilt chalice given to the Community by Sr Elizabeth in 1856 is now in the care of the Victoria & Albert Museum. Sr Elizabeth's Bible and Rule Book are now in the care of the National Trust at Little Moreton Hall. (For further information about Sr Elizabeth, her family and her generosity to the CSJB, see Appendix 6.)

On Christmas Day 1912 Sr Katherine Mary, first Superior of the London work, died at Clewer aged 90 years. And on February 22nd 1913 the death occurred of Sr Ann, an old lay Sister who, before entering the Community had been in domestic service to the Revd John Keble, one of the founders of the Tractarian, or Oxford, Movement. She had nursed Mr Keble and his wife during their last illnesses.

The Edwardian era has been seen by historians as a last spell of economic prosperity and social stability before the deluge of 1914–18, after which the world was changed forever. Within the Community itself the period was equally stable, reflecting in general terms the state of society. Numbers of Sisters continued to increase until 1911, the optimum year. In 1901, the year of Canon Carter's death, there were 274 Sisters, plus thirty-eight in the American Affiliation. In 1911 there were 302 Sisters, consisting of 205 choir Sisters, sixty-one lay Sisters, thirty-three choir and lay novices and three Second Order Sisters; plus thirty-nine in America. It was not until the 1920s, when the effects of the Great War became generally manifest in society, that there was any marked change in the Community or its work.

Mother Betha, who had been Superior since November 1889, was not re-elected in the 1907 Chapter of election, the office falling upon Sr Evelyn, who had joined in 1883, the year of Mother Harriet's death. Professed in 1885, Sr Evelyn had succeeded Sr Elizabeth as Novice Mistress in 1889 and remained so until her election as Superior. She was to fulfil the demanding duties of Superior for the next twenty-one years, steering the Community through the Great War and its aftermath with all the changes it was to bring about. But the Community was constantly adapting itself to changing needs, and the *Annals* record that the Constitutions were revised once more and finally signed by the Visitor in 1908, and *The Day Hours of the Church of England* were revised in 1909.

The buildings of the Community and House of Mercy were by now beginning to show signs of their age. The new century had brought new standards and it was essential to keep abreast of them. In 1907 the telephone had been installed and a year later the lengthy process of connection to the main Windsor drainage system was embarked upon, involving considerable upheaval and even greater expense. The new century had brought motor transport, and many enterprising tradesmen were using these means for fast and efficient delivery. By this time other laundries were being set up locally so that it was essential to maintain efficiency, and in 1912 a "fine motor van" was purchased for the House of Mercy laundry with part of a legacy. In the spring of 1914 it was decided to install electric lighting in the House, starting with the chapel. In fact the onset of War intervened, but a start was made, which is more than happened with the Sisters' Infirmary. The decision to build this had been taken in May 1914 just before the War broke out because there were an increasing number of aged and infirm Sisters, and the limited number of beds reserved at St Andrew's Convalescent Hospital was no longer sufficient. Although £1,500 had been received for this project nothing more was done until the early 1920s.

1911, Coronation year, once more saw a change of both Warden and Visitor. Bishop Paget died in August and his successor as Bishop and Visitor was Charles Gore, a founder member of the Community of the Resurrection at Mirfield. He paid his first visit to Clewer on December 18th, when three choir Sisters and one lay Sister were professed. In July 1911 the Revd G S Cuthbert had resigned as Warden and was succeeded by the Revd Bernard Moultrie, who took up his duties in April 1912.

Just before Fr Cuthbert retired the Community decided once again to use incense at the Sung Eucharist on Sundays and festivals but the experiment seems to have been shortlived. Also at this time (mid-1912) the Community began taking lessons in Plainsong, and the visitors on Commemoration Day 1914 were able to hear the results of their endeavours. The *Annals* note: "The music, which was strict Plainsong, was admired by some who thought the voices sounded very pure and sweet, but by others it was felt to be feeble and rather depressing."

Bernard Moultrie's time as Warden was undistinguished in all except the manner of his departure, which came suddenly in May 1915. This was due to one of those doctrinal disputes which afflict Anglicanism every few years. The last straw for Moultrie came as the result of the so-called 'Kikuyu affair' and what many saw as the unsatisfactory action on the part of Archbishop Randall Davidson. (In 1913 a missionary conference of Anglicans and Non-Conformists was held at Kikuyu in East Africa, at which a federation of the constituent Churches was proposed, including recognition of common membership together with inter-Communion. Many Anglicans objected to the scheme and Bishop Frank Weston of Zanzibar appealed to the Archbishop of Canterbury, Randall Davidson, who gave his opinion that Non-Conformists might be admitted to Communion in Anglican churches, but that Anglicans should not seek Communion from Non-Conformist ministers.) Following his resignation on May 23rd 1915, Moultrie severed all ties with Clewer and on June 6th was received into the Roman Catholic Church. This dealt a crushing blow to the Community because at this time it was still considered an act of betrayal when someone left the Church of England and joined the Roman Catholic Church. But when that person held a position of authority it had wider implications, so that for the Warden to resign in such circumstances was a matter of great embarrassment to the Community. Moultrie was replaced in October 1915 by the Revd Arthur East, who had been Sub-Warden since 1912, and he was assisted by a new Sub-Warden, the Revd George Bernard Hardy, who now began an association with the Clewer Sisters which was to last for many years.

The Great War was the first time such a conflict had directly affected the Community, the Victorian years having been peaceful except for a few skirmishes in the outposts of Empire. The Boer War had been marked by special prayers in the Community Chapel for the duration, and a Te Deum was sung after the relief of Mafeking. But with the onset of this, the most catastrophic war in history, the Community found itself involved in a way it had never known before. On August 4th 1914, the day England found itself at war with Germany, Mother Evelyn went to London to see a Sister who was ill. When she returned to Clewer she reported that Londoners had been awake all night, the crowds singing "Rule Britannia" and "God save the King". It was this early euphoria which made men respond in their thousands to Kitchener's request for recruits. It was the same patriotic euphoria which made women urge their menfolk to join up, not knowing of the horrors which trench warfare would unfold before many months had passed. But this was a war which, so everyone believed, would all be over by Christmas.

The Sisters too were caught up in the euphoria. For instance, Sr Etheldreda made it known that no former St Augustine's Home boy would be welcome there if he had failed to serve his country. In fact over fifty had joined up by the end of 1914. Sr Helen Rachel had taken over the Guards visiting from Sr Georgina Mary, and, like her predecessor, threw herself wholly into the work. She returned from her rest period early to bid farewell to her guardsmen in the British Expeditionary Force before it crossed to France, and in addition to her regular visiting made herself the "scourge" of the Westminster War Pensions Office where she soon became known as "the Guards' Nun". A former clerk there later recalled, "Her visits always inspired us to fresh efforts ... when tempted to treat as 'cases' and 'files' the mass of suffering humanity that was daily passing through our hands ... Often she would sit at my table ... always ending with the same stern command, 'Something must be done,' and it gives me an odd thrill of pleasure to think how many times we dodged the regulations so that the 'Guards' Nun' might not be disappointed."

But for most of the Community the War meant an extra discipline of prayer and intercession rather than active war work. This round of dedicated intercession was additional to the normal daily round of Eucharist, Divine Office and private prayer, and took two forms. Firstly, there were corporate prayers at the end of the daily Office, and secondly, days were set apart for special prayer and intercession which would be divided into set periods, each Sister having a time assigned to her. Some of these days were also National Days of Prayer designated by the Archbishops and observed in churches everywhere. January 3rd 1915 was such a day and was kept by Christians of all denominations, a rare example of ecumenical co-operation. But there were many more, including the much heralded National Mission for Repentance and Hope in 1916.

A tragic accident befell one of the Sisters in London. On October 10th 1915 Sr Sophie was knocked down by a motorbus. Some soldiers saw the accident and they carefully carried her into the mission room at St Barnabas Pimlico and administered First Aid. Then she was taken to St George's Hospital, but she never regained consciousness and died at 11.30 pm. She had taken an old lady home after Evensong, fearing she might be knocked down by the traffic, little thinking that the same kind of accident would befall her.

In 1915 Commemoration Day was cancelled and not held again until 1919, and other festivities were severely curtailed. For the first time in history there was danger in the skies: the Zeppelin raids were a grim foretaste of an even deadlier war to come, and blackout precautions were introduced in January 1915. Although Clewer remained free from attack, there were raids on Folkestone and Leytonstone as well as in London, but fortunately none of the Community houses were damaged. Twenty children and two novices were evacuated from Leytonstone to St John's Home, Clewer. It was, however, a solemn reminder of how much the world had changed since the Community's early growth and expansion.

There was not only peril in the air but also at sea. This had two direct effects. Firstly, it made communication with the overseas work both difficult and dangerous, and secondly, food rationing was introduced. Hitherto there had been frequent comings and goings to and from India and America, but German submarines made the voyage perilous, and in April 1918 the ship carrying three Sisters home from India was torpedoed—but there will be more about that in a later chapter. Such was the food situation that two 'meatless' days a week were introduced for a time during 1917, and afternoon tea was only taken on major festivals. January 1918 saw the postponement of the Sisters' retreat because of the food shortage. Sisters coming from far-flung branches would have strained the catering beyond its means.

In June 1917 the Sub-Warden, Fr Hardy, left temporarily to become an Army chaplain and was sent first of all to Strensall Camp near York, where he had several thousand men in his spiritual care. The officers gave him the use of a bell tent which he named 'The Vicarage' and invited the soldiers to call on him when they were off duty. An increasing number took up his invitation as their time to embark for the Front drew near. In September 1917 Fr Hardy returned to Clewer for a short period of leave before embarking for France on September 11th, where he served until September 1918. During his time abroad he wrote a number of letters to the Community describing his experiences at the Front and the men to whom he ministered. A letter in the Community *Annals*, described the plight of the men as they emerged from the trenches. "Days and nights in mud and water are very trying … I shall never forget a Mass in a crowded dug-out the day before they went into action. Halfway through the service two Officers managed to slip into the doorway, there was no other spot. I remember them so well, crouching in a very uncomfortable position shutting out all of what little light could get in. Only the two candles on the altar gave light. They made their Communions. It was their viaticum [last Communion]—God rest their souls."

Just before Christmas the Sisters received several more letters which the Sister-Secretary transcribed into the *Annals* thus ensuring their survival. "This morning," wrote Fr Hardy, "I had an hour's walk through mud and trenches delayed for a time by the unwelcome attention of a German aeroplane … At last I arrived at a certain dugout. Down about 20 feet ran a steep staircase onto a square flat … On the flat I arranged a little altar. Men all up and down the stairs crouched to one side so as to leave me room to pass to Communicate them. A few outside in the trench [were] kneeling in the mud. At the bottom were a few un-Confirmed Officers who were very interested and reverent. I reminded them that Our Lord chose a dugout when he first came to earth. It was all very suggestive of Bethlehem except for the noise of the guns outside."

A few days later he wrote, "We have discovered a large cellar beneath ruins close to the lines [ie the line of battle]. There is plenty of room for a canteen, reading room and a chapel. The chapel is to be dedicated to St John Baptist. I wonder if the Community would furnish the altar for us. I said Mass here this morning. Sixty men came and were very reverent and appreciative." The Sisters responded to this request by sending an altar frontal, and in his next letter Fr Hardy was able to report on its use. "The frontal came today and all is quite beautiful. Thank you so much. I have two candlesticks made out of biscuit tins. The men are immensely proud of them. They are making also a tabernacle [for reserving the Blessed Sacrament] and a Cross."

Fr Hardy was in a different part of the front line when he wrote to the Sisters on Christmas Day. "This morning my first Mass was said in a barn. The altar was set up against the door surrounded by straw [and] piled up arms. So again there was no room for Him in the inn. The service over, I rode to a neighbouring village, my servant following on a bicycle with the bag of sacred vessels. There in a hall I had a whole battalion, the band played the hymns." There are no further letters in the *Annals* except a note stating that Fr Hardy returned to Clewer on September 9th 1918.

During Fr Hardy's absence the Warden was assisted by the Revd G S Cuthbert, who came out of retirement. (The Revd G S Cuthbert died on December 14th 1918, just two months after his last visit to Clewer.) The war years were an unsettling time and there was a very slight downward trend in Community numbers. In 1914 there were 294 Sisters (plus forty-one in America); by 1919 there were 281 (plus forty-three in America). It might be easy to suggest that women did not test their vocations because of the War, and yet the choir noviciate rose slightly whilst the lay noviciate dropped. But the war years saw a number of professed Sisters leave to join the Roman Catholic Church, and one left to join the Eastern Orthodox Church, which helps to account for the drop, and deaths account for the rest. It would also be easy to suggest that the secession of Bernard Moultrie had something to do with this, but there is no real evidence to support the idea especially as there were secessions in the 1920s too.

The Sisters for the most part fought the War with prayer and fasting but there were some whose active work won tangible decorations, which was an honour for all. In October 1917 Sr Laura Jane, Sister Superior of St Andrew's Convalescent Home, Folkestone, was awarded the Royal Red Cross decoration by His Majesty King George V in recognition of the work for convalescent soldiers at the Home. In 1918 the King of the Belgians bestowed the *Medaille de la Reine Elisabeth* on Sr Edith Katherine in recognition of help given to Belgian refugees and soldiers during the War. In the same year Sr Mary Victoria was awarded the Kaisar-i-Hind decoration in the King's birthday honours.

November 11th 1918, Armistice Day was marked by the singing of a Te Deum at Evensong. Next day there was a Choral Eucharist of thanksgiving at 8.30 am after which the Warden gave a general dispensation from silence.

The penitents had a 'talking' dinner and a free evening, and throughout the Community the following Sunday was kept as a day of special thanksgiving.

A brass plaque in Bayton church in Worcestershire commemorates a Clewer Sister who, though she has passed into obscurity, was one of the large number of Sisters who served God faithfully, but not in a leadership role. She was Mary Elizabeth Wicksted, and at Clewer she was known as Sr Mary Verena. Her death occurred in the final year of the Great War.

The inscription is as follows:

> To the Glory of God
> And in memory of
> MARY ELIZABETH
> SISTER MARY VERENA CSJB, CLEWER
> DAUGHTER OF
> CHARLES WICKSTED of Shakenhurst
> BORN 1841 DIED 1918
> HIS SERVANTS SHALL SERVE
> HIM AND THEY SHALL SEE
> HIS FACE

Sr Mary Verena's family home, Shakenhurst Hall, an elegant, predominantly 18th-century Grade 2* mansion, fell on hard times in the late 20th century and was on the market in 2010 for £12 million.

But there was a new peril as deadly as war: influenza. The epidemic swept across Europe, taking its toll on a war-weary and debilitated population. In England and Wales alone more than 150,000 people died from influenza, and the worldwide mortality rate has been put as high as 30 million. Windsor and Clewer did not escape the scourge, all churches and schools being affected. But this did not dampen the spirit of thanksgiving which all felt for the coming of peace. The Treaty of Versailles was signed at the end of June 1919, a Te Deum of thanksgiving was sung after Evensong, and for the first time since 1915, Commemoration Day was kept. Bishop Gore preached on what was also his last day as Bishop of Oxford and Visitor of the Community. But there were some absent friends too: Colonel the Hon Charles Hay-Drummond, member of the Council of the House of Mercy since 1875 and sometime Treasurer; Victor Myddleton Biddulph, member

of the Council since 1891, and server in the Community chapel; and the
Revd G S Cuthbert had all died since the War ended. In addition, the War
had taken its toll on Fr Hardy and early in 1919 he had to receive treatment,
having been gassed in the trenches.

As 1919 gave way to a new decade the Community entered a new phase.
The Edwardian period had been an extension of the Victorian heyday; now,
as the 1920s dawned, the Community was to be increasingly affected by the
social changes which came in the aftermath of the War.

14

SUNDRY AND MANIFOLD CHANGES

As the 1920s dawned there was a tendency within society to resume life from where it had been in August 1914, but it soon became obvious that this would be impossible. There were too many homes bereft of fathers, sons and brothers; too many rolls of honour cataloguing a lost generation. Those who came back found a changed world: the War had strained the economy so that recovery was to prove difficult and make the 1918 General Election promises of "a land fit for heroes" difficult to keep; it had changed the relationship between the social classes so that while the poor remained poor, the rich found themselves not quite so rich; it had undermined Christianity, many men losing their faith after Ypres, Passchendaele and Gallipoli; and it had changed the role of women forever. All these factors were to have a bearing on Religious Communities, on their potential membership, their secular benefactors and consequently on their active work.

1920 was an important year in the life of the Community. Firstly, the new Visitor, Bishop Herbert Burge, sanctioned Reservation of the Blessed Sacrament (the consecrated bread from Holy Communion) in one of the chapels. (His predecessor Bishop Gore was well known for his steadfast refusal to allow Reservation in all chapels and churches within his jurisdiction.) The Blessed Sacrament was reserved in the old chapel until Easter Sunday, when it was transferred to the tabernacle on the high altar of the Chapel of St John Baptist at the end of High Mass. The only condition made by the Bishop was that the Eucharist should not be celebrated at the same altar. Secondly, on October 1st 1920 there was a profession service at which the vows were made during the service in the presence of the Bishop for the first time rather than privately to the Warden before the Service. The Bishop of Buckingham (the Rt Revd E D Shaw) officiated and received the vows of Sr Beatrice Miriam and Sr Helen Muriel.

In January 1922 the Warden, the Revd Arthur East, resigned and was replaced by the Revd G H Tremenheere, who was installed on September 21st. Relations between Community and Warden had changed since Carter's well nigh autocratic rule, but the Sisters were still subject to the Warden's word to a large degree. For instance, in 1918 East had refused to allow the

Sisters to sign Bishop Gore's petition protesting against the consecration of Hensley Henson as Bishop of Hereford (on the grounds of his unorthodox beliefs), adding that by signing it himself he was signing for the Community. Similarly in 1924 Tremenheere expressed his disapproval of Sisters who worked in parishes becoming members of Parochial Church Councils. (These were a recent innovation introduced by the Church Assembly, itself a creation of the Church of England Assembly [Powers] Act of 1919.)

It seems as though Tremenheere failed to achieve any rapport with many of the Sisters, so much so that the Chapter felt it was causing harm. This situation could not continue and in May 1926 the Chapter voted for his removal: this was ratified at a second chapter in August, a hitherto unprecedented step. A further break with tradition was made when the Bishop of Buckingham, the Rt Revd Philip Eliot, was elected as the first non-resident Warden. Bishop Eliot was an old friend of the Community, having been Rector of Slough from 1896 until his consecration in January 1921. There had been some doubt whether having a non-resident Warden would be successful and at first the appointment was made for a year, commencing in August 1926, before becoming permanent. But there seems to have been a good relationship, though there were still times when the Warden took the initiative. For instance, at the time of the 1929 General Election Eliot made it known that he disapproved of Sisters voting, so none of them did so. This was a year after the voting age for women had been lowered from 30 to 21, but it is not clear whether any Sisters had voted in the General Elections from 1918 onwards (though it is unlikely).

In June 1923 HRH the Princess Christian of Schleswig-Holstein died. Born in 1846, HRH the Princess Helena Augusta Victoria was the seventh child of Queen Victoria. In 1866 she married the Prince Christian of Schleswig-Holstein and together they did much philanthropic work. Nursing the sick poor was of especial interest to the Princess. St Andrew's Convalescent Home, Folkestone, enjoyed her special patronage, and she founded two hospitals in Windsor. These were the Princess Christian Maternity Home in Alma Road, which closed in the late 1970s and was subsequently demolished, and the Princess Christian Nursing Home, founded in 1904 and closed in 2005. (After standing empty for five years the nursing home underwent redevelopment as luxury apartments.) During the Boer War the Princess had sent a hospital train to South Africa and both the

Sisters and the penitents had made shirts and dressing gowns for the men.

The Clewer Sisters were therefore greatly honoured when they were asked to undertake a night watch by the Royal coffin in the Albert Memorial Chapel, Windsor Castle, on June 14th. Mother Evelyn and three Sisters took the first watch from 11.00 pm until 1.00 am, and sixteen other Sisters watched in two-hourly shifts consisting of four Sisters at a time. At 9.00 am Mother Evelyn and three Sisters arrived for the last watch, and at 11.30 am the King, Queen and other members of the Royal Family entered the chapel. The daughters of the Princess shook hands with Mother Evelyn and thanked her warmly for what the Community had done. The coffin was then carried into St George's Chapel for the burial service, the Sisters having been allocated seats where they would see the Royal procession. A few days later the Community received a letter from HH the Princess Helena Victoria: "May I thank you and all the Sisters from my heart for what you did for my dear Mother on Thursday night. It was such a comfort to my Sister and myself to feel that those loving prayers were going up to the Throne of God. I can never thank you enough."

In fact the Community was asked to undertake a night watch in the Albert Memorial Chapel before two other Royal funerals, in 1931 and 1935. In January 1931, by the desire of HRH the Princess Arthur, the Sisters kept watch by the coffin of her mother HRH the Princess Royal (Princess Louise). The watch was kept on two successive nights—January 8th from 8.00 pm until 8.00 am and 9th from 10.00 pm until 11.30 am. When their Majesties entered the chapel the four Sisters were presented and the Queen shook hands with each of them.

Similarly, on December 6th 1935, by the desire of HM King George V, the Sisters watched by the coffin of his sister HRH the Princess Victoria from 5.30 pm until 11.30 am. The King, Queen and the Queen of Norway (another sister) all shook hands with the Sisters and expressed their gratitude. (In 1906 the Princess Victoria had visited St Andrew's Convalescent Hospital with her mother Queen Alexandra after which they sent a large box of toys to the children's ward.)

The slight downward trend in numbers which became apparent in the Great War became more pronounced afterwards. In 1920 there were 276 Sisters, plus forty-three in America; by 1930 there were 240 Sisters, plus thirty-eight in America; and by 1937 there were 203 Sisters, plus thirty-seven in America. (Figures are not available for the period 1938–41.) The fall in numbers was most pronounced amongst the choir Sisters, the number of lay Sisters being fairly stable. During the immediate post-War years a number of choir Sisters left, some to join the Roman Catholic Church.

There can be little doubt that the War accounted for some of the unrest and uncertainty which many Christians were feeling, and that members of Communities were not immune from the general crisis. Also, the War had seen the beginning of newly found freedom for women. Their role in keeping the Country going while the men were away had resulted in the opening of doors which had always been closed. It now became possible for women to do dedicated work without making the sacrifices which the Religious Life demanded. Also, there were many more opportunities in professional and academic life which tended to divert women away from Communities. In addition, a number of new contemplative Communities had been founded in the immediate pre-War years which offered an alternative to the older active Orders. Thus many active Communities began to experience a falling off in vocations from this time onwards which, coupled with the deaths of older Sisters, helps to account for the fall in numbers. This caused some concern at Clewer, and from 1923 onwards there were periodical Novenas of Prayer [nine days of prayer] for an increase in vocations. The natural consequence of there being fewer Sisters was the closure of branches. But the crisis with the branches arose not only through the fall in vocations but also because of the passing of Associates and other benefactors.

As well as the fall in vocations there were an increasing number of elderly and infirm Sisters who needed special care. Plans for building an Infirmary wing had been shelved due to the Great War but by the mid-twenties it was felt expedient to go ahead. Accordingly, on March 19th 1925 the Bishop of Buckingham (who had not yet become Warden) laid the foundation stone of the new building in the presence of a large number of Sisters, the chapel choir stalls being almost full. On February 2nd 1926 the Bishop blessed the Infirmary (which had been designed by Cecil Hare) amidst a large gathering of Sisters, Associates and other friends, and the building came into use in April. The new L-shaped wing joined the Community chapel and Sisters' refectory (which later became the Community Library), thus forming a quadrangle. The principle material was red brick and the new wing ably complemented the existing buildings. Not only was there an Infirmary, but also an oratory [small chapel], and new premises for the noviciate. On March 15th 1926 Mother Evelyn herself placed the cross on top of the east gable of the oratory. This involved a perilous ascent via an open window up a sloping plank to a small railed gallery where there was just enough room for herself, the foreman, labourer and stonemason! Thus completed, the oratory was dedicated to St Joseph by Bishop Eliot on July 13th 1926.

In March 1925 the Charity Commissioners agreed to the Community purchasing the land on which the convent buildings stood, plus the field adjacent to the chapel, together with St John's Home and the land adjoining it, all of which hitherto was the property of the House of Mercy. Until this time the premises of the Community as well as the Penitentiary had been known as the House of Mercy because the rescue work pre-dated the Sisterhood. Purchasing the land was a legal safeguard so that should the House of Mercy close, the Community would still be secure. From March 1926 the Community buildings became known as the Convent of St John Baptist, whilst the Penitentiary buildings retained the title of the Clewer House of Mercy. Also from this time the Superior became known as the Reverend Mother Superior rather than Mother Superior.

The inter-War years were not renowned for ecumenical relations, so it is perhaps all the more remarkable that during this period the Community received a number of visits from leaders of other churches. July 6th 1920 was kept as Commemoration Day and the Community were honoured by the presence of His Grace the Metropolitan of Demotica and his contingent. They formed the delegation from the Patriarchate of Constantinople to the Lambeth Conference and were accompanied by the Revd Henry Joy Fynes-Clinton and Mr Athelstan Riley. They were present at the Eucharist, at the end of which His Grace gave a blessing in Greek. (In fact this was not the first visit by an Eastern Orthodox bishop, the Archbishop of Belgrade, Metropolitan of Serbia, having been to Clewer in April 1916 when he gave each Sister his blessing and also visited the hospital and orphanage.)

On July 2nd 1925 no less than eight Eastern Orthodox bishops visited Clewer accompanied by Fr Douglas and Athelstan Riley. The most senior were His Beatitude the Lord Photios, Patriarch and Pope of Alexandria, and His Beatitude the Patriarch of Jerusalem. They were in England for the anniversary of the Council of Nicaea (325 AD). Each gave Mother Evelyn his blessing before entering the chapel, and kissed the ivory crucifix used at clothings and professions. Then they were censed and as they entered the chapel by the west door the choir sang an anthem. They kissed the altar and the Patriarch of Alexandria gave his blessing to the Sisters in choir.

September 8th 1937 saw a visit by the Abbé Paul Couturier who was brought by Dom Benedict Ley from Nashdom Abbey in nearby Burnham, where he was a guest. The Abbé was a prime mover in Roman Catholic/ Anglican relations and did much of the groundwork for later dialogue. He also promoted the Octave of prayer for Christian Unity which the Community had observed since 1926. At Clewer he went to the chapel to pray for unity with many of the Sisters and took photographs of the convent away with him.

The strikes which beleaguered the 1920s were met in the Community by days of prayer and intercession for the welfare of the nation, especially during the coal strike of 1921 and the General Strike of 1926. In the wider Church, efforts were being made to inject new life and enthusiasm into Anglo-Catholicism as an antidote to the loss of faith caused by the horrors of the War. To this end a series of Anglo-Catholic Congresses were held, starting in 1920. Mother Evelyn and some Sisters went to the opening service of the second Congress in 1923 and the Community undertook a chain of continuous prayer from June 10th–12th. On February 8th 1924 a day of prayer for the conversion of England was held. As an outcome of the Congress, Religious Communities were asked to keep continuous intercession for the year: the Clewer Sisters undertook responsibility for an hour each day and every Friday from 6.00 am–10.00 pm. Similarly, a day of intercession was held at the time of the 1930 Lambeth Conference. The Oxford Movement Centenary was widely celebrated in July 1933 and at the convent there was a High Mass followed by lunch and a procession to Clewer church, where a pilgrimage was made to Canon Carter's grave. Clearly the Community had become more advanced in Anglo-Catholicism in the immediate post-War years, influenced largely by their choice of Wardens.

Mother Evelyn resigned in 1928 after twenty-one years as Superior, in which she had held the Community together through the Edwardian summer, the dark days of war and the grey aftermath. One of her achievements has not been mentioned so far because it will be dealt with later: the undertaking of work in Barbados in 1926. But it may be said here that it gave the Community a fresh impetus at a time when spirits were low. Mother

Evelyn was a kind and wise Superior, an able leader with a great sense of the spirit of Mother Harriet, and she continued to be spoken of with affection within the Community long after her time. She was an inveterate traveller, visiting India in 1910 and Barbados prior to the Community accepting work there. Following her resignation she went to Torquay, where she spent the remaining fourteen years of her life.

Mother Evelyn was succeeded as Superior by Sr Katherine Maud, who was installed on November 27th 1928. Professed in February 1899, she had undergone training at Guy's Hospital before being sent to Calcutta in 1902 to work in the recently rebuilt Presidency General Hospital. She worked there until 1920, when she returned to England to take charge of St Andrew's Convalescent Home, Folkestone, where she was working when elected Superior.

As the Community moved into the 1930s many of the older Sisters who remembered the Victorian years had died. Some had died during the Great War, such as Sr Selina, pioneer of the work in Newport, who died on December 16th 1916. Sr Helen Rachel, for fifteen years the "Guards' Nun", died on February 17th 1924. There were many guardsmen at her funeral, which took place at St Barnabas Pimlico. Two Grenadier Guardsmen and two Life Guardsmen carried the coffin from the church to the hearse. Also in 1924 the death occurred of Sr Jane Frances, Sister Superior of the Indian work until 1918, and before that Mother Superior of the Community. She died at Torquay on July 6th and was buried there on July 10th.

In 1926 a piece of land on the opposite side of Hatch Lane to the convent had been set aside as a burial ground to be known as 'The Garth.' This had become necessary owing to the closure of Clewer churchyard for burials in new graves. The first Sister to be buried there was Sr Mary Elizabeth, who was laid to rest on October 30th 1926. January 21st 1931 saw the death of Sr Fidelia, who had been professed in 1875 and whose life's work had been at the Manor House, Oxford. April 24th 1936 saw the passing of Sr Annie Constance, who had worked in Gloucester for many years and who had done such sterling work in the smallpox epidemic of 1895–6. Sr Isabel Walker, the last but one of the Second Order Sisters, died in September 1938 aged 95. And June 28th 1939 saw the ending of an era with the death of Sr Amabel, Mother Harriet's niece. (But in 1957 another O'Brien was professed in the Community: Mother Harriet's great-great-niece, Sr Sheila.)

As the 1930s dawned, a number of changes took place in the Community. The Constitutions were revised again, together with the Rule, in 1934. In 1930 the scapular had been adopted as part of the habit and in April 1939 wimples were worn for the first time. Also in 1930, the lay Sisters' habit was altered. July 1932 saw the introduction of Devotions to the Blessed Sacrament on Thursdays before Vespers, and a Candlemass procession was first held in 1933. At the end of 1934 the restoration of the old chapel was begun. On March 1st 1936 Mass was said for the first time according to the 1549 Prayer Book (though it is not clear whether this became the general use), and the same year saw the veiling of the reredos [behind the altar] during Lent. 1937 saw a new edition of *The Day Hours of the Church of England* and in 1938 the two non-Scriptural Stations of the Cross were placed in chapel. During Lent that year, the Holy Hour was observed for the first time. Also in 1938 the order of precedence was changed both in chapel and refectory, so that lay Sisters now came before choir novices, and the Consultative Council and Finance Committee both underwent reforms.

The 1930s was the decade of three Sovereigns for Nation and Empire, and three Mothers for the Clewer Community. 1935, the year of King George V's Silver Jubilee, saw the untimely death of Mother Katherine Maud. Her short time as Mother Superior had been an exacting one during which she had carried the burden of falling numbers and the closure of branches. In addition she had visited India in 1931, Barbados in 1932 and America in 1934. On November 16th 1934 Mother Katherine Maud sailed for India, but between Bombay and Calcutta she contracted a severe cold together with dysentery and entered hospital upon arriving in Calcutta. She started for home in February 1935 accompanied by Sr Hilda Frances, but a cable arrived at Clewer with the alarming news that Mother had been taken ashore at Port Sudan for an emergency operation.

Two days later a further cable stated "Danger over," but the surgeon advised a quick passage back to England as soon as possible in order to seek further advice. They arrived at Marseilles on March 15th and were met by a nurse from St Bartholomew's Hospital who accompanied them the rest of the way. Mother Katherine Maud never returned to Clewer. After three weeks at 'Bart's' she appeared to be making progress but on April 9th she collapsed again and died peacefully the next day. The coffin was received at Clewer on April 12th and a watch kept until 8.00 pm by the novices.

The night watch was kept by the Sisters until the first requiem at 7.00 am, which was said at the high altar. This was followed by the solemn requiem at 8.30 am, the Sub-Warden celebrating and the Warden (Bishop Eliot) pontificating. Burial in the Garth followed at 10.30 am; there were many Associates, clergy and friends present including the Abbot of Nashdom, Dom Martin Collett OSB.

Between the death of Mother Katherine Maud and the election of Sr Frances as her successor, the King kept his Jubilee with great rejoicing. Despite their recent bereavement the Sisters entered into the spirit of things. And, thanks to the advent of sound broadcasting they were able to do this in an entirely novel way. On May 6th they gathered in the recreation room to hear the thanksgiving service in St Paul's Cathedral. It must have seemed like a miracle! In the afternoon there were sports for the penitents followed by the distribution of prizes and Jubilee medals. In the evening all listened to the King's speech to his people.

On July 25th 1935 Mother Frances was installed at High Mass in the presence of a large number of Sisters. The Abbot of Nashdom and a monk from Alton Abbey were present, and Mother Frances' own brother was deacon. Mother Frances was not in good health, suffering as she did from severe rheumatism, which became increasingly worse and which prevented her from travelling as extensively as her predecessors. The *Annals* sum up 1935 thus: "So closed for the Community a year of deep sorrow and sore trial. May it fulfil the purpose of God in the year to come."

1936 dawned with the illness of King George V, and at 11.55 pm on January 20th he died peacefully, just five minutes before the thirty-fifth anniversary of his grandmother Queen Victoria. On January 28th there was a solemn requiem in the Community chapel, and then at 2.30 pm the whole household gathered to hear the broadcast of the funeral in St George's Chapel. 1936 was marked by the constitutional crisis which culminated in the abdication of King Edward VIII, but May 1937 saw the Clewer household listening to a happier broadcast—the Coronation of their Majesties King George VI and Queen Elizabeth.

Mother Frances' short time as Superior saw the Indian work become a Province in November 1938 rather than a branch work of Clewer as hitherto. Sr Dorothy Frances, Sister Superior in India since 1931, now became Mother Provincial, and Mother Frances now became Mother General. Also, there were thoughts in Chapter regarding the title 'Magdalen' but nothing was done until after the War. The recently renovated old chapel was fitted with new hangings, altar frontal, candlesticks and tabernacle in memory of Mother Katherine Maud and dedicated on October 20th 1935. Despite worsening health Mother Frances was re-elected Mother General in November 1938 but resigned in February 1939. In May 1939 Sr Dorothy Frances was elected Mother General just six months after being elected Mother Provincial of India. She was installed at Clewer on July 7th 1939 and remained in office until 1958. Sr Frances retired to the Infirmary and died there very peacefully on November 10th 1940.

Mother Dorothy Frances had entered the Community in 1911 and was professed in 1913. Within a matter of months she had the unenviable task of steering her Community through a War which would force the closure of many branches, followed by the coming of the Welfare State which would alter the rest of the active work, and the inevitable crisis which would follow. But there was the Centenary, too, and the challenge of starting new work in a new world. But before we turn to all that we must look at the branch work from the death of Victoria until 1939.

15

OLD WORK IN A NEW WORLD

Although the Community of St John Baptist undertook a wide variety of work, the principal activity was always rescue work together with preventive work as its counterpart. By 1900 it is true to say that most of the penitents were not prostitutes, though a few were. But as pointed out in chapter 4, this was also true of the work in the earlier days.

The Clewer casebooks have not survived after 1918, though similar records for some of the other Houses of Mercy have done so. All have very similar case histories irrespective of admission dates. By 1900 the number of penitents at Clewer averaged eighty, and the annual number of admissions was slightly fewer than a few years previously, mainly because more stayed the whole two years. Although most women were in their 20s and 30s a few were younger and some were older. But the older cases were by far the most difficult to reform and train, though there were always exceptions.

This sample of cases from 1900–18 is typical of those received at Clewer, the names being those given during their stay: Laura, aged 31, went to service but returned to drink. Alice, aged 24, showed incipient mental symptoms and was sent to the Workhouse. Edith, aged 30, a slight alcoholic who came for one year. Was sent to service and in 1903 was doing very well as a private nurse. Charlotte, aged 18, transferred to Highgate from whence she was sent away for violence. Ellen, aged 33, did very well in service and after six or seven months married. Then took to drink, since reformed again.

Maria, aged 26, violent temper, transferred to Great Maplestead and dismissed from there for temper. Constance, aged 34, sent to friends, emigrated to Canada. Doing well in 1911. Frances, aged 27, left of her own free will. Had been in remand Home previously. Violent temper. Now on 'Cautionary List'. May, aged 40, sent to service but proved unsatisfactory and was discharged August 1910. November 1911 we heard that she had drowned herself. Florrie, aged 20, sent to service. April 1911 was sent away from her second place having 'fallen' again and expecting confinement. 1913 in prison.

Florence, aged 17, did well in service, then left in February 1912 to find work for herself. Later heard of in Lewes Prison. Sarah, aged 29, sent to service, proved unequal to the work. May 1916 heard of doing very well as Matron of a Girls' Hostel. Mabel Maude, aged 19, sent to service. In 1914 heard of as doing very well as a clerk in an Insurance Office. Lisa, aged 27, a maternity case, sent to Windsor Union Workhouse. Behaved very wrongly and deceitfully. Mabel, aged 23, mental symptoms. Removed to Workhouses and later to County Asylum.

These cases are similar to those cited in chapter 4, there being very little to indicate that they belong to the 20th century. There are many others very similar, but they are striking in one particular aspect. These women were obviously not prostitutes: some were servants who had become pregnant, often as the result of rape or assault at their place of work. Some were mentally ill or had learning difficulties, many were alcoholics, a few were so burdened with problems as to be suicidal, some were consumptive or had poverty-related diseases, a number had been involved in petty crime and were sent by the Probation Service as an alternative to prison. All were in need of refuge and a fresh start. Although many were still sent by individuals who were prepared to pay for their upkeep, an increasing number were now sent by welfare workers, and this trend was to increase. But it is obvious that many women, especially difficult cases, were still passed from one institution to another. This must have been very demoralising. And a few were not 'fallen cases' at all but came simply to train as servants and laundresses.

The onset of the Great War does not seem to have made a great deal of difference to the type of cases received at Clewer despite there being a national increase in the illegitimate birth-rate. A few girls did War Work upon leaving: Lily aged 20 left Clewer in 1917 for service and in 1918 joined the WAAC. Lavinia aged 18 left in 1917 and a year later was working in munitions but wanted to get into service. Rosalie aged 27 was a married woman with four children whose husband was a prisoner of War in Germany. She left Clewer in August 1917 of her own free will and went to the Winchester Refuge. A few cases were received of married women who had been unfaithful during their husbands' absence in the War.

The routine at the Clewer House of Mercy was the same as in Victorian days. The penitents were still trained as servants, and a dim view was taken of anyone who wished to do anything different upon leaving. They were still called penitents until 1928, after which they were generally referred to as 'the girls'. Even so, such a label still seems patronising, though it may not have seemed so at the time. There seems to have been some resistance to the changed world by the Sisters, but some outside influences had to be recognised. For instance, new factory legislation meant that the laundry had to re-organise its long hours and the premises became subject to government inspection. Otherwise the daily routine was the same as ever, with a strict rule of silence except at certain permitted times, and marks to be earned for good behaviour and lost for bad. There was also a rule that no one must ever mention their past life. There was a certain logic in this: women who had led bad or abused lives might by their conversation lead the more innocent astray. But nowadays, understanding as we do the need to confront the past in order to overcome problems, we might question the wisdom of imposing an absolute ban which excluded any counselling process.

There were occasional treats which made a welcome break from the daily routine, notably the Christmas party with a tree laden with useful presents followed by an entertainment; and the traditional outside tea party and fireworks at St John Baptist-tide (June 24th). During the Great War the penitents voluntarily gave up their Christmas tree and presents, donating the money thus saved to helping war victims. The Magdalens continued to provide a firm support to the Sisters and a good example to the penitents. Their training, dress and Rule remained the same as in the early days and it was not until 1946 that they were reconstituted as a Third Order.

The 1920s saw the beginning of problems for the Clewer House of Mercy. The *Annual Report* for 1920–1 revealed a financial deficit of nearly £900, which had gradually accumulated. An appeal was launched which wiped out the debt, but it was a symptom of a problem which was to afflict much of the Community work—the falling off in annual subscriptions and other regular sources of income. This was due partly to the post-War economic crisis, partly to the deaths of many of the older Associates and benefactors, and to the lack of interest in this type of work on the part of the new generation and their subsequent failure to assist financially. The wealthy who had previously supported rescue work, both financially and by employing the women thus trained as servants, now found their own wealth sorely stretched. One of the side effects was that whereas previously they had owned several houses many were forced to sell some of their property. Therefore they no longer needed as many servants.

The inter-War years saw the rise of the 'new rich' City workers who took advantage of the suburban housing developments to commute to their business. These smaller homes had no need for an army of servants, though many had at least one and some had two. But even more importantly, such homes were increasingly equipped with electricity, and many had the latest labour-saving devices such as vacuum cleaners and washing machines. Now for the first time it became possible for one woman to run the house unassisted (although of course the poor had always had to do so). The advent of the domestic washing machine helps account for some of the fall in the workload of laundries run by Penitentiaries, though the growth of commercial laundries with the latest equipment is also a factor.

Not only was there a fall in the demand for servants in post-War Britain, but also there was a feeling of resentment amongst young women towards domestic service. The wages were very low, whilst factory and office work was far more lucrative. Many women who had done war work had no wish to return to domestic service which they now saw as servitude. The post-War years saw the beginnings of women's liberation and this was seen by many as a farewell to inequality. But the change was not easily accepted in all quarters. For instance, those who saw the training of servants as part of a higher discipline found it difficult to understand why women now sought freedom and equality. Writing in the *Associates' Newsletter* for October 1921 a Sister stated, "The foolish idea so prevalent among the people that domestic service is degrading makes us feel the increasing importance of encouraging girls to train for this kind of work, and the need to teach them to look upon domestic service as an honourable and not a despicable career."

By the early 1930s the finances at the Clewer House of Mercy were grave. The laundry had great need of new customers, having recently lost Eton College after many years. Both laundry and needlework departments were losing revenue due to the general economic depression. Also there was increasing pressure from welfare workers and other external sources to reduce the period of training. But the Sisters resolutely defended their position, maintaining that little could be done with the penitents in less than two years. And whilst there was still a high failure rate, yet there were many who made a good life after leaving Clewer and were grateful for what the Sisters had done for them. Many kept in touch over the years in a lasting link that only death would sever. When the first edition of this book was being prepared a number of former penitents contributed some of their memories and spoke not only of the strict discipline, but also of its value, even though they did not always appreciate it at the time!

The rescue work at Clewer and elsewhere survived until the coming of the Welfare State, though some of the smaller houses were given up much earlier: Newark House, Gloucester, in 1912, the Stone House Refuge, Pimlico, in 1919, and St Mary's Home, Stone, Kent in 1926. This still left several major Houses of Mercy under Community care: the Devon House of Mercy at Bovey Tracey, the Diocesan Houses at Oxford (since 1929 removed from the Manor House at Holywell to Littlemore), Leamington, Salisbury, Great Maplestead and Highgate. The problems arising from changing social patterns were the same at these regional Houses as they were at Clewer. Over the years some of these houses had specialised in a particular type of case, although general cases were taken too: Leamington took girls between 14 and 17 who were either preventive cases or were on probation; Littlemore was mostly for those who had various types of learning difficulties; Great Maplestead mainly took girls who had been involved in petty crime. In 1923 the Community withdrew from the Home for Working Girls in Nelson Square, Blackfriars. This was not a Penitentiary, being a hostel for homeless girls in work. High rates, increased running costs, lack of benefactors and the fact that the Home was half empty due to unemployment forced its closure.

Closely allied to rescue work was preventive work which included work with orphans. This underwent dramatic changes in the inter-War period. At the turn of the century the Clewer Sisters ran several orphanages: St John's Home, Clewer; St Barnabas Orphanage, Pimlico (closed 1913); Rose Street, Soho (which in 1899 removed to Leytonstone); All Saints' Home, Hawley; St Lucy's Home, Gloucester; and St John Baptist Home, Newport. All these were girls' Homes, the only work for boys being St Augustine's Home, Clewer. Much of the work with orphans had been put into the Sisters' hands by the original benefactor, and the work flourished while that person lived. But keeping the funds coming in for such work proved very difficult afterwards. As the larger children's charities such as Dr Barnardo's Homes (later known as Barnardo's) and the Waifs and Strays Society (later known as the Children's Society) became more highly organised, many people gave them their support rather than the smaller private Homes. But it must be said that the large charities themselves saw the value of the smaller Homes and sometimes referred cases when they thought a child might be happier there.

The work with orphans was of great importance even though nowadays the idea of such institutions is somewhat abhorrent. There are casebooks surviving from the 1920s and 30s which (like the Penitentiary records) have very little to show that they do not date from the Victorian period, so awful are the backgrounds of poverty, overcrowding and cruelty which they describe. Of particular importance in this field was St John Baptist Home, Newport, South Wales, which was a preventive Home. The girls were not orphans, most having one parent and some having both living. These were mostly the victims of sexual abuse and other forms of cruelty and when brought to the Home they were so traumatised that they seemed unreachable. The fact that many of them were quite different people when they left the Home says a great deal for the quality of care given them by the Clewer Sisters. By the 1920s and 30s the Sisters increasingly worked in liaison with welfare workers and there is evidence that in some instances not only medical but also psychiatric help was sought. The Home closed at the end of 1939 with the Sisters' withdrawal from Newport.

But times were changing, and whilst many secular orphanages survived the birth of the Welfare State, the economic problems of the inter-War years made their management untenable for the Community. The first to be closed after the Great War was St Augustine's Home, Clewer, in 1921. The main house, though purpose built, was found to be badly constructed and ill-drained; consequently it was condemned. A smaller house opposite Clewer St Stephen was taken for the younger boys, but lack of funds and the falling number of supporters forced the final closure.

In 1934 the Sisters withdrew from St Lucy's Home, Gloucester, due mainly to the pressing need for Sisters elsewhere. In addition to the orphans there was also a small ward for incurable women; these were found alternative accommodation. Two other orphanages changed their work completely in the 1930s and became guest houses for ladies: St John's Home, Clewer, in 1932 and All Saints' Home, Hawley, in 1937. Once again falling revenues and premises which no longer met Government standards forced the change. Many of the orphans had been free cases and there were no funds available for the upkeep of the buildings. As a guest house it was hoped that both establishments would remain solvent. Work was put in hand for the necessary alterations and both houses proved highly successful and fulfilled a need. These guest houses augmented the longer term accommodation provided for elderly ladies at St Andrew's Cottage and Almshouses, Clewer, and St Basil's Home, Oxford. St John's Home also provided accommodation for the Church Workroom which had removed from Gower Street in 1927. This left just one orphanage under the care of the Clewer Community when War broke out again in 1939: the Home of the Good Shepherd, Leytonstone.

One of the consequences of the fall in vocations was the enforced closure of branches, irrespective of the social changes which were taking place at the same time. Sometimes the Sisters thus released were sent to other branches, sometimes back to the Mother House at Clewer. This in itself led to difficulties, for in many cases Sisters had not worked at Clewer since their noviciate and upon their return found themselves virtual strangers. Many of the withdrawals from parish mission work between the Wars came as the consequence of there being fewer Sisters. But there had been withdrawals from some parishes before the Great War, notably St Mary's Vincent Square, Westminster, in 1910 and St Frideswide Poplar in 1914. The large crucifix above the rood screen in the Chapel of St John Baptist at Clewer was given as a thank-offering by St Frideswide's clergy for the Sisters' work in the parish. The inter-War years saw withdrawals from the parishes of Bovey Tracey (1922), All Hallows' Southwark (1930), Clewer St Stephen (1931), St Barnabas Pimlico (1933), St Mary and St John Cowley (1937), and St Eanswyth's Folkestone (1937).

Such mission work was never given up without deep sadness but when the Community took up this work many of the parishes were new. The Sisters had stood beside the clergy in all their early struggles but now the time seemed right to withdraw. The Great War had taken its toll on the parishes too. There was hardly a church in the whole land which had not lost young men from its midst: choirmen, altar servers, prospective ordinands were all depleted through war loss and post-War agnosticism. Pre-War State benefits for the poor (the Pensions Act 1908, the Labour Exchanges Act 1911 and the National Insurance Act 1911), combined with post-War hard times, made the poor begin to look to the State for help rather than exclusively to the Church. Whilst the Church was still to provide relief to the poor and needy who attended services regularly by means of benefit clubs and guilds, Church resources were to become increasingly stretched as the wealthy benefactors of bygone days died.

Closely associated with parish missions in the early days were the schools.

St John's School, South Hampstead, closed in 1907. This had originated in the parish of St Barnabas Pimlico where it grew into a respectable girls' school and had moved to Hamilton Terrace in 1877 and to South Hampstead in 1899. Changing educational standards were to make a difference to many smaller private schools as the century progressed.

St Stephen's College moved to West Folkestone in August 1919 after enduring cramped conditions at Clewer for many years. Fr Nicholas, the first vicar of Clewer St Stephen, had reluctantly retired in 1917. He was to be a familiar figure locally until his death in 1932 in his 96th year, having been in Holy Orders for seventy-two of them. He had conducted a love-hate relationship with the Community, and especially with the College, whose students attended the church and helped fill it. Now, two years after his departure, they left too, but the premises did not stand idle. St Stephen's High School was pleased to occupy the empty classrooms known as St Stephen's House. The College flourished in its spacious new quarters at Folkestone and remained there until the outbreak of World War II forced the evacuation to Taplow Court near Maidenhead.

In the meantime St Stephen's High School was in deep financial trouble and by 1931 the Sisters were faced with the possibility of the school's closure. They were extremely reluctant to do this and were therefore pleased to accept an offer which enabled the school to become part of the Imperial Service College, Windsor. The continuance of the school thus seemed assured, albeit in different hands. Accordingly, the Sisters withdrew in 1931, but by 1934 the fortunes of the school had not improved and the ISC announced the closure forthwith. This was met with deep sorrow and some anger from pupils and ex-pupils who remembered the sterling work of Sr Miriam and Sr Mary Susanna, not to speak of the lay teachers, Miss du Pré, Miss Commins, Miss Porcher and others. A large chair with the daffodil motif which came from the High School was given to St Andrew's Clewer. The site of the school was redeveloped and was incorporated into the Windsor Boys' School.

The last major school to be opened by the Clewer Community was St John Baptist High School, Newport. This was opened in 1901 by Sr Selina and consisted of a High School and an Intermediate School under one roof. Both grew simultaneously and soon the Intermediate School was given up to make way for the High School, which developed along the lines of

St Stephen's College. By 1916 there were thirty boarders paying £40 per annum and 100 day girls paying £5–£10; by 1920 there were 160 day girls and the boarding fees had risen to 60 guineas (1 guinea = £1 1 shilling, or in modern sterling currency £1.05). But there was trouble ahead. Although it reached the educational standard demanded under the 1918 Education Act, the school was reluctant to accept the Government grant lest it should lose its distinctly Church character. In fact in 1923 the school relinquished the grant on those grounds and the governing body (known as the Council) raised the fees to make up the loss. This was an extremely short-sighted act which lost many pupils who could go elsewhere for less fees. From then onwards the school had an increasing financial struggle together with diminishing numbers until it finally closed in December 1939. It was a sad end to an extremely good and well equipped school.

There was one other category of work in which the Community was involved: hospitals. For many years Sisters had been undergoing professional training in nursing, and at least one Sister (Sr Bertha Margaret) was a qualified doctor by the time of the Great War, and there have been others since then. During the Great War St Andrew's Convalescent Hospital, Clewer, took many patients suffering the after-effects of the Zeppelin raids on London, a new and terrifying experience. At St Andrew's Convalescent Home, Folkestone, wounded soldiers and sailors were taken in large numbers, which affected the civilian capacity. The work in peacetime was mostly with convalescent patients, but it has already been noted that many were terminally ill with consumption.

Even in the Victorian period St Andrew's Convalescent Hospital, Clewer, and the sister Home at Folkestone had struggled to survive financially. This became increasingly a problem as older subscribers died and new ones failed to take their place. Also, medical research was making strides and standards were changing rapidly. Older premises such as those at Clewer and Folkestone became increasingly substandard, especially that at Clewer, which had been designed by Henry Woodyer to match the convent rather than to fulfil the purpose of a hospital. But it was the coming first of the War and then of the Welfare State which sounded the death knell for these two hospitals which, despite all their shortcomings, had served the sick poor so well.

The children's hospital at Gloucester (St Lucy's) had been given up in 1921 because there was no fully trained Sister available; then in 1928 the

Community had resumed work there. It was finally given up in 1939 when the Nursing Sisters of St John the Divine took over. The three Homes in Torquay, St Raphael's, St Luke's and St Barnabas remained with the Community until 1959.

Before examining the progress of the Community and its work from War to Welfare State it is necessary to look at the overseas work from 1900 onwards.

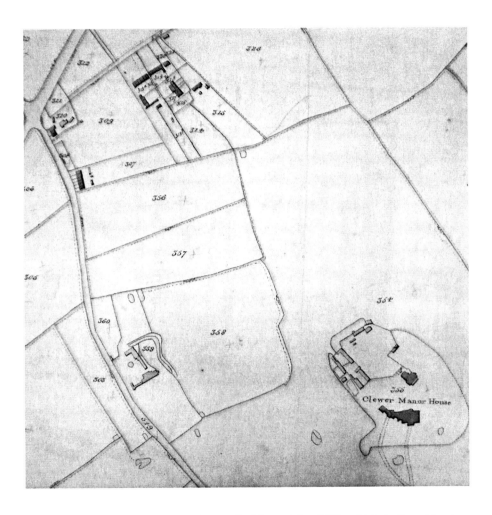

1841 Tithe Map showing Nightingale Place (plot 359) which is listed in the schedule as Nightingale Lodge.
The road in front of the property is Hatch Lane.

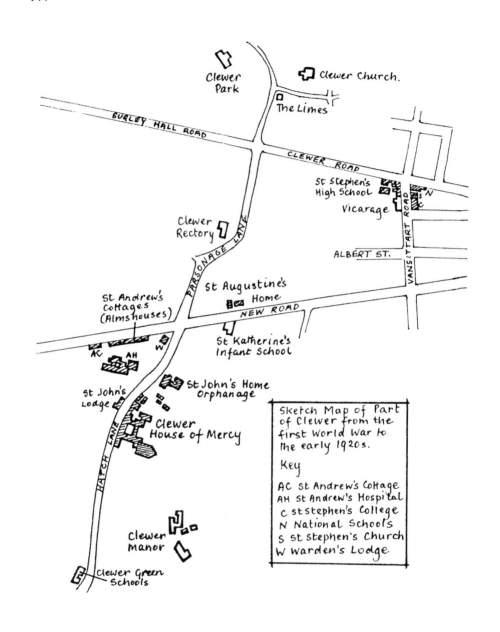

Sketch map showing CSJB work in Clewer between World War I and the 1920s

Blue plaque at 'The Limes' commemorating the work of Mariquita Tennant

The Revd T T Carter, Rector of Clewer and Co-Founder of CSJB

Mariquita Tennant

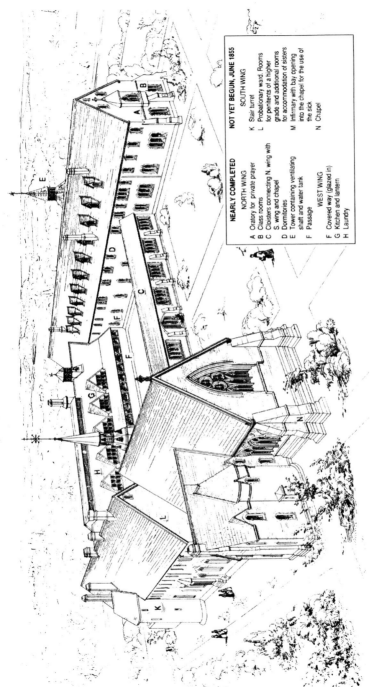

Line drawing of the Clewer House of Mercy, 1855–8

NEARLY COMPLETED

NORTH WING

A Oratory for private prayer
B Class rooms
C Cloisters connecting N. wing with S. wing and chapel
D Dormitories
E Tower containing ventilating shaft and water tank
F Passage

WEST WING

F Covered way (glazed in)
G Kitchen and lantern
H Laundry

NOT YET BEGUN, JUNE 1855

SOUTH WING

K Stair turret
L Probationary ward. Rooms for penitents of a higher grade and additional rooms for accommodation of sisters
M Infirmary with bay opening into the chapel for the use of the sick
N Chapel

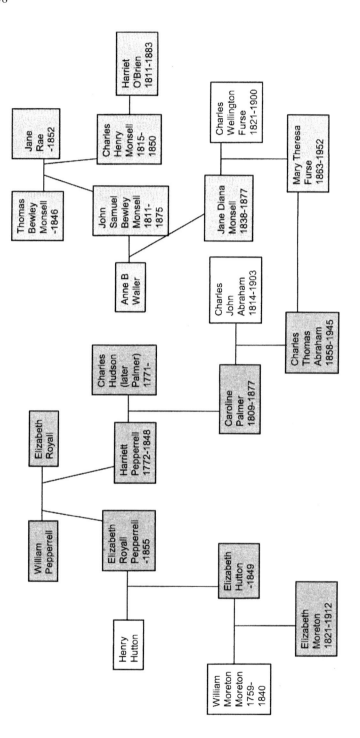

Sr Elizabeth Moreton's family tree

Sr Emma, foundress of St Augustine's Home for destitute boys and collector of English folk songs

Sr Elizabeth (Moreton) with an unknown companion

A group of early Sisters (1870s)

Sr Helen Margaret, foundress of the work in New York

Appeal leaflet for St Augustine's Home

St John Baptist House, East 17th Street, New York

ORDINARY DIET TABLE, S. ANDREW'S HOSPITAL.

MEN.

BREAKFAST. 8 a.m.	LUNCHEON.	DINNER. 12.30 p.m.	TEA. 4 p.m.	SUPPER. 8 a.m.
Bread unlimited. Bacon, 2 oz. Butter, 1¼ oz. Coffee and Tea with Milk and Sugar		Cooked Meat, 1 lb. Potatoes and green Vegetables. Beer or Porter, ½ pint. *Sundays.*—Cold Meat and Vegetables with puddings or fruit pies.	Bread unlimited. Butter, 1¼ oz. Tea with Milk and Sugar.	Meat, Fish, or Soup. Bread and Cheese. Beer, Porter, or Milk.

WOMEN.

BREAKFAST.	LUNCHEON. 10.30 a.m.	DINNER.	TEA.	SUPPER.
Bread unlimited. Bacon, 1½ oz. Butter, 1 oz. Tea with Milk and Sugar.	Cocoa, or Beef Tea, Bread.	Cooked meat, ¾ lb. Potatoes and green Vegetables. Beer or Porter, ½ pint. *Sundays as above.*	Bread, *ad lib.* Butter, 1 oz. Tea with Milk and Sugar.	Milk or light Puddings, Cocoa, Coffee, or Beef Tea.

CHILDREN. From 4 to 14.

	LUNCHEON.	DINNER.	TEA.	SUPPER. 7 p.m.
	Cocoa, or Beef Tea. Bread.	Cooked meat, 1½ oz. Potatoes and green Vegetables. *Sundays as above.*	Bread with Butter, *ad lib.* Tea with Milk and Sugar.	Milk Puddings. Milk and Water.

UNDER 4.

	LUNCHEON.	DINNER.	TEA.	SUPPER.
	Bread and Milk. Milk, Bread.	¼ less of Meat, with Gravy and potatoes. Rice or Sago Puddings. Children too young for Meat have Broth or Beef Tea.	Bread and Butter. Milk and Water.	Cocoa or Milk.

Girls from 14 to 18 years, have the same diet as the Women, with the exception of Beer, unless this is ordered by the Medical Officer.

Extras, as Fish, Eggs, Beef-tea, Milk, Arrowroot, Porridge, etc., may be ordered at any time, as may Wine, Spirits, or an increase in the ordinary allowance of Beer or Porter for any Patient for whom the Medical Officer thinks fit to prescribe them.

Night Drinks, such as Toast, or Barley-water, Milk, Lemonade, etc., are provided for any Patient needing them.

Diet sheet for St Andrew's Convalescent Hospital, Clewer, 1883

St Andrew's Convalescent Hospital, Clewer

St Andrew's Convalescent Home, Folkestone, c1910

Orphans at All Saints' Home, Hawley, circa late 1890s,
with Sr Emilia and Sr Sarah

The 'Wash House' in the laundry at St Lucy's Home, Gloucester, supervised
by a Magdalen, back row extreme left

Clewer St Stephen interior 1871. Fr G D Nicholas on the left and two Sisters on the right, one of whom would probably have been Sr Emily.

Clewer St Stephen exterior 1871, showing completed chancel and temporary nave

The main entrance to St Stephen's College, Clewer, on Oxford Road. The priest is likely to be Fr G D Nicholas; the Sisters may be Sr Emily, the Sister Superior, and Sr Alexandrina, the Sister Headmistress.

The College, Clewer

St Stephen's College, Clewer. The buildings on Oxford Road (to the right) were later demolished and houses built on the site. The church and the range of buildings on Vansittart Road (to the left) still exist.

St Stephen's College senior students on a summer outing, 1900. The Sister may be Sr Alexandrina.

Sr Lucy, first Sister Superior of the work in India, 1881–9

Mission boat in the Sunderbuns with Sr Jane Frances, 1890s

Diocesan Girls' High School Darjeeling after the landslip, 1899

CSJB Chapel of St John Baptist exterior, completed 1881

The Clewer chapels: St John Baptist on left, Chapel of the Forerunner on right

The convent main entrance when Hatch Lane was a country lane

The Sisters' garden

The Ironing Room at the Clewer House of Mercy laundry, 1928

Another view of the Ironing Room at Clewer

The London Diocesan House of Mercy, Park House, North Hill, Highgate

A day off: haymaking at the Highgate House of Mercy, 1930s

The Devon House of Mercy, Bovey Tracey, in 1940

In the laundry at the Devon House of Mercy. Note the row of wooden wash tubs and the mangle.

Some of the Community of St John Baptist in the late 1980s

Modern technology comes to Clewer: Sr Pamela and Sr Jane Olive word processing in the 1980s. Note too the cordless telephone.

The convent buildings at Mendham, New Jersey

The CSJB Sisters at Mendham, NJ, in 2010

Sr Jane and helpers at the Good Shepherd Home in the Cameroon, which is supported by the CSJB

Sr Mary Lynne and children at the Good Shepherd Home, Cameroon

Begbroke Priory

A group of Sisters at Begbroke

Sr Anne CSJB, Mrs Rosita Chrestien (Lady Principal) (4th from left, wearing glasses), and staff of St John's Diocesan Girls' Higher Secondary School, Kolkata (formerly Calcutta)

The 'Sister Eudora block' at St John's School, Kolkata

Bishop Michael Perham and Bishop John Pritchard blessing the Foundation Stones for the Bishop Edward King Chapel and Harriet Monsell House, Ripon College, Cuddesdon

The Foundation stone of the new buildings at Cuddesdon

Harriet Monsell House, Cuddesdon (from architect's drawing)
(see back cover for photograph of building in progress)

The Bishop Edward King Chapel, Cuddesdon: exterior

*The Bishop Edward King Chapel, Cuddesdon: interior
(from architect's drawing)*

HOME AND COLONIAL

When Sr Mary Angela became third Superior of the American Affiliation in 1903 there were thirty-five Sisters. In 1904 the Community was asked by the Bishop of the Diocese and school Trustees to undertake the supervision of St Helen's Hall, a Diocesan day and boarding school for girls at Portland, Oregon. This had been founded in 1869 and was the oldest Episcopalian school on the Pacific coast, five days' train journey away from the Mother House in New York. The work was accepted in earnest and in due time flourished.

In 1914 a fire seriously damaged part of the buildings after which the decision was made to sell the site and build a new school not far away. A year later, Mother Mary Angela resigned as Mother Superior and took charge of St Helen's Hall until 1922. During this time she strengthened and developed the work in Oregon, the school at last finding a permanent home after the fire and reaching academic excellence with a roll of nearly 200 day pupils and fifty boarders by 1921. In addition to the school there was also a small Penitentiary for fifteen girls called St Elizabeth's Home, which was begun by the Sisters in 1909.

The varied work in New York continued despite changes in the social and economic patterns of life. In 1911 the Holy Cross Mission, originally founded to minister to the German immigrants, was changed into a Home for Working Girls, aiming at providing a safe haven for up to thirty-four low-paid girls who would contribute $7 a week towards their upkeep.

In 1913 Mother Evelyn visited the American Affiliation and was present at the laying of the foundation stone of the new Mother House at Ralston in New Jersey. This was the very first visit by the Mother Superior from Clewer and she was able to see the work in Oregon as well as in the East. Building work at Ralston was slow and it was not for another two years that the Community was able to move in; during the long wait they had been living nearby at St Anna's Cottage. The convent was blessed on June 8th 1916. America was not yet at war, but war conditions in England prevented Mother Evelyn's presence on this great day, the first time that an international situation had affected the Community in this way. The new convent was constructed from concrete and terracotta in Gothic style with red tiled roofs, and was built on a hill top site with commanding views of the surrounding countryside.

The move to Ralston was accompanied by St John Baptist School, which had previously been based in New York. (St Marguerite's Home and St Anna's Cottage had already moved there.) St John Baptist School for girls moved from Stuyvesant Square, New York, to a rented house in Bernardsville near Ralston during 1914–15. In September 1915 the school moved to Ralston, and an appeal was launched to enable the erection of a new building. This was blessed on June 5th 1929 and the school, like its counterpart in Portland, continued to maintain a high standard. It survived all the vicissitudes of the twentieth century until the 1980s. In January 1987, following extensive refurbishment, the premises were renamed 'The Shire' and became New Jersey's first residential treatment centre for teenage alcoholics.

St Marguerite's Home was a continuation of the work begun in 1880 as a boarding and day school at St Hilda's Morristown, New Jersey. In 1897 it changed to an orphanage and industrial school, but a country site was thought desirable. A new house was built at Ralston and occupied on St Margaret's Day (July 20th) 1909, near where the new Mother House was eventually built. Thirty-five girls aged from 3–18 were cared for and educated at St Marguerite's. In 1960 St Marguerite's became a retreat house and still fulfils that purpose.

St Anna's Cottage, Ralston, was the direct descendant of St Anna's Cottage, Farmingdale, Long Island, the summer home for women, girls and children connected with the Holy Cross Mission. This was abandoned in 1898 because of typhoid fever and temporary accommodation was found at Mendham in New Jersey. A plot of land was acquired nearby at Ralston, a house was built, and blessed on the eve of St Anne's day (July 25th) 1905. This was to provide the Sisters with temporary accommodation while their new Mother House was being built at the top of the hill. (Mendham and Ralston are fairly closely situated and in 1955 the convent's official postal address was changed from Ralston to Mendham.) By 1915 the work at St Anna's had changed to that of caring for up to thirty-five girls and young women with behavioural problems, aged from 14–21, and was by then occupying a wing of the convent.

The effects of the Great War and its aftermath on the Community were very similar in America to those in England. Although America did not join the conflict until 1917, the loss of communication was felt keenly on both sides of the Atlantic. As at Clewer, intercession was constantly made for the ending of hostilities, and America's delay at joining what was seen as a European conflict was the occasion of deep pain to the Sisters at Ralston. On a more personal note, several of the Sisters lost loved ones in the War, and the role played by the Sisters, especially at Portland, in the post-War influenza epidemic was nothing short of heroic. The economic boom of the 1920s, followed by the Wall Street crash and the great economic depression of the 1930s, was to have similar effects on the American Community to those already discussed as affecting Clewer. Social changes made a difference to vocations, not least the changing role and status of women, which was to increase in momentum as the years passed.

1918 was the peak year for the American Affiliation, with forty-five Sisters. No figures were kept for 1923–5, 1933 and 1938–41, but in 1930 there were thirty-eight Sisters. In 1940 the choir and mission Sisters were amalgamated into one main Order and by 1942 there were thirty-five professed Sisters but no novices.

The inter-War years had allowed communications and visits to be resumed with Clewer. Sr Evelyn, formerly Mother, was able to visit in 1929, and in March 1934 Mother Katherine Maud stayed for nearly two months. The outbreak of World War II once more put an end to communications and the American Affiliation became more and more isolated. Nevertheless during this time one of the English Sisters found herself working at Ralston. Sr Eudora had been working first in India and then in Barbados, but the Battle of the Atlantic prevented her from getting back to England and so it was decided that she should go to America. This was accomplished with difficulty but she finally arrived at Ralston and spent the next two and a half years in most of the major works. When the first edition of this book was published in 1989, Sr Eudora was still alive, the only surviving Sister at Clewer who had worked in all three overseas branches.

During Sr Eudora's American interlude the Community suffered a sad loss: in 1942 Mother Florence Teresa (who had succeeded Mother Mary Angela in 1915) resigned and was replaced by Sr Alice Ursula. In May 1943 Mother Alice Ursula visited Portland, Oregon, and on May 26th she died suddenly from heart failure. She was in her late fifties and had held office as Mother Superior for just six months. All were deeply shocked, both in England and America. Even the death in office of Mother Katherine Maud in 1935 had been forewarned by illness. In accordance with Community tradition Mother Alice Ursula was buried at Portland where she had died. Sr Waldine Lucia, who had been in charge of St Helen's Hall since 1922, was elected Mother Superior in July 1943 and was installed a month later.

Mother Waldine Lucia had the difficult task of steering the Community through the war years and the immediate aftermath. Falling numbers in the Community made it necessary to withdraw from St Helen's Hall in Portland, Oregon, for the sake of the work in the East. (In 1964 the school was forced to move to its present location and in 1972 it merged with Bishop Dagwell Hall, a boys' school, to become the Oregon Episcopal School.) Some Community work had already closed before the War due to economic and other difficulties, notably St Michael's Home, Mamaroneck, in 1939. In March 1949 the ageing St Andrew's Convalescent Hospital, New York, was sold and a move made to a mansion at Poughkeepsie in New York; the rest of the New York work was given up soon afterwards.

But the War had made a difference to the Community in other ways and it was perhaps inevitable that the English and American houses should grow apart. So it was that despite negotiations which attempted to ward off the move, the American Affiliation severed its connection with Clewer in May 1949, just a few months before Mother Waldine Lucia resigned from office. The dedication, habit and cross of the Community of St John Baptist were retained, but otherwise Ralston was now independent and remained so until the two Houses were reaffiliated in February 1974.

*

In India the Raj was still flourishing at the turn of the century, and although the winds of change would soon begin to blow there were still a few years of prosperity left. The 1902 Delhi Durbar, which celebrated the Coronation of the new King-Emperor Edward VII, showed the Raj at its most splendid. In Calcutta itself the Edwardian years were characterised by growing political strife. This was not new; there had been rioting between Muslims and Hindus in 1895, and the continued growth of Nationalism was to see the situation worsen, especially after the Great War. December 1911 saw a Durbar in Delhi to celebrate the Coronation of another King-Emperor, George V. This time the monarch and his Queen were both present, and it was the King-Emperor himself who dropped a bombshell: the seat of Government was to be removed from Calcutta to Delhi, the ancient capital of India. India was jubilant, but many of the British in Calcutta were enraged at the downgrading of the city.

But for the Clewer Sisters life went on as before. Their work in Calcutta flourished and the schools in the rebuilt mission compound at Ballyganj maintained a good reputation. In 1909 the Diocesan Mission High School became known as the Diocesan Collegiate School and later became St John's Diocesan High School; also in 1909 the Diocesan College became affiliated to Calcutta University. At Darjeeling the girls' school, so disastrously demolished in the landslip of 1899, was rebuilt and reopened as St Michael's School at Michaelmas 1904. Thereafter this became an increasingly prestigious school with a high educational standard. The mission work in the Sunderbuns villages went on apace. The hospital work also made progress, the Presidency General Hospital being rebuilt around the turn of the century.

The coming of the Great War did not affect the Indian work at first but this state of affairs was not to last for long. In 1916 four Sisters arrived home safely after perilous voyages through the Mediterranean. Then on December 17th 1916 Sr Katherine Hope and Sr Georgina arrived home, their ship having struck a mine about one and a half hours from Marseilles. All the passengers were put into life boats but two of the crew lost their lives. The Sisters were picked up by a destroyer who took them to Marseilles. The worst was yet to come. Sr Alexandrina, accompanied by Sr Marian Edith and Sr Edith Helen, finally arrived in England on April 26th 1918 after what they called an 'adventurous voyage'. Their ship was torpedoed in the Mediterranean and they spent about two hours in open boats on a rough sea before being picked up by a British sloop-of-war. They landed at Bizerte, on the coast of Tunisia, and remained there four days before being taken on board a French troopship bound for Marseilles.

In 1916 the Clewer Chapter accepted the work of St Thomas' School, Kidderpore, on the outskirts of Calcutta but were unable to begin before January 1919 on account of the War. This school had its origins in the days of the East India Company when it began as the Calcutta Free School for poor children of mixed European and Indian parentage. In 1915 the Government of India gave Kidderpore House at Alipur, formerly one of the mansions of Warren Hastings, to the Governors of the school. The junior section of the school was removed there and the Sisters renamed it St Thomas' School. Building work was soon begun and by 1924 older girls were also taken so that there were about 185 girls and fifty small boys.

The Pratt Memorial School faced increasing difficulties as the new century progressed. By 1910 the buildings were again totally inadequate and in 1912 they were partially demolished and rebuilt, the operation being completed towards the end of 1913. At that time there were well over 200 pupils, more than 100 of whom were boarders. By the 1920s many former pupils were working as nurses and teachers, and the high standard, so long part of the school's ethos, was well maintained. But the finances were a constant anxiety, especially the debt which accrued after the rebuilding, and the school never quite recovered.

Finance was also causing anxiety at the Pipalpatti Mission, which had undergone major rebuilding in the early 1920s leaving a heavy debt, and there was more to come as several of the schools in the compound also needed urgent repairs.

In 1910 Sr Jane Frances had been awarded the silver Kaisar-i-Hind medal for her work, an honour which reflected on the whole Community. This was a decoration awarded by the British monarch from 1900–47 to civilians for distinguished service to the Raj. The silver medal was presented by the Viceroy. In 1918 Sr Jane Frances laid down the office of Sister Superior, which she had held since 1889, and her place was taken by Sr Margaret. Increasing attacks of bronchial asthma had made life in the uncongenial Indian climate very difficult for Sr Jane Frances during the last few years, but she had continued to visit all the work, including the villages, which had a particular fascination for her. Her return to England marked the ending of an era not only personally but also for the work itself. When she died at Torquay on July 6th 1924, there was deep and genuine sorrow in India among those with whom she had worked. Happily her release came before the ending of the Raj and wholesale withdrawal of the Community.

The hospital work was gradually given up from 1910 onwards. Mother Evelyn visited India from December 1909–March 1910 and in November it was decided that the Sisters should withdraw from the Medical College Hospital and also the Eden Hospital. Both had been greatly enlarged since the Community had gone there so that a larger nursing staff was required than Mother Evelyn felt she could supply. Also standards were rising continuously so that it seemed appropriate that professional nurses should take over. Accordingly, in November 1910 nurses arrived from the London Hospital to take up the work. The Eden Sanatorium at Darjeeling was relinquished as from Easter 1923, leaving the Presidency General as the only remaining hospital work. Reluctantly, in 1928, after forty-seven years, the Community also withdrew from the Presidency General Hospital, its original Indian work. When they came to Calcutta in 1881 the Sisters had found just seventeen nurses; when they left there were over eighty.

Both the Medical College and Presidency General Hospitals were very important and flourished under the Sisters' management. And some important medical breakthroughs were made there, though the Community did not make them. In 1883 Robert Koch began research at the Medical College Hospital and identified the cholera bacillus as having its source in polluted water. From 1906–20 Sir Leonard Rogers worked on a cure for cholera at the Medical College Hospital and developed a saline treatment. In 1901 Surgeon-Major Ronald Ross, working at the Presidency General Hospital (now called the Seth Sukhlal Karnani Memorial Hospital), discovered that malaria was caused by mosquitoes. This breakthrough gained him the 1902 Nobel Prize for medicine, and a nasty attack of malaria for his servant Mahomed Bux, who had the task of collecting the mosquitoes!

In 1928 an important development took place in the village work. In 1922 the Society for the Propagation of the Gospel had offered the Community a mission house and compound at Baruipur, a predominately Hindu locality seventeen miles south of Calcutta. After various difficulties the offer was accepted, and in 1928 a school was opened there for about twenty-six girls aged 5–13 years. The school was named St Peter's after the nearby church and was at first run by Associates until a Sister could be spared from Calcutta. The Sisters withdrew from Baruipur in 1934, handing it over to Fr Balcombe, who had been with the Oxford Mission and who now worked for the SPG.

The 1930s brought changes to India, with the promise of more to come. Politically it was the era of Gandhi, civil disobedience and the policy of non co-operation. Within ten years or so this would crystallise into the 'quit India' campaign and the agonised wranglings between the Congress party and the Muslim League which finally resulted in the partition of India. The Government of India Act was passed in 1935, committing the British

Government to Indian independence within a generation. In fact it was to come much sooner.

In 1930 Mother Katherine Maud made the first of her two visits as Mother Superior to India, the second being in 1934 during which she was taken ill and died on her return journey to Clewer. 1931 saw the Golden Jubilee of the beginning of the Indian work, as well as of the dedication of the Chapel of St John Baptist at Clewer. During the intervening fifty years, seventy-eight Sisters had worked in India and five had died there. There were at that time fourteen Sisters and the Superior, fewer than at the turn of the century, when there were twenty or more, but new work in Barbados had necessitated the withdrawal of some of the Indian contingent.

The 1930s were to see further withdrawals from various works and the coming of War was to force still more. It was with great regret that the Diocesan College was closed in 1935, due mainly to the inadequacy of the buildings and the lack of funds with which to run them. This had been one of only two Anglican women's colleges in India and the only one in Bengal. Although it was hoped that the work might continue elsewhere in other hands this did not prove possible. Meanwhile the College premises were taken over by St John's Diocesan High School, formerly known as the Diocesan Collegiate School.

Ironically, the Clewer Chapter decided to make the Indian work a Province in 1938. This had first been discussed as far back as 1925, but the time was not thought to be right. Now, on the eve of India's independence and the Community's withdrawal, the work became a Province. Sr Dorothy Frances, Sister Superior since 1931, became Mother Provincial in November 1938 until she was recalled to Clewer following her election as Mother General in May 1939. (The title Mother General was accorded to the Clewer Mother following India's elevation to Provincial status.) She was succeeded in India by Sr Hilda Frances.

The onset of War once again stopped communications with England and the general movement of Sisters, and there was the threat of invasion as Burma fell into the hands of the Japanese. The schools in the mission compound were closed and part of it walled off to make an ARP area, but the Sisters managed to keep some of the work going. By 1942 Mother Hilda Frances had been allowed to open a few classes for the St John's High School children in the building formerly occupied by St Elizabeth's Middle

English School, previously called the Lower or Vernacular School. The latter school had been evacuated to Thakurpukur, a village outside Calcutta, and here the congregation of Calcutta Cathedral had established a food depot to help combat the suffering caused by the rice shortage. 15,000 people came in one day, but many were already too ill from malnutrition to use the food provided.

During the twenty years in which the Community had run St Thomas' School at Kidderpore, it had been transformed from an old-fashioned charity school where the pupils wore long uniform frocks into a modern school with a good educational standard. Shortage of Sisters forced the decision to close at the end of 1939. The end of 1940 saw the withdrawal of the Community from the Pratt Memorial School. The *Associates' Newsletter* for October 1940 commented, "It is probably time that we left the work to those we have sought to train. Many old pupils are competent teachers and it is for them to rise up now and carry on those principles and traditions which have been established."

Independence followed the ending of the War and the Sisters prepared for the final homecoming. Many Indian people had found Christianity through the Community and its work, but Indian vocations had not been forthcoming. There were however two exceptions: Sr Susila, a former pupil of Sr Eudora at the Pratt Memorial School, joined the Oxford Mission Sisterhood of the Epiphany. In 1970 she founded a Community called the Christa Sevika Sangha (the Handmaids of Christ). This was under the care of the Oxford Mission Sisterhood of the Epiphany until 1986, when its own Constitution was passed and Sr Susila was elected as Superior. It is now an indigenous Bangladeshi Community which retains close links with the Oxford Mission. The headquarters are at Jobarpar, where the Sisters supervise girls' hostels and a play centre for small children. They also help in St Gabriel's School and supervise St Mary's Asroi (Home) at Barisal. Numbers in the Community remain around twenty Sisters. In 1987 Mother Susila and some of her Sisters visited England and spent several days at Clewer, and have made several subsequent visits. Mother Susila died in May 2011. Secondly, Sr Dipika came to Clewer for her noviciate and was professed in Calcutta in 1939, but remained in India after the Community's final withdrawal. She lived alone for the rest of her life.

Withdrawal was inevitable after Independence, primarily because of the political situation, but also because the work needed strong, healthy Sisters and these were fewer in number. The remaining work was transferred into other hands whenever possible. The village work in the Sunderbuns was very similar to that of the Society for the Propagation of the Gospel, whose missionaries now took responsibility for it. The Oxford Mission was working in the same area too. St Michael's School, Darjeeling, closed in 1948. It had been hoped that another Community would run it, and the Community of the Companions of Jesus the Good Shepherd took over for a few months, but changes introduced by the new Indian Government would have completely altered its character and so it was closed. Also, many English people were leaving India which meant a drastic drop in the number of boarders. But the school has not been forgotten and the diminishing number of former pupils remember it with affection. The buildings became a training college run by the Indian government and were later absorbed into the Indira Gandhi National Open University.

And so the Sisters came home, the last being Sr Georgina and Sr Lilian Mary, who arrived at Clewer from Darjeeling on Easter Sunday 1946. The Sisters in Calcutta had left there in February 1945. Two of the Sisters who worked in India were still at Clewer when the first edition of this book was produced: Sr Gladys who worked there from 1933 until 1945 at St Elizabeth's Middle English School and in the Sunderbuns villages, and Sr Eudora who was there from the end of 1933 until 1938 working at the Pratt Memorial School and St Thomas' School, Kidderpore, before being sent to Barbados. Both have died in the intervening years.

It is impossible to feel sad at the passing of the Indian work because so much was achieved during those years. Sixty-five years of teaching, nursing and ministering has left an indelible mark on the life of India which has manifested itself in those who came under the Sisters' influence and their succeeding generations. In the 21st century their work in the schools of Calcutta is still remembered with affection.

*

At the beginning of 1925 the Clewer Chapter refused work in Queensland and Accra, but was seriously considering a request first made in 1923 to undertake mission work in Barbados. There was some debate whether Sisters could be spared for new overseas work at a time when other work was being given up, and some Sisters did not favour the idea. In November

1923 Mother Evelyn and Sister Susan visited Barbados and received an enthusiastic welcome from the Bishop, who was anxious for them to accept his invitation as soon as possible. Nevertheless the Community did not finally accept the work until May 1925, when Chapter voted with a clear majority. On January 30th 1926 the first four Sisters sailed. They were Sr Anita, Sr Mary Joyce, Sr Agnes Jean and Sr Dorothy Maude.

The work consisted very largely of missionary activities similar to those carried out in England: house visiting, running parish guilds, Sunday Schools, moral rescue and, in the course of time, retreats and quiet days. The mission house was at Bridgetown not far from the Cathedral and the Sisters were fully supported by the Bishop, clergy and many of the English population. It was, however, fraught with difficulties, not least the influence of American religious sects and a high illegitimate birth rate. When the Sub-Warden of Clewer (the Revd K McMaster) visited Barbados in 1934, he laid the blame for the latter firmly at the door of the English planters who, until the abolition of slavery just 100 years previously, had denied marriage to the indigenous people. But poor housing and overcrowded conditions did not help matters either.

The War effectively cut off communication with England. It had a sinister side too, as Sr Eudora found when visiting the nearby island of St Vincent: some of the islanders decided that she was a German spy disguised as a nun! It was with great difficulty that she obtained a passage back to Barbados and she only achieved it by signing on as the ship's cook!

The ending of the War saw great changes within the Community and it was decided to withdraw from Barbados. Accordingly, on November 7th 1946 Sr Agnes Jean, Sr Dorothy Maude and Sr Marian arrived home after an uncomfortable voyage. The work had made great headway over twenty years and was now undertaken by the Community of the Companions of Jesus the Good Shepherd, whose Mother House was at West Ogwell in Devon. Founded in 1920 from a group of teachers, the Community was very closely allied with the Community of St Mary the Virgin, Wantage, in its early years. It was this Community which had hoped to take over St Michael's School, Darjeeling.

So the aftermath of World War II saw the ending of the Clewer Sisters' overseas connections, but it is now time to see how the War affected the work at home.

17

FROM WORLD WAR TO WELFARE STATE

When Sr Dorothy Frances was installed as Mother General on July 7th 1939 there were barely two months' peacetime left. Exact statistics are not available for 1938–41 inclusive, but there are likely to have been a little under 200 Sisters, of whom about fifty were lay Sisters. In 1942 there were 173 Sisters altogether against 203 in 1937. As England stood once again on the brink of war, the Community still had a considerable amount of branch work: hospitals and convalescent homes at Clewer, Folkestone, Gloucester (the latter given up in December 1939) and Torquay; penitentiaries at Clewer, Bovey Tracey, Highgate, Great Maplestead, Salisbury, Littlemore and Leamington; schools at Folkestone and Newport (the latter given up at the end of 1939); parish mission work in Folkestone and Holborn, as well as the House of Charity in Soho (the Sisters withdrew from the latter in August 1939); guest houses at Clewer, Hawley and Oxford; orphanages at Leytonstone and Newport (the latter was closed at the end of 1939); and the overseas work. Most of this would have changed hands by the time of the Community's Centenary in 1952.

The outbreak of the War was met by the Community with the closure of some houses and evacuation from others. It is quite likely that some of the closures or withdrawals would have happened in any case. For instance, St Andrew's Convalescent Hospital, Clewer, had reached a crisis point by the end of 1939 brought about by chronic financial problems, inadequate facilities to meet Government requirements and a shortage of qualified Sisters to run it. The outbreak of war dashed all hopes of reconstruction for the duration, so the Council of the hospital decided to close it forthwith. It was requisitioned by the Government, who used it as a nurses' hostel, ownership being retained by the Trustees, who hoped it would revert to its former use with the coming of peace.

Within the first week of the War nearly one and a half million people were evacuated from the big cities for fear of wholesale bombing and gas attacks. Of these, 8,000–9,000 women and children, mostly from London, found themselves in Windsor. The safety of those under their care must have been a considerable anxiety for the Clewer Sisters, who wisely decided to join the fray and evacuate some of their more vulnerable houses. Accordingly, the residents at Hawley (by now a guest house for elderly ladies) came to the safety of Clewer—the Sisters going to the convent and the ladies and staff to St John's Home.

The Sisters working at St Alban's Holborn bravely soldiered on even through the Blitz, during which the church was destroyed. Their mission house was saved, but life for the Sisters held no privileges and they took their place alongside everyone else sleeping in the public air raid shelters at night and ministering by day to those who had lost everything. This was the only work in central London, but there were two branch houses on the outskirts, at Highgate and Leytonstone. These were both closed in 1940 as the so-called 'phoney War' ended and the situation across the Channel worsened, making the threat of invasion and intensive bombing a reality.

The House of Mercy at Highgate closed in June 1940, the women and girls being found places in similar institutions and the Magdalens going to other houses or to Clewer. The orphanage at Leytonstone was evacuated wholesale to Burton Latimer Hall near Kettering in May 1940, and at first all seemed well, once the Sisters had persuaded the local residents that they were not German spies! Then winter set in and the many shortcomings of the house, such as inadequate lighting, bad drainage, gas leaks and non-existent heating, became apparent. All attempts to find alternative accommodation were thwarted and so in September 1942 the Sisters were forced to close the work.

But life at Burton Latimer was not all hardship, as Wynne Malpass, one of the former girls, later recalled. "My best memory is of the garden; it was a delight. We played under the enormous horse chestnut tree making 'little gardens' ... We attended the village schools. My sister was an infant ... I was across the road ... We did not join in village life at all except to attend church. We walked to school and church in a 'crocodile'. Sr Elizabeth Helen had a budgerigar called 'Joey'. It used to sit on her head even in chapel. At meal times he said grace with us. When he died we buried him in a cardboard box under the horse chestnut tree. We tried to dig him up when we were leaving the Hall but there was nothing in the ground. (Had he gone to heaven?) Sr Dorothy, in charge of the kitchen, one morning came into the refectory at breakfast time after the first chapel service of the day (there were seven services every day). She let fall from her sleeves windfall apples onto the tables. She had them under the wide sleeves all through the service and as a consequence of this generosity she was stung by wasps many times."

The Devon House of Mercy at Bovey Tracey was another work for which the War proved to be the last straw. It closed in January 1940, the women and girls being dispersed to other Houses, and the Magdalens to Clewer, Salisbury and Littlemore. This was traumatic for the Magdalens, many of whom had never been to Clewer; they were to find a much stricter régime there than the one they had known hitherto. But the closure of Bovey was perhaps fortuitous, because a landmine later fell at the back of the house, causing extensive damage. The house was commandeered by the Army for the duration, after which it was finally converted into flats.

At the end of 1943 the Sisters left St Mary's Home, Great Maplestead, which now passed to the Waifs and Strays Society (later known as the Children's Society). By this time the girls were mostly young offenders under 17 and needed a large staff of Sisters to cope with them. This was no longer feasible for the Community; also Henry Woodyer's building was large and impractical and needed considerable financial outlay to bring it up to the required standard.

When St Andrew's Convalescent Home, Folkestone, had been built in 1875, no one had imagined flying machines hurling bombs at these shores. Situated on the East Cliff overlooking Folkestone harbour, St Andrew's now found itself an uncomfortable target for aerial warfare. As soon as War was declared the Ministry of Health commandeered the Home for emergency casualties, but when the French Channel ports fell at the end of May 1940 it was considered to be in a danger area and the claim was rescinded. The Council of the Home closed it in June 1940. There had already been some damage caused by a mine exploding down in the harbour, the blast from which broke over thirty windows. The War Department continued to make use of the premises until 1943, after which it stood empty until the end of the War. But there was other work in Folkestone too, notably St Stephen's College, which was evacuated to Taplow Court in Buckinghamshire in March 1940. The mission work at St Saviour's Folkestone was maintained, being some distance from the town centre and harbour.

Meanwhile at Clewer the Community was coping with the War as best as it could. Sisters, Magdalens and girls were arriving from closed houses and this must have brought difficulties at a time of food rationing and general deprivation. The difficulties of achieving blackout conditions in the Chapel of St John Baptist, together with the expense of heating it, forced the Sisters to abandon its regular use in favour of the old chapel, which from October 1940 became known as the Chapel of the Forerunner. This was in good order having been recently refurbished. Commemoration Day was not held during the War but an annual appeal was made for funds for the House of Mercy and the response was generally good. As in the Great War, the girls did without their Christmas tree and presents, although they had their traditional entertainment in which they all participated.

Air raids were very much part of the War in Windsor and the convent was a large target. Unlike its near neighbour Eton College, the buildings escaped major damage in the extensive bombing raids which rained incendiary devices all over the town. The Community did not evacuate the convent and House of Mercy, although they took the precaution of not using the top floors. The girls slept in the Magdalens' dining room, the workrooms and classrooms, whilst the Sisters slept in the library, retreat room and other sitting rooms. But the Sisters were well prepared, having special ARP practices and being well drilled in fire watching, especially on the chapel roof, tin hats on top of their veils being the order of the day! Hardly anywhere in Windsor escaped unscathed when a flying bomb fell in nearby Dedworth in July 1944. The convent sustained a number of broken windows in the blast but nothing more serious.

As the War progressed the Sisters continued their work to the best of their ability, notwithstanding all the difficulties of blackout, rationing, sleepless nights and the general anxiety which everyone felt for the progress of the conflict. Two former Mothers Superior died during the War: Sr Frances died in the Infirmary on November 10th 1940 and Sr Evelyn died at Torquay on May 25th 1942. In October 1940 the Community took charge of Bapsey House at Taplow for mothers and babies evacuated from London, but it was handed over to two Sisters from the Community of St Michael and All Angels, Bloemfontein, on January 30th 1941. Also during the War, Chapter decided not to accept two bequests of new work: in 1941 the London Mothers' Convalescent Home at Sunningdale, and in 1942 the Oakdene School at Beaconsfield, there being no spare Sisters to run them.

War conditions did not entirely quench all festivity within the Community or the wider Church. Some important commemorations were observed in the 1940s and were attended by members of the Clewer Community. In June 1941 the centenary of the profession of Marian Rebecca Hughes, the first nun in the Church of England since the Reformation, was celebrated in Oxford with a procession from the Convent of the Society of the Holy and Undivided Trinity to St Barnabas, where the Bishop of Oxford pontificated at High Mass. Nearer home, January 24th 1944 saw celebrations at St Andrew's Clewer to mark the centenary of the induction of the Revd T T Carter as Rector. There was High Mass, the preacher being the Rector, the Revd Cyprian Dymoke-Marr. On January 29th there was a service in the convent chapel, followed by a procession to Carter's grave in Clewer churchyard and finishing with solemn Evensong. The Bishops of Oxford and Buckingham and Bishop Vibert Jackson were participants. Finally, on April 4th 1945, the Warden (Bishop Eliot), Mother Dorothy Frances and two Sisters went to Ascot Priory to celebrate the centenary of the foundation by Dr Pusey of the Sisterhood of the Holy Cross at Park Village, Regent's Park, the Community at Ascot Priory being the lineal descendant.

Even while the War showed no sign of ending it was becoming clear that the world would be a different place afterwards. Social patterns had changed since the ending of the Great War and this had affected the whole of society. Legislation passed during the inter-War period had gone some way to easing the lot of the poor and to taking away the social stigma which attached itself to unemployment and sickness benefits, which many still regarded as poor relief. But there was a long way to go: poverty remained a serious social problem, unemployment and low wages being responsible for more than half of it when the War broke out.

1942 saw the publication of the Beveridge Report, which advocated a comprehensive policy of social insurance which would ensure benefit in all circumstances of need, from the cradle to the grave. The Report was not implemented until the coming of peace but the legislation which finally arose out of it laid the foundation of the Welfare State: the National Insurance Act, the National Assistance Act and the National Health Service Act, all of 1946. Also there was the Education Act 1944, the Family Allowances Act 1945, the Housing Act 1946, and others. The pre-War privately run orphanages, penitentiaries and voluntary hospitals were suddenly part of history, whereas less than ten years before they had all been part of the fabric of society.

The Religious Communities had realised that times were changing and that much of the work previously done by them would ultimately pass to the State. If there was any regret it was simply because the State would not lay the same emphasis on religious principles. In 1943 it was decided that the name 'Clewer House of Mercy' should be altered to 'St John's Training Home'. In October 1945 two Clewer Sisters attended a conference at the Community of the Holy Name, Malvern Link, in which members of Communities met with professional welfare workers. As a direct result of this the Clewer Community drastically restricted laundry work in the training home, and in 1946 it was given up completely. In fact this added to the growing financial burden, the laundry being the chief source of income, although the Community was able to claim state assistance for each girl's upkeep. The War years had seen a rapid decrease in numbers at the Clewer training home, many girls opting for war work, and many petty offenders being sent to borstal instead, so that by 1945 there were only about twenty-five girls. Also, welfare workers were pressing for shorter periods of training, which the Sisters did not altogether agree with.

1946, the year which saw the birth of the Welfare State, saw the failure in legal terms of St John's Training Home. The Council held a special meeting on October 24th and decided that the institution had failed in that the funds available were insufficient for the maintenance of the Charity as a separate entity. The institution was thereby dissolved as from March 31st 1947. The Home would now be the responsibility of the Community of St John Baptist, who would maintain it for as long as it was possible to do so, but the buildings would revert to the Community in the event of the Home finally closing.

The immediate post-War years were important for the Community itself. The Warden, Bishop Eliot, resigned as from February 1st 1945 after eighteen years in office: he died on April 1st 1946. The new Warden, the Revd G B Hardy, was no stranger to Clewer, having been Sub-Warden from 1915–19, after which he became vicar of St Peter's Plymouth, which had recently been destroyed by the Luftwaffe. Fr Hardy was installed by the Bishop of Oxford, Dr Kirk, on March 16th 1945 at High Mass, after which the Bishop addressed the Sisters.

The time now seemed right for the Community to review its own structure, which had remained largely unchanged since the earliest days, consisting as it did of choir and lay Sisters (the Second Order having died out with the passing of Sr Catherine Seal in February 1940, just a few weeks before her 106th birthday). But by the end of the Second World War this division had become anachronistic, smacking of the Victorian social system. A number of Communities, including the Society of St Margaret and the Society of All Saints, had already merged their choir and lay Sisters during the 1930s; now the Community of St John Baptist began to consider taking the same action.

Throughout 1945 Chapter worked towards the changes which would bring the Community into line with many of its contemporaries. On May 2nd 1946 the choir and lay Sisters merged into one Order. It had been decided that the new habit should be an amalgamation of the previous two: the long veils of the choir Sisters were retained by all, combined with the simpler habit of the lay Sisters with their narrower (and more economical) sleeves. In January 1947, the first year after the amalgamation of choir and lay Sisters, the Community numbered 145.

In addition there were the Magdalens, a quite separate Order which had grown out of the original rescue work because the Founders had felt it inappropriate for former penitents to join the Community, yet acknowledged that some felt called to a dedicated life. By the 20th century some women were offering themselves as postulant Magdalens without having been through the House of Mercy. They saw the Magdalen Order as simply another Religious Order, perhaps as an alternative to being a lay Sister. The second major change came on November 16th 1946, when at a Low Mass in the Chapel of the Forerunner the Magdalens were reconstituted by the Visitor as a Third Order of the Community, to be known as the Society of St John the Forerunner. There were at that time twenty-one in final vows, four renewing their vows annually, and three novices. Out of this total, nineteen were resident at Clewer. The SSJF had its own Rule and Constitution, and its own Mother Superior from CSJB. The SSJF Sisters now dispensed with the somewhat dated Magdalen's habit and adopted a grey habit with black veil and distinctive cross.

These changes within the Community necessitated a revised Constitution and Rule, both of which were ratified by the Visitor in 1947. A year earlier, on June 29th 1946, a Sister had been professed in first vows for the first time as a preliminary to life vows. The office book *The Day Hours of the Church of England* was also undergoing yet another revision and this was ready for use soon after Easter 1950. A new departure for the Community was the introduction of Oblates. Many Communities make provision for clergy and laity living in the world to adopt a rule of life in conjunction with the ethos of the Community. The Clewer Sisters had always had Associates, whose prayers and benevolence had been a great support, but in 1949 provision was made for those who would like a firmer rule and closer spiritual connection. The first two Oblates were received as probationers in September 1949.

The years up to 1950 saw some more withdrawals from branch work, as well as the return from India and Barbados and the breaking of the American Affiliation. The Community withdrew from the Homes at Salisbury in 1946, Littlemore in 1949 and Leamington in 1950. In each case the circumstances were similar: fewer Sisters, changing standards demanded by welfare workers, and the advent of the Welfare State. The Community rightly recognised that having done the work when there was no one else to do it was no justification for clinging to it now. The world was changing and the Community must adapt to its needs. But there were still some loose ends to tie up after the War. St Andrew's Convalescent Home, Folkestone, was sold in 1946, having sustained damage which would be too costly to repair. Its namesake at Clewer was still requisitioned by the Ministry of Health and would remain so until the early 1950s, by which time the coming of the National Health Service would render it obsolete.

But not all the work was obsolete. Although the Community had withdrawn from St Saviour's Folkestone in 1945, there were still mission Sisters at St Alban's Holborn. St Stephen's College had left its wartime refuge at Taplow Court in 1946 and moved to Broadstairs. In the summer of 1949 the Community contributed to a local history exhibition called 'Bygone Windsor'. This coincided with the Centenary of the founding of the rescue work by Mariquita Tennant and aroused much local interest, including an article in the *Windsor and Eton Express*, which proved to be the first of many in the succeeding years. But the work which was beginning to thrive in these early post-War days was that of receiving retreatants at the former St John's Home, which by 1946 was being referred to as St John's

Retreat House. There were still permanent guests but an increasing number of groups and individuals began to discover the value of a retreat. So it was that as the sun set on the original work after the first hundred years, so it arose on new work which would become a major focus of Community work in the next generation.

18

MAKING ALL THINGS NEW

As the Community of St John Baptist approached the Centenary it found that the rescue work which had been its *raison d'être* was coming to an end. St John's Training Home was still in existence but it was clear that its days were numbered. This must have been rather disheartening and could have cast a shadow over the very real achievement of having existed a whole century. Certainly it implied the need to think and pray very deeply about the future role of the Community in the wider Church. This process had already begun as far back as November 1945, when the Chapter had discussed with the Warden (Fr Hardy) the balance to be kept between active work and the obligations of the Religious Life. Fr Hardy favoured a change towards the contemplative life, and the introduction of Oblates may well have reflected this line of thought. But after due consideration the Community decided it would be wrong to change the ethos; after all, the contemplative and active vocations are quite different. And so the Community approached the Centenary in thanksgiving for the past and with a spirit of openness for the future.

There were in fact two jubilees in the early 1950s: October 28th 1951 marked the 50th Anniversary of the death of Canon Carter; and November 30th 1952 marked the Centenary of Harriet Monsell's profession and installation as first Mother Superior, the date always taken by the Community as their starting point. Canon Carter's anniversary was kept at St Andrew's Clewer on October 27th with a special Mass at which the Bishop of Oxford, Dr Kenneth Kirk, preached and members of the Community were present.

The Centenary celebrations were held throughout the summer of 1952, the main observances being two Commemoration Days on June 24th and 26th. These were both well attended by Oblates, Associates and friends, as well as clergy and other Religious, and on both days the sun shone too. In addition, there was a parish day with High Mass and an open afternoon which was attended by a large gathering, many of whom had never seen behind the high wall of the convent and were amazed at what they found! The Church Workroom and wafer bakery were open for inspection, the chapels and gardens were on view, and there was a dancing display by the girls from the Training Home. In addition the visitors could buy a copy of the Centenary book *The Founders of Clewer*, written by one of the Sisters, which had been published in February. Also, two reunions took place: the Old Girls' Associations of St Stephen's High School and College respectively. One of the old College girls had left in 1881—what memories she must have had!

At the time of the Centenary there were 120 Sisters in the Community and the total number was to drop to 99 by 1959—the first time there had been less than 100 Sisters since the early days. This dramatic fall in vocations was felt throughout the Church both in Anglican and Roman Catholic Communities, and in these post-War years many smaller Communities were forced to close. The fall in numbers can again be ascribed to changing social patterns as well as to the deaths of older Sisters. Post-War society had continued to open up the professions to women, who found that they could become teachers, nurses and doctors without making the sacrifices demanded by the cloistered life. Also, society was becoming increasingly secular with a whole new set of ideals, which was further enhanced by the spread of television. The post-War increase in private cars and paid holidays saw Church attendance fall dramatically. Increasing home comforts now became the norm so that young women became reluctant to leave their modern homes for those great Victorian convents which presented a draughty prospect. Communities such as that at Clewer needed to bring their buildings up to date, but the immediate post-War days were still fraught with deprivation and strictures which prevented early action.

The first year of the new century in Community life was also Coronation year and the Sisters entered into the spirit of things in two ways. Firstly they kept an all-night vigil of prayer for the new Queen, taking turns in the chapel. Secondly they listened to the Coronation service on a wireless set especially installed in chapel for the occasion. Then there was a tea party for the whole household, but the sports arranged for the girls in the evening had to be cancelled because of the bad weather, although they improvised indoors.

The early 1950s bade farewell to St Andrew's Convalescent Hospital, which was finally released by the Ministry of Health but was in such a poor state of repair that demolition seemed the only course. The Community had realised the impossibility of using it as a hospital again; professional standards prevented this in any case, and the use of penicillin had revolutionised medicine so that long-term convalescent care was becoming a thing of the past. In August 1954 the hospital was sold to developers and was subsequently demolished to make way for the houses of Carter Close. Victorian architecture was not highly regarded so few mourned the loss of Henry Woodyer's very impractical, but nonetheless important, building. Doubtless it was a millstone around the Community's neck, but one cannot help feeling a twinge of regret at its passing. It would be another decade or so before Victorian architecture began to be championed by John Betjeman and others, and many buildings were subsequently saved from destruction.

In 1954 the Community withdrew from All Saints' Home, Hawley, the elderly residents having returned there after their wartime evacuation to Clewer. On May 1st 1954 it was handed over to the Royal United Kingdom Benevolent Association, who planned to enlarge and restore the house and to adapt a neighbouring one for those needing nursing. The adjoining chapel had served as a church for the neighbourhood but post-War development resulted in the focus of population now being elsewhere. Therefore in 1975 the chapel was closed but the altar and reredos were later given to St Andrew's Clewer, where they were placed in the Lady chapel.

1954 also saw the final closure of St John's Training Home. The Sisters had endeavoured to work in accordance with modern methods favoured by welfare workers, but this was governed by a totally different philosophy. Short-term training without religious influence was now the order of the day. The Community decided that the time had come to leave the work to its new advocates and develop new work in the old buildings. The former House of Mercy/training home buildings were adapted and made into a Retreat Wing, the work being blessed in March 1955. This took pressure off St John's Home, which was really meant for permanent guests, though retreatants had been taken there. Also, the Church Workroom moved from St John's Home to the convent and in 1958 the wafer bakery was extended. A side effect of the ending of the training home was the ending of the farm in 1955. From the earliest days of Nightingale Place there had always been a small farm with a dairy herd which grazed the nearby meadows. But now that Hatch Lane was part of suburban Windsor, it was thought appropriate to give up the farm and sell some of the pastureland for building.

In 1958 Mother Dorothy Frances resigned after nineteen years in office and was succeeded by Sr Annys who was installed on September 15th. (Sr Dorothy Frances died in April 1974.) Very soon after taking office Mother Annys had to close the work in Torquay. It was now impossible to run the three convalescent homes, due to lack of Sisters and the decline in demand for such institutions. (Three years previously there had been a disastrous fire at St Luke's which had cost £14,500 to restore, the home being underinsured.) But as one door closed so another opened, and in 1959 the Community returned to Salisbury. The former Diocesan House of Mercy (St Mary's Home) had been made into a retreat house after the Sisters' withdrawal in 1947. Sisters from the Community of St Peter the Apostle, Laleham, had been running it but had to withdraw in January 1959, and the Clewer Sisters took up the work with Sr Eudora in charge. After extensive refurbishment the retreat house was reopened in September 1959.

The 1960s was an important decade for the worldwide Church. At Clewer the 1950s had been a time of throwing off old work and taking stock of the changing needs of the world. Now the 1960s heralded a new outward-looking approach, the impetus for which came from outside. The second Vatican Council came to a conclusion in 1964 and its repercussions were felt far beyond its own denominational boundaries. Two of the most far-reaching effects were the ecumenical and liturgical movements which affected the Anglican Church very deeply. Such changes as these were not without chaos, and many people deeply regretted some of the changes which took place. Nevertheless there was undoubtedly a deep renewal in the spiritual life of the worldwide Church.

The liturgical movement was not wholly born of Vatican II, some reforms having been made in the 1950s. Indeed the Church of England Liturgical Commission was set up in 1955 and its work led eventually to the *Alternative Service Book* of 1980. In 1958 the Community used the revised rite for Holy Week for the first time, but generally it was the 1960s which saw the most radical changes. On Advent Sunday 1960 the first changes were introduced in the form of the omission of the preparation prayers before Mass and the reading of the Last Gospel [the first fourteen verses of St John's Gospel]. As from June 1962 the ministry of the Word at High Mass was said from the sedilia [the priest's chair] rather than from the altar, thus emphasising the difference between Word and Sacrament. March 1965 saw the introduction of general Communion at High Mass: formerly no one except the celebrant would receive Holy Communion, all having previously done so at Low Mass. (Commemoration Day that year saw a general Communion for the first time.) There were still more changes in October 1965, when a portable nave altar was introduced for Low Mass instead of the altar in the side chapel, and a three-month experiment in standing to receive Communion was begun. The latter practice was continued, and the nave altar was occasionally moved into choir for use at High Mass.

Extra-liturgical services such as Devotions to the Blessed Sacrament were given up at this time in order to emphasise the centrality of the Mass and Divine Office. The natural progression of these reforms continued in the revival of the westward facing position of the celebrant [ie facing the congregation]. This was introduced at Clewer in May 1966 and soon after Christmas the High Altar was moved forward. This necessitated the rehousing of the Blessed Sacrament, which had formerly been in a tabernacle on the High Altar. The sanctuary lamps were removed at this time except for the central one, which was converted into a hanging Pyx to contain the Blessed Sacrament and was blessed on August 24th 1967. The Series II Eucharistic rite was introduced on Advent Sunday 1968, and from September 30th 1969 the daily Mass was celebrated in the choir.

These changes must be seen in the light of similar events in the wider Church, and although it was painful to lay aside long cherished customs, it was deemed necessary in order to be part of the living Church. This decade also saw some other changes in the Community: in 1960 *The Day Hours of the Church of England* was revised again; there was a new edition of the Customary, and the Constitutions were once more revised; in 1967 the revised Rule was ratified by the Visitor; and on Advent Sunday 1968 wimples were abandoned in favour of caps and roll collars.

But more than anything else, the 1960s were the years of ecumenism and travel. In May 1962 Mother Margaret Helena from the CSJB in Mendham came to Clewer for a month, on a visit which was to begin the healing process between the two Houses. In June 1963 Sr Eudora and Sr Helen Muriel started on an ecumenical tour of the Continent, staying at Roman Catholic, Lutheran and Russian Orthodox convents—an experience of deep and lasting spiritual renewal. Also in 1963 two CSJB Sisters from Mendham came to Clewer and in October 1964 Mother Annys and Sr Catherine paid a return visit. In 1964 Sr Letitia went on a pilgrimage to Rome, and Mother Margaret Helena revisited Clewer. There was also the chance to meet with other Religious: Sr Helen Muriel attended several conferences for Novice Mistresses in France; in July 1965 over 200 Anglican Religious met at Oxford to consider 'The Religious Life and the World of Tomorrow', and this was repeated in 1967. The Fellowship of St Alban and St Sergius held its conference at St Stephen's College and began a lasting link. In addition, an increasing number of ecumenical visitors came to Clewer, for some of whom the discovery of a Community within the Anglican Church was altogether new. This is just a sample of the meetings and journeys experienced by the Sisters at this time.

The spirit of renewal which pervaded the 1960s also affected the work. The Retreat Wing continued to be a success, 800 women and girls being catered for in forty-nine retreats in 1962 alone, and the end of the decade saw it being opened up to laymen (clergy had already been permitted to make private retreats). Ecumenical conferences were also held there, and a growing number of groups and individuals came to appreciate the sharing of ideas and spirituality. Nearby, St John's House for elderly ladies was renamed St Anne's House on January 1st 1961, to avoid confusion with St John's Lodge in Hatch Lane. Active work also increased for the Sisters, a number becoming involved in parish work again. (The Sisters had withdrawn from mission work at St Alban's Holborn in 1955.) At Salisbury, too, the retreat house flourished, but the 1960s saw two more openings for mission and renewal. In 1964 the Community took over Neale House in Cambridge from the Society of St Margaret. This was a relatively small house where students could stay and from whence the Sisters did pastoral work within the student body, parish and hospital visiting, and running quiet days. And for a brief time from January 1967 until July 1968 the Sisters shared mission work in Reading with members of the Society of St John the Evangelist, Cowley (known as the Cowley Fathers).

There were a few withdrawals too. In July 1965 the Sisters withdrew from the teaching at St Stephen's College, Broadstairs. The College now passed into the control of a Board of Governors on which the Community was to be represented. Many people regretted this action, but it was felt by the Community to be in the best interest of the school, there being fewer qualified Sisters to teach the girls. In fact the links between the Community and College did not suffer. In 1968 the College celebrated its Centenary and marked the occasion with the official opening of the new hall by a former pupil, the writer Margaret Lane, Countess of Huntingdon.

In Oxford, St Basil's Home was finally closed in 1966 after a long financial struggle. The house was sold and the proceeds used towards improving St Anne's House, Clewer, which was itself showing its age. Five residents from St Basil's came to St Anne's, where the Community hoped to concentrate its work with the elderly. But St Andrew's Lodge (formerly called St Andrew's Cottage) should not be forgotten. Situated on the Dedworth Road, this work went along quietly, supervised by a long line of secular ladies. The last of these was Mrs Mary Littleton, daughter of Fr Hardy (Sub-Warden 1915–19 and Warden 1945–57) and herself a Clewer Oblate. Mrs Littleton took care of the Lodge from 1967–77, after which the Abbeyfield Society took the buildings over. Nearby stood the Almshouses originally confusingly known as St Andrew's Cottages. These were demolished in 1984.

Windsorians are accustomed to the residential home known as Warden's Lodge on the corner of Hatch Lane and Dedworth Road. This occupies the site of the house called 'The Warden's Lodge' which was actually the residence of the Sub-Warden of the Community: the Warden lived opposite the convent at St John's Lodge. As the years passed neither house was needed and so the Community sold them for redevelopment. The Warden's Lodge was sold in 1954 and the name retained in the residential home which was built there in 1962. In 1963 St John's Lodge was demolished and a new house built nearby called St Augustine's. This was used by the convent chaplain for some years but was later sold.

As the 1970s dawned, the problem of falling vocations seemed to necessitate a two-fold action: to close the remaining branches, thus concentrating the work at Clewer, and the daunting prospect of bringing the buildings up to an acceptable standard. In 1959 there were ninety-nine Sisters, in 1969 there were seventy-six, and in 1979 there were forty. In accordance with this policy the Sisters withdrew from the retreat house at Salisbury in 1971. Likewise the Sisters gave up the work at Cambridge, Neale House being sold to Fitzwilliam College in 1976.

The first phase in the redevelopment of the convent buildings was completed in December 1970 when the ironing room of the former laundry was transformed into a new hall available for public use. This was blessed by the Warden (the Revd F P Coleman) and named Carter Hall. At 7.30 pm on December 11th the Mayor declared the Hall open in the presence of a large gathering including the local press. But this was only the beginning: towards the end of 1971 a firm of architects surveyed the convent buildings and made recommendations for their future use, presenting their findings in the spring of 1972. The kitchen was to be completely reorganised and modernised—the *Associates' Newsletter* of July 1967 had wryly remarked: "If Henry Woodyer had had to do any cooking, [he] would not have designed his own kitchen after the style of the Abbot's kitchen at Glastonbury as he did the Convent one." Once the kitchen was completed, a new Infirmary block was planned for the ground floor of the former House of Mercy/ training home with the Retreat Wing above. This would release the Infirmary on the far side of the convent, which would thence be taken over by St Anne's House, the old premises of which would be sold to help finance the project.

Work did not begin until April 30th 1974, but once begun there was to be no turning back. In order to enable the work to proceed, a good deal of internal moving about had to be done and this necessitated the closure of the Retreat Wing for a considerable period. With the kitchen still in ruins the work began simultaneously on the new Infirmary. Bedlam reigned briefly, and then order began to surface out of the chaos. Writing in the *Associates' Newsletter* of December 1973 Mother Annys commented, "We are mindful that this House was built to serve God and His people and we hope that all we are doing may enable us to serve more fully."

But there were other problems besides noise and rubble. Victorian architecture was now in favour, and whilst St Andrew's Convalescent Hospital had disappeared without a tear being shed, St Anne's House, formerly St John's Home, found itself the subject of a preservation order which a heritage group had obtained. The problem was that the heritage group had no use for the building, nor funds to buy it: they simply wanted it to stay there. So it did—empty and forlorn, providing a magnificent target for local vandalism. What had previously been an impressive building now became a derelict eyesore. This situation remained until 1981 when the property was sold to developers who transformed it into office accommodation whilst retaining Henry Woodyer's architectural features.

Because the money was not immediately forthcoming from St Anne's House, the Sisters had to resort to appeals in order to complete the rebuilding. An appeal in *The Times* brought in a mere £278, but Rosamund Essex had more success when she spoke on Radio 4's *The Week's Good Cause* and managed to bring in £3,000 out of the estimated £30,000 required. By the end of 1975 the dust was beginning to clear and most of the work was done. Some of the land around St Anne's House was sold and subsequently developed as Bridgeman Drive. By March 1976 the Retreat Wing was again fully open, and the ladies from St Anne's House took up residence in their new quarters.

Ever since 1958 a number of women and girls with learning difficulties had been taken at the convent. They had originally come from Leavesden Hospital and were for the most part wrongly placed in such an institution, not being mentally ill but in need of sheltered care. Some had been there for years, reflecting the lack of understanding surrounding people with special needs. At Clewer they had been known as 'the Staff' and helped in the house and kitchen in return for a home with the Sisters. In May 1976, following the improvements to the buildings, the Sisters were registered as running a hostel for mentally handicapped women (as they were known at the time), which henceforth became known as St John's Convent Home.

The period under review saw the passing of a number of older Sisters who had worked in the branches and overseas. This included Sr Edith Emily in 1965, in her 98th year and her 67th year in Community, who had worked in India (five times between 1900 and 1928) and also at Folkestone and Hawley; Sr Helen Muriel in November 1968, professed in 1920, had worked in India twice from 1920–26 and 1927–29, at St Stephen's College 1933–60, as Novice Mistress 1960–67, and at Neale House, Cambridge; Sr Georgina, who died in 1969 soon after her 97th birthday, had been for many years at St Michael's School Darjeeling; Sr Grace Dorothea on November 9th 1972, sometime Sister Secretary and Bursar, and for the last fourteen years Assistant Superior; Sr Ida died happily on December 14th 1972, just ten days after enjoying a tea party to celebrate her 100th birthday; also at this time Sr Dorothy Florence died; Sr Waldine Lucia, who was Mother Superior in America when the Affiliation was severed, died towards the end of 1975; and there were others, all of whose names were inscribed in the Chapel of

St John Baptist. This period also saw the admission of many new Sisters, among them Mother Harriet's great-great-niece Sr Sheila, who made her Final Vows on Ascension Day 1961, 110 years after Mother Harriet's clothing on Ascension Day 1851.

One of the most important achievements of Mother Annys' time as Superior was the restoration of the Affiliation between Clewer and Mendham. The two Houses had grown apart so that severance had seemed inevitable, but there had always been some contact. As noted earlier, visits began to be exchanged from 1962 onwards and this did much to heal the breach. At the end of 1973 it was decided to renew the Affiliation and this took effect from February 1st 1974, which also marked the American Centenary. The Centenary Mass, which was attended by Mother Annys and several Sisters from Clewer, was celebrated on February 5th. It was preceded by a Seminar for Religious which was attended by members of most of the American Communities. At the time of the break with England there were thirty-one American Sisters including two novices; now in 1974 there were fifteen Sisters and no novices.

Ever since the momentous visit to the House of Mercy by Queen Victoria there had been 'Royal occasions', and happily this has continued in recent times. On April 24th 1966 the Community was honoured by a visit from HRH the Princess Andrew of Greece. Mother Annys escorted the Princess on a tour of the Convent and Chapel, picking their way through the darkness due to the rewiring. During tea the Princess told the Sisters about her own efforts to found a Community in Greece, and how, despite failing to do so, she lived as a Religious, saying, "I have no Community but I still have my vocation." After tea the Princess continued her tour, visiting the Church Workroom and wafer bakery, and then joined the Community for Vespers. At the end she came out in the procession with Mother Annys and left at 6.00 pm.

On May 21st 1973 Mother Annys and Sister Violet Anne had the honour of being presented to Her Majesty the Queen when she visited the King George VI Club in Windsor. Similarly, in 1987 Mother Edna Frances and Sr Gina were presented to the Queen at the official opening of the Thames Valley Hospice.

On August 10th 1978 Mother Edna Frances was installed by the Bishop of Reading (the Rt Revd Eric Wild), Mother Annys having laid down her office after twenty years' service. It had been an eventful twenty years, starting with reconstructing the Community work in the late 1950s, a task begun by Mother Dorothy Frances; moving through spiritual renewal and builders' chaos to the point where the Community could begin to build on the fruits of this labour. Mother Annys had some difficult decisions to make but by the time she laid down her office the Community, though smaller in numbers, was equipped for ministry in the modern Church.

19

ADAPTING AND DEVELOPING

The close of the 1970s saw not only a new Mother Superior but also a new Visitor, Warden and Chaplain. Bishop Kenneth Woollcombe resigned as Bishop of Oxford in 1978 and was succeeded by Bishop Patrick Rodger, who also became Visitor to the Community. In 1979 Fr Coleman ceased to be Warden after eleven years and was succeeded by Fr Austin Masters SSM, who was installed on September 21st 1979. The Chaplain, Fr Bulley, also left at this time to become Chaplain to the Sisters of Charity at Knowle. He was succeeded by Fr Robert Gould, who held the post until 1986.

The advent of the 1980s saw two important events. Firstly, the Community of Reparation to Jesus in the Blessed Sacrament moved from their large house in Rushworth Street, Southwark, to Clewer. This was accomplished in gradual stages commencing in 1980. The first CRJBS Sisters had served their noviciate at Clewer, and in the days when the Clewer Sisters worked in the parish of All Hallows' Southwark the two Communities had been near neighbours. There had always been a bond between them, and now this was to be strengthened by the CRJBS sharing in the life and work at Clewer whilst still maintaining its own identity. Thus the CRJBS Sisters retained their own habit and Rule, and until failing health forced Mother Eunice's retirement they had their own Mother Superior. On November 1st 1987 Mother Edna Frances CSJB became the CRJBS Superior too. The arrival of the CRJBS added a new dimension to the Clewer Sisters' work, for although few in number, the Sisters brought their own ethos. The work with the deaf and deaf/blind to which Sr Katherine Mary CRJBS had devoted much of her life was henceforth to be shared with the CSJB. And other CRJBS Sisters began ministering to those in the care of the Clewer Community and in the local area, especially at the Dedworth Day Centre. For a well established Community to join with another might have been a difficult process, but it turned out to be a happy and deeply enriching relationship for both Orders.

The second important event was the Centenary of the Chapel of St John Baptist in 1981. The Bishop of Oxford presided at the Sung Eucharist at 11.00 am on October 20th and also received the first vows of a Sister. This was a great day in Community life, uniting as it did the present-day Sisters with all who had gone before them. Many Oblates, Associates, and other friends were present. Of special interest was an exhibition in the Chapel of the Forerunner consisting of vestments, holy vessels and Henry Woodyer's original plans of the chapel, and this was much appreciated by all who saw them.

Another Centenary fell soon afterwards: that of Mother Harriet's death on March 25th 1883. The actual Centenary was kept as a quiet Community festival at Clewer, the main observance being at Folkestone where Mother Harriet had died and was buried. This took the form of a Sung Eucharist on June 22nd at the parish church of St Mary and St Eanswythe. Twenty Sisters, together with the Sub-Warden (Canon Perkins) and other friends, went by coach. The vicar of the parish (Canon Cole) was the Celebrant and Canon Allchin was deacon at the Eucharist. Later the Sisters visited St Saviour's Church and said Vespers there, and before leaving Folkestone they made a pilgrimage to Mother Harriet's grave.

The renewed Affiliation with the CSJB in America bore fruit during the years which followed, Mother Edna Frances visiting Mendham several times, the first of which was in 1979. These visits have been reciprocated by the American Sisters and in July 1985 the whole Community visited Clewer. For three weeks the convent took on a trans-Atlantic air, the newly restored entrance lodge being adorned with a large Union Jack and the Stars and Stripes. During their stay the Sisters were able to share and exchange ideas on the Religious Life, but there was some light relief too. They visited Hereford by the invitation of the Warden, who was a Canon in residence at the Cathedral; there was a visit to Canterbury culminating in the singing of Vespers in the Chapel of Our Lady of the Undercroft; a pilgrimage to Folkestone where they saw the places associated with the earlier Community; and nearer home, a visit to St George's Chapel. Fr Alan Harrison conducted a Quiet Day, Dr Paul Rampton gave a talk about Canon Carter, and I talked about the research which has since culminated in this book. It was a deeply rewarding time which touched all who had a part in it.

The post-War years have been a time of great testing for all Religious Communities. Falling numbers have left many with large buildings they can no longer fill, and in some cases without the active work they once had, although the life of prayer goes on. They have tackled the problem in different ways: some have sold their property and moved to smaller, more manageable quarters, such as the Community of the Holy Cross who moved from Hayward's Heath to Rempstone near Loughborough, and the Benedictine monks who moved from Nashdom Abbey near Burnham to Elmore at Speen near Newbury, and thence to Salisbury. Others, such as the Society of St Margaret at East Grinstead, built new accommodation in the grounds of their old convent; they subsequently moved to a smaller house at Uckfield. And some have closed altogether.

However, in 1985 the Clewer Sisters decided that the time had come to think and pray deeply about the future. It was not a question of closure, but rather a question of whether they too should move, or stay and rebuild in the grounds, or do yet more work on the buildings so as to make the whole plant serve the wider Church more effectively. After a long period of prayer, reflection, discussion and consultation with various experts, the Community decided to stay at Clewer, to retain the present buildings and to further adapt and modernise them. So once more the convent resounded to the noise of workmen who were improving the living quarters. This would make more space available for the Retreat Wing which became increasingly busy as people attempted to cope with ever noisier and more stressful lives. The long-term plan for reconstruction and development was to take the Community well into the 1990s. But the buildings which so easily could have become a millstone (and would soon do so) were being adapted as the means of bringing the Gospel to a wider group of people. The Sisters were attempting to use their vast buildings for the mission of the Church as they approached the final decade of the 20th century. This positive outlook reflects the hopefulness so characteristic of Mother Harriet and which has always been the hallmark of the Community of St John Baptist.

During Mother Edna Frances' period of office a number of Sisters kept their jubilees, including Sr Annie Maud and Sr Annie Jean, both sixty years; Sr Gladys, Sr Eudora, Sr Annys, Sr Edith Ursula, Sr Alison and Sr Gladys Mary, all fifty years. In addition there were a number of silver jubilees.

As well as jubilees there were a number of deaths, including Sr Hilda Frances in February 1981, Sr Alice Mabel in April 1983, Sr Priscilla in July 1985, and Sr Verena in April 1987. Also several CRJBS Sisters had died since moving to Clewer. On September 12th 1983 Mother Elizabeth Anne from Mendham died there after a fairly short illness: she was succeeded as Sister Superior by Sr Suzanne Elizabeth (the title having been changed at this time from Mother Superior). The death at Clewer in June 1988 of Sr Charlotte Rand SSJF in her 98th year saw the passing of a great character whose connections with Clewer stretched back to 1908. She had entered the House of Mercy aged 18 years ("though I wasn't one of them bad girls," she told me). She was received as a postulant Magdalen on November 30th 1920 and became a consecrated Magdalen on October 6th 1927. As a Magdalen she worked at Oxford Manor House and Littlemore as well as Clewer. In 1946 she became a member of the Society of St John the Forerunner. Her death left just one member of SSJF, Sr Beatrice Kitchener, whose main work was in St John's Convent Home. The reinstallation of Mother Edna Frances for her third term of office was overshadowed by the death, after a very short illness, of Sr Sheila Mary on August 29th 1988. Her death at the age of 59 years came as a deep shock to the Community and she was greatly missed.

A number of faithful friends of the Community also passed to their rest during this period. In June 1981 Eric Crook, Associate and organist for twenty-one years, died after a short illness; and March 1982 saw the sudden death of another server and Associate, George Dann. On January 25th 1984, Janet Norman, the wife of Derek the convent maintenance engineer, died from cancer. The Norman family have had a long connection with the Sisters, Derek's father having worked for them at Highgate until it closed in 1940, after which he came to Clewer. On Commemoration Day 1985 Ernest Day collapsed in the sanctuary at the Sung Eucharist soon after censing the congregation, and died shortly afterwards. He had served at the Clewer altar for sixty-four years and died in the place he loved. A memorial tablet was placed in the Chapel of St John Baptist.

During the 1980s the Community continued to adapt and develop internally according to the changing times. The habit was now much simpler and more economical to produce than of old, and a further adaptation to the head dress was introduced in April 1984. The Daily Offices were fully revised, a new six-fold office using modern language having replaced *The Day Hours of the Church of England*. The *Alternative Service Book* (published in 1980) was adopted, the Community using the 'Rite A' form of the Eucharist, and in addition, the rites for Lent, Holy Week and Easter authorised by the House of Bishops in 1986. The daily Eucharist was once more celebrated at a nave altar, the Sisters and congregation sitting together in the nave. (This was the original altar from the House of Mercy.) On major festivals the Sung

Eucharist was celebrated at the High Altar with the Sisters sitting in choir.

By this time the Community governed itself, the Warden having more faith in women's ability to make their own decisions than Canon Carter had! But times change and Communities are no longer the daring innovation that they were in Carter's time. The Visitor has always been the Bishop of Oxford, though few have kept as tight a rein on things as Samuel Wilberforce, but as noted before it was quite revolutionary for a Diocesan Bishop in the 1850s to associate with a Religious Community. During the 1980s two successive Bishops of Oxford came to Clewer: from June 1st–3rd 1983 when Bishop Patrick Rodger conducted a Visitation; and on Ascension Day 1988 when Bishop Richard Harries celebrated and preached.

The active work of the Community took many forms but remained faithful to Mother Harriet's belief that Sisters should exercise their talents (although some of the work may have brought otherwise latent talents to the fore). Some of the older established work continued: St John's Convent Home provided a safe haven for the residents who helped both in the convent and at the Dedworth Day Centre. But it wasn't all work: outings were arranged for them and some also attended adult literacy classes. The management of St Anne's House for elderly ladies had passed to a secular Council of Management, but the Community had three representatives on it. The Sisters maintained pastoral oversight, visiting the residents daily and joining them for meals. There was a mid-week Eucharist in the small oratory dedicated to St Joseph, and the residents were able to join the Sisters in the Community chapel. The Sisters' Infirmary continued to care for the sick and aged Sisters and was also available for members of other Communities. A trained secular nursing staff helped in this work, which was supervised by the Community. Some of the Sisters in the Infirmary were able to attend chapel, but for those unable to do so there was the oratory of St Mary Magdalen close by. The Church Workroom continued to produce high quality ecclesiastical embroidery and took orders from all over the world. The wafer bakery closed at the end of 1988, a victim of competition from commercial producers.

The links with St Stephen's College continued to be strong, members of the Community serving on the Governing Body and making frequent visits. Nearer home, the Community had connections with several local schools. A Sister was a Governor of the Princess Margaret Royal Free School, the

Church of England senior school in Windsor; Haileybury Junior School, near neighbours of the convent at the former Clewer Manor house, used the Community chapel on Sundays after the Sisters' Mass had ended; and the top class from Clewer Green Church of England First School periodically used the Chapel of the Forerunner for their Eucharist.

Individual Sisters continued to be engaged in many and varied activities ranging from the artistic and musical to the pastoral. Sr Katherine Mary CRJBS and her work with the deaf/blind has been briefly mentioned: this included teaching Braille at Broadmoor Hospital, and a long-standing association with St John's Guild for the Blind. Sr Sheila was Treasurer of the Guild of Church Braillists and had transcribed several books. Sr Doreen had attended a 'signing' course in order to interpret for the deaf, and Sr Olga, who was profoundly deaf, had written on the subject. Many Sisters went out to give talks, to lead prayer groups, to preach or to take part in parish missions, and one Sister was a parish worker at All Saints', Dedworth. A great deal of visiting the sick and elderly was being undertaken, besides the caring work of the Dedworth Day Centre and support for the local Guideposts project. A Sister regularly visited the patients in the Thames Valley Hospice not far from the convent. Visits to other Communities, meetings of bodies such as the Communities' Consultative Council, the Association for Promoting Retreats, the Women's World Day of Prayer Committee, attendance at conferences of Superiors, Novice Guardians, and monastic musicians were all part of the ongoing work of the Community in the 1980s.

Beyond doubt the growing work of the Community was that of the Retreat Wing. The demand for retreats, quiet days or even quiet evenings had increased tremendously as the pace of life in the outside world had become faster, noisier and more competitive. When the work with retreatants was first introduced only women were taken, but by the 1980s the Retreat Wing was open to all and catered for a wide variety of needs. At first all the retreats were led by outside conductors, but the renewed interest in Ignatian methods led some of the Sisters to be trained in retreat conducting, and individually guided three-day retreats were conducted by members of the Community. Sisters were also going out to parishes in order to conduct retreats. The Sisters also became involved in a new concept, the 'open door' retreat, designed for busy people who have no time to get away for any appreciable space but who might manage an hour or two once a week in their own parish. The conductor would guide the retreatant during the time allowed and leave an exercise to be prayed through during the coming week, at the end of which there would be another session.

Another successful extension of the retreat work was the introduction of 'drop-in days' where the facilities of the convent were made available for people to leave the frenzy of everyday life and 'drop into quietness'. Except for a Mass at mid-day nothing was organised; participants would be free to read, write, pray and relax in whatever way they wished. This met a genuine need especially for those unable to get away for longer.

The published retreat list may not have looked exhaustive, but these were the 'spare' times, practically all the rest of the calendar being occupied by parish or group bookings. And happily the ecumenical links fostered in the 1960s were still bearing fruit, many of the groups consisting of Christians from other denominations. The Chapel of the Forerunner, which was thoroughly refurbished in 1985, was made available for retreat groups. The following is a sample of the retreats in 1988, excluding parish and other private groups: three 'drop-in days'; three open retreats; two 'training the trainers' weekends (for prospective leaders of retreats, quiet days etc); an eight-day individually guided retreat led by Bishop Graham Chadwick and Sr Gina CSJB; 'Do you have a Religious Vocation?'—a chance to explore the Religious Life; a beginner's retreat; a prayer and painting retreat; and a Gregorian Chant retreat. Early in 1989 the Convent hosted a quiet day for 130 priests from the Willesden Episcopal area of the London Diocese.

In addition to retreatants the Convent also welcomed many individual visitors throughout the year. Commemoration Day was well established and there was always a full Chapel for the Sung Eucharist. But in 1979 an additional open afternoon was held in August to allow local people to see the convent. This became an annual event and proved to be highly successful. It did much to bring the Community to the notice of a wider public.

In 1988 the Community of St John Baptist numbered twenty-eight, the CRJBS eight and the American Affiliation nine. Like many Religious Communities at the time, the Sisters at Clewer desperately needed vocations, but there were a few novices and the Sisters hoped that this was a good sign for future growth. But the most optimistic thing was the Community itself. As a result of prayerful self-examination regarding the future life and work, a spirit of renewal had gone through the Community. Something far deeper had emerged than simply a decision to stay at Clewer and refurbish the Victorian buildings. Admittedly, there was a reluctance to walk away from the buildings that so enshrined the life and history of the Community. But there was a strong sense of going forward in the same spirit which Mother Harriet described as "the sparkle", ie the ability to change when necessary in order to meet changing needs. This is what Mother Harriet meant when she told the Sisters, "We must keep ourselves ready to answer God's call … for we cannot tell what He may do with us."

At the end of the 1980s there was still work to be done at Clewer even though the Sisters would find it increasingly challenging. Once upon a time the Clewer Sisters encircled the world from Calcutta to Oregon, answering God's call in many and various ways. Now the world was coming to Clewer and Mendham, to rest and be renewed and to go back to the noise and chaos. The work had changed outwardly, but the Religious vocation: the living of the life with God, the readiness to answer God's call, and the willingness to serve God wherever, whenever and in whoever, is still essentially part of the Clewer ethos, and indeed of all Religious.

And so in 1989 the Sisters at Clewer prepared themselves to go forward into the future in a spirit of thankfulness for the undoubtedly glorious past, a spirit of joy for all God's blessings at the present time, and in the sure and certain knowledge of the continued love and prayers of those who had gone before. The next decade would bring them their greatest challenge—to face the inevitable decision to leave Clewer and to move on into the unknown.

20

TOWARDS THE MOMENTOUS DECISION

The first edition of *A Joyous Service* was published in June 1989 amidst a spirit of optimism for the future of the Community. The decision made a few years previously, to remain at Clewer and improve the facilities there for use by the wider Church, seemed to be right and work was in progress when the book was launched. There was a sense of excitement and of looking forward to renewed life at Clewer, but as the Community entered the 1990s and moved towards the new Millennium so it became clear that the Sisters must grasp the nettle and move on. To take such a radical step was probably the most painful decision the Community has made in all its long life. In the next three chapters we will look at the life and work of the Community in those last years at Clewer, follow them through that momentous decision to move, see them settled into their new home at Begbroke Priory near Oxford, and the exploration of a final move to Ripon College, Cuddesdon. And we shall also look at the work of the American CSJB, based at Mendham in New Jersey.

The final year of the 1980s was marked by reconstruction work on the kitchen wing in order to improve the facilities of St John's Convent Home. The eight residents had previously lived on the second floor above the visitors' and retreat wings, in rooms which no longer reached the rigorous standards then required. The new facilities, consisting of sitting room, dining room, new bathrooms and showers, and individual bedrooms, all newly furnished, were opened by Mr Tony Ellam, senior social worker, and blessed by the Sub-Warden, Canon Eric Perkins, on July 5th 1989. Sister Zoë continued to be the Sister responsible for the care of the residents, who continued to do light duties in the convent buildings.

The external work of the Community continued at a rapid pace and included preaching engagements, retreat conducting in parishes as well as at home, talks to local clubs about the Religious Life, visits to other Communities, and visits to local schools. And there was more specialised work too such as Sr Catherine Mary's work once a week at St Martin-in-the-Fields, where she was helping in the office of the social care centre. Mother Edna Frances and Sr Jane Olive had begun studying reflexology and this alternative therapy was in due course offered to patients at the nearby Thames Valley Hospice. Sr Katherine Mary CRJBS was still very busy with her work with the deaf and blind and in August 1989 took part in a Radio Oxford 'phone-in'. Sr Pamela had been adapting the plainchant traditionally used in chapel for use with the text of the *Alternative Service Book*. Members of other Communities had expressed an interest in this work, the fruits of which was published in 1991 under the title *An English Kyriale*. This represented several years' collaboration between Sr Pamela, Dr Mary Berry, Dr David Hiley and Fr Peter Allen of the Community of the Resurrection.

It is a sad fact that an ageing Community sees more deaths than new vocations, and consequently both Communities (CSJB and CRJBS) were saddened by the passing on January 9th 1990 of Mother Eunice CRJBS. She had been in the Community Infirmary for a long time. Her death was followed on May 5th 1990 by that of Sr Gladys after a severe heart attack in January, from which she never fully recovered. Sr Gladys had a varied Community life, having worked in India from 1933–45, and then at St Stephen's College, Broadstairs, before returning to Clewer to be in charge of St Anne's House. Her final years saw her in charge of the wafer bakery, where she became a well-known figure locally.

But although the 1990s had begun on a note of sadness through the death of these two well loved Sisters, the 1980s had closed with bright hope for the future. There had been the profession in first vows of Sister Veronica Joan on December 21st, the clothing as a novice of Sr Elizabeth on December 31st, and the reception of Angela Hughes as a postulant on December 30th followed by her clothing as a novice on August 15th.

The renewed relationship with the Community of St John Baptist in Mendham, New Jersey, continued to flourish. In June 1989 Mother Edna Frances, a stalwart supporter of women's ordination, had visited the American Sisters and was present at Sr Barbara Jean's ordination as a deacon in Trenton Cathedral. Her visit was followed in October by a two-week visit by Sr Zoë and Sr Sheila. And there have been many visits from Sisters from both sides of the Atlantic since then. One such visit by two of the American Sisters gave the indomitable Sr Eudora a unique opportunity to fulfil a life-long ambition. Sister Suzanne Elizabeth and Sr Mary Lynne had come over for a three-week visit in July 1990 and the latter had asked to visit Iona. The trip was planned but there was a last minute hitch because Sr Sheila, who was

due to accompany them, fell ill at the last minute. Writing in the *Associates'*
Newsletter for Autumn 1990 Sr Eudora took up the story: "I, Sr Eudora,
having a rest morning to 7 am, was in bed at 6.50 when the Infirmarian
came to say, 'There's a crisis, Sr Sheila cannot go. Will you—leaving 8.15?'
Me (aloud) 'Yes' (under breath) 'not half.' Mother [Edna Frances] appeared
from nowhere with a bag and began to pack. Sr Zoë produced breakfast.
Mother and Sr Zoë made the bed … Then 'booted and spurred' I stood by
the car at 8.15 … and with Mother at the wheel—'poop, poop' like Toad
we were off …'"

More work was done on the buildings during 1990. For twenty years Carter
Hall had served the public for recreational activities, but during that time
other meeting places had become available, making Carter Hall superfluous.
Therefore it was decided to convert part of the Hall into a dwelling, to be
named Carter House, for the use of Derek Norman (Community engineer)
and his family. The other part of the Hall was converted into garaging for
the Community. Within the convent itself, the chapel bell was taken down,
repaired and rehung by the Whitechapel Bell Foundry at a considerably
larger expense than the original £105 4s 4d of 1899.

The spate of postulants continued during 1991 with the admission of
Daphne Hutchieson on February 1st and Mary Britt on February 8th, the
latter being clothed as Sr Mary Stephen on August 6th. (Daphne Hutchieson
later left the Community and became an Associate.) At the other end of the
scale Sr Annie Maud, who was in her 95th year, celebrated her sixty-eighth
anniversary of profession on April 28th. Meanwhile, Sr Eudora was about
to celebrate her 90th birthday. She did so in her usual flamboyant style;
her appetite for Iona having been whetted the previous year, a friend paid
for her to make a return visit for a whole week. A Sister from Mendham,
Sr Katherine Veronica, who was professed in 1940, died at this time after a
long illness. Sr Doreen and Sr Pamela had spent three weeks at Mendham
in the summer and were present at the clothing of Sr Margo Elizabeth.
Sr Catherine Mary, another well known Clewer Sister, died peacefully on
October 14th 1991. Before joining the Community she had been a mission
doctor in Assam where she met Frances Wood (Oblate CSJB) and Cicely
Workman (Associate CSJB), who were nurses at the same mission station.
It was through them that she heard about the Community which she later
joined.

In May 1991 Sr Susila, Superior of the Christa Sevika Sangha in Bangladesh, together with Sisters Anima, Agnes, Margaret and Dorothy, came to England and visited Clewer. They had previously visited in 1987 when they had spent several days at Clewer and had met Sr Eudora, who had recently returned following the closure of the retreat house at Salisbury. This connection had begun in the 1930s when Susila was a pupil at the Pratt Memorial School in Calcutta and Sr Eudora was teaching there. The Sisters' 1991 visit was overshadowed by news from Bangladesh of a hurricane that had wrought much havoc on crops and housing.

In July 1991, after 123 years of its existence, St Stephen's College, Broadstairs, was closed. The Sisters had withdrawn from the teaching in 1965 but retained a presence on the Governing body. At the time of their withdrawal they had vested the college in the care of two separate bodies—the Trustees who would control the property, and the Governors who would be responsible for the running of the school. There had been a number of problems, chiefly relating to finance and falling numbers on the roll, and consequently the school was becoming less viable. The decision by the Governors to close the college was not taken lightly but in view of a deficit of £100,000, which had accrued by the end of 1990, there seemed to be no alternative. A number of last-ditch attempts to save the school were made by concerned parents and former pupils, but to no avail. The college closed at the end of the summer term 1991 following a thanksgiving service and open day. Archive material was removed to Clewer for safe keeping and was later deposited in the Berkshire Record Office. In 1994 the Old St Stephenites' Society published *The Story of St Stephen's College*, researched and written by former student Jenny Balston, whose forebear, Harriet Ann Balston, was Canon Carter's sister.

1992 began with the major refurbishment of the Chapel of St John Baptist. Initially the chapel was to be rewired, but as this involved the use of scaffolding it was decided that the chapel should undergo a complete cleaning. As the wiring was almost sixty years old it was long overdue. During the course of the cleaning process, paintings of angels holding musical instruments were revealed on the vaulting above the apse. 110 years of candle smoke and incense had completely obscured these lovely paintings. It was also discovered that the web of the vaulting was made of canvas.

In June 1992 the second volume of Community history was published under the title *A Place in Life: the Clewer House of Mercy 1849–1883*. The original intention had been for a single volume, but during 1988, just as I was about to write up all my research, Mother Edna Frances asked me to sort through a cupboard in her office during her holiday and dispose of anything no longer required. What I discovered was a complete and hitherto forgotten archive of the original House of Mercy founded at 'The Limes' by Mariquita Tennant in 1849. There were also documents relating to the early Community, including Mother Harriet's manuscript Rule in her own handwriting. It felt like walking into Aladdin's Cave: it also meant we had to rethink the book project because what I had found amounted to a book in itself. So, after taking advice from Canon Donald Allchin, the decision was made to publish a general history (*A Joyous Service*) followed by the more detailed account of the House of Mercy, with 1883 as the 'cut off' date, this being the year of Mother Harriet's death.

In August 1992 Mother Edna Frances laid down the office of Mother Superior a year early, and was succeeded by Sr Jane Olive who was installed in August. Mother Edna Frances had served the Community in this way for fourteen years, having been installed on August 10th 1978. During that time she had led the Community through a further period of improvements to the buildings, having grappled with the decision to remain at Clewer. Some of her predecessor Mother Annys' work was now bearing fruit, notably the renewed friendship with the American affiliation. There had also been changes to the habit and to the Daily Office and Eucharist, and to the way in which the Community governed itself.

Mother Jane Olive therefore had a good foundation on which to build her own leadership. But the fact remained that the Community was an ageing one, and the question of how long the Sisters would be able to sustain life in the vast buildings at Clewer was never far away. In January 1993 the Bishop of Oxford, the Rt Revd Richard Harries, carried out a Visitation. One of his recommendations was that the Community should have a 'fallow period' of three months during which time the Sisters would think, pray and discuss aspects of their life and work, and try to discern where God might be leading them. It was therefore decided not to take visitors or lead retreats from the end of June until the beginning of October.

There were a number of comings and goings within the Community in the first part of the 1990s. On January 17th 1993 Sr Philippa Irene was clothed as a novice and on April 1st Sr Margaret Ruth was clothed. December 22nd 1993 saw the profession in final vows of Sr Veronica Joan. On May 25th Sr Margo Elizabeth had been professed in first vows at Mendham. On October 24th Sr Eudora had celebrated the diamond jubilee of her profession.

As well as arrivals in the Community, there were also some departures, because the idea of testing a vocation is to discern whether there is a calling from God to Community Life. For this reason it is a gradual process over a number of years. Sometimes the discernment process may lead away from the original Community and into something slightly different. Sr Angela had been a novice for two or three years but decided that she was being called to a more contemplative form of the Religious Life. She transferred to the Society of the Precious Blood at Burnham Abbey and was clothed as a novice there on October 30th 1993, some of the Clewer Sisters being present. Sr Gina, a longstanding member of the Community, had also been reviewing her calling and early in 1992 had gone to test her vocation with the Community of St Francis. At that time the Community was based at Compton Durville in Somerset, and had Sisters working in many parts of England. Early in 2010 the Community of St Francis announced its impending departure from Compton Durville for a new house in Lincolnshire and at the time of writing Sr Gina is still with the Franciscans.

*

These same years saw the deaths of more Sisters. Sr Emma Clare, well known for being in charge of the Church Workroom, died very suddenly on August 8th 1992, a week after the death of Sr Annie Jean in her 97th year. The sudden death of Sr Olga on July 10th 1993, four days after a triple heart bypass operation, came as a great shock to the Community. Sr Olga was a very gentle person, profoundly deaf and very artistic. She provided some of her delicate line drawings for the chapter endings of *A Joyous Service* and *A Place in Life*. Sr Annie Maud, a well known former parish Sister, died on November 18th 1993 in her 96th year and in the seventieth year of her profession. The death on April 7th 1993 of Sr Beatrice Kitchener, aged 90, saw the end of an era. She had been received as a postulant Magdalen on October 12th 1938 and was consecrated on May 31st 1944. In addition to serving at Clewer she also served at the Devon House of Mercy until it closed in 1940. She was the last member of the Society of St John the Forerunner, which had been formed in 1946 as a Third Order of the Community when the Order of Magdalens was reconstituted. February 1994 saw the death of Sr Edith Ursula, and in March Sr Lillah, the latter having once been the portress whose cheery smile welcomed many visitors into the convent. Also, two members of the CRJBS had died—Sr Francesca in December 1993 and Sr Lydia in January 1994.

The whole question of the meaning of 'ordained ministry' was very much to the fore in the first part of the 1990s. The Episcopal Church of the USA, to which the Mendham Sisters belonged, was ahead of the Church of England in ordaining women to the priesthood. Many traditionalists within the Church on both sides of the Atlantic had assumed that women Religious would oppose the ordination of women. By making this assumption they failed to understand that Religious Communities from the earliest days had been pioneers, doing something very radical, and therefore might not be opposed to women priests. So there was a sense of shock in some quarters when some Communities failed to oppose the opening of the priesthood to women. On November 11th 1992 the General Synod of the Church of England voted in favour of ordaining women as priests. At Clewer, some Sisters were in favour, others had reservations and a small number were against. The Community maintained a spirit of prayerful discernment, respecting both viewpoints, and this led to the present position where two Sisters, Sr Anne and Sr Mary Stephen, have been able, with the blessing of the Community, to become priests. Meanwhile, on March 19th 1995, Sr Anne (who had been received as a postulant on February 7th 1994) was licensed as a Reader in the New Windsor Team Ministry, having been a licensed Reader before coming to Clewer. In America, on February 19th 1995 Sr Barbara Jean was ordained to the priesthood by the Bishop of New Jersey at the convent in Mendham. Mother Jane Olive and Sr Marjorie had flown over for the occasion, braving very bad weather conditions and disrupted flights.

An outcome of the three-month period of reflection and discernment in 1993 had been the revision of the Community Rule. A further outcome had been a firm resolve to stay at Clewer, and to this end more work was planned to improve the facilities. This would mostly affect two areas of the convent—the Sisters' infirmary and the retreat wing. Under the guidance of Sr Pamela, the work of the retreat wing had grown and expanded in recent years. Many types of retreat were now being given, ranging from traditional preached retreats led by a number of well known leaders, to themed retreats such as painting and prayer, or embroidery and prayer, to Ignatian individually guided retreats. Several Sisters were involved in this growing work, which was fast proving to be one of the most important ministries exercised from the convent. But the retreat wing was in need of upgrading—health and safety standards were rising, and people were now having higher expectations of the facilities.

At the same time there was a growing concern about the Sisters' infirmary, which occupied the ground floor of the former west wing underneath the retreat wing. Fewer Sisters within the convent needed the infirmary and fewer Sisters from other Communities were using it. Consequently it was becoming uneconomical to run as a separate entity and there was a real danger of a financial crisis. It was therefore decided to relocate the infirmary to St Anne's House in the convent. This would enable the premises to be renovated and used as part of the retreat wing. It was a difficult decision because it involved the loss of three nurses who had worked in the infirmary for many years. The first Sisters moved into St Anne's House in March 1994. Work began on the former infirmary and the resulting improved facilities were renamed the Clewer Spirituality Centre. On December 15th 1994 the Bishop of Oxford came to bless the new Centre. As well as providing extra bedrooms, the new facilities included a dining room, retreatants' coffee-making area, sitting rooms, a chapel with view over the garden, and the chapel of St Mary Magdalen. The Sisters were still very much involved with the retreat work, but two secular administrators, Sue Armstead and Robert Langton, were appointed for the running of the Centre.

After finding the extra archive material which formed the basis of *A Place in Life* I had decided that there was also enough material for a short third volume devoted to the work in India. Then one day Mother Edna Frances came into the parlour where I was working and said, "Er, I've found these!" She was clutching a large portfolio which on further investigation proved to be the letters sent to Clewer by Sr Jane Frances, who was Sister Superior in Calcutta from 1889 until 1918. Mother then produced a wonderful album of photographs of the Indian work. This was in addition to the large volume of photographs of the buildings where the Sisters worked in Calcutta and Darjeeling. I then asked the inevitable question, "Is there any more, and if so may I see it now?" "Oh no, there's no more," she replied, and *Sisters of the Raj* was duly published in 1997. But just before we went to press I asked Mother Jane Olive a question about one of the Sisters who had worked in India. "Oh, I'll look it up in the India book," she replied. Bombshell! With sinking heart I said, "Did you say 'India book'? What India book?" "Oh, it lists all the Sisters who worked there; would you like to see it?" "Yes, Mother, and anything else relevant, before it's too late!" The book was duly produced, and what a mine of information it was—not only the name of every Sister who worked in India, but the dates of departure and return and even the name of the ships they sailed on. Roger Cullingham, who typeset the book, was able to reproduce it as an appendix.

Canon Donald Allchin, who had written the preface for the first two books, had suggested that I should visit the places in India where the Sisters had once worked. At first the very idea seemed impossible but as I delved further into the Indian archives I fell under the spell of India just as Sr Jane Frances, whose letters I was reading, had done before. I was able to talk to Sr Eudora about her experiences, and clearly she too was still in love with India, sixty years after returning. (Although Sr Gladys had died some years previously, I had interviewed her when researching the Indian work for *A Joyous Service*.) So I decided to take the plunge, and accompanied by Joyce Sampson, a friend from Windsor, I visited Calcutta and Darjeeling in February 1995. Our visit is recounted in the final chapter of *Sisters of the Raj*. Whilst in Calcutta I missed Mother Susila by about two hours but I was able to meet her at Wantage when she came to England in the summer of 1996.

One of the most impressive things about the Indian visit was how much the work of the Sisters was still valued at St John's Diocesan Girls' Higher Secondary School, even though they had left in 1947. Mrs Chrestien, the Lady Principal, had been in touch with Sr Eudora during the year before my visit, and on the day we visited the school we were laden with gifts to bring back to her. Sr Eudora was longing to go to India with us, but her physical health was too frail even though she would have gone given half the chance! So it was good to bring back a positive report about the Calcutta schools she knew so well. And then in the autumn of 1995, Mr and Mrs Chrestien came to visit their daughter who was at London University, and came to Clewer to see the convent, and they met Sr Eudora.

On October 5th 1995 Sr Katherine Mary CRJBS died peacefully aged 93. She had been an experienced parish mission Sister, braving all types of urban deprivation, no challenge being too great for her. She had an irrepressible sense of humour and was always very good company. Nor was she afraid to laugh at herself—her work at Broadmoor, teaching Braille to the inmates, frequently drew the comment from her that she had only just come out of Broadmoor! The reaction from visitors to the convent who did not know her reason for going was interesting, and she would enjoy every moment. She also did a lot of work with the St John's Guild for the Blind, accompanying them on their annual Walsingham pilgrimage, as well as local work with the deaf/blind. The death of Sr Katherine Mary meant that only one Sister remained of the twelve members of the Community of Reparation to Jesus in the Blessed Sacrament who had come to live at Clewer in 1980. Sr Esther Mary, the last Sister, was still very active and was at this time Chair of the Dedworth Day Centre, and a representative (with Sr Sheila) for Churches Together in Windsor.

On October 1st 1995 Canon Austin Masters SSM retired as Warden of the CSJB on health grounds, and the Sisters decided that the time had come to dispense with the office of Warden with its Victorian overtones. In his place, Fr Lister Tonge was appointed residential Chaplain, though due to prior overseas engagements he did not take up his duties until February 1996.

The Community of the Companions of Jesus the Good Shepherd, in common with many Religious Communities, was dwindling in numbers and finding the large convent at West Ogwell in Devon difficult to maintain. There had been a tentative connection with the Clewer Community, inasmuch as the CJGS had briefly taken over the running of St Michael's School, Darjeeling, in 1946, following the withdrawal of the CSJB, and then had also taken over the CSJB work in Barbados in 1946. In 1996 it was decided that the CJGS should come and live at Clewer alongside the CSJB, whilst retaining their own distinctive brown habit, their Rule, Mother Superior and Warden. They would share with the CSJB in their daily life, work and worship. Mother Ann Verena and four Sisters duly arrived at Clewer, two other Sisters having opted to live with other Communities. The Community of the Companions of Jesus the Good Shepherd was a much 'newer' Community than the CSJB, having begun in 1920 as an association of schoolteachers who wished to share aspects of the Religious Life together whilst continuing to live within their own homes. They would meet together in the school holidays and live as a Community but disperse in term-time. But they failed to win recognition as a Religious Community from the wider Anglican church authorities because none of them lived permanently in community. In response, some members decided to take life vows and live together in community, whilst others continued to work in the teaching profession. The teaching mission expanded to South America, India and the West Indies. Sr Ann Verena had joined in 1964, having had wide teaching experience ranging from teaching prep school boys to science teaching, and retained a lifelong speciality in science subjects, including the relationship between science and religion. She became Mother Superior of CJGS in 1996 just before the move to Clewer.

Two professions took place in the summer of 1996. On August 6th Sr Mary Stephen was professed in final vows and on August 24th Sr Anne was professed in first vows. Both Sisters were by this time deeply involved in mission and retreat work at Clewer and in parishes further afield.

On September 6th 1996 Sr Mary Theresa died in St Anne's House aged 88 years. She joined the Community in 1948 and was professed in 1954. Ten days later, on September 16th, Sr Annys died aged 85. She joined the Community in 1931, aged 20, and was professed in 1934. During the early years of World War II she had read for a degree at London University. She had many stories to tell of her early years in the Community, including fire-watching duties on the chapel roof, wearing a tin hat over her veil and balancing precariously with only the fragile parapet preventing a fall to the ground. After the War she taught at St Stephen's College, retaining a life-long interest in the school, and only returning to Clewer upon her election as Mother Superior in 1958. These were changing times both in terms of falling numbers in the Community and changes in the wider Church; Mother Annys steered the Community through both, managing at the same time to maintain the ethos of the Community. She had taken leadership reluctantly but did not fail to grasp the nettle when difficult decisions had to be made, such as the closure of branch houses and the redevelopment of the convent buildings. She was an ecumenist at a time when there were great hopes for Christian unity—Sisters were sent on visits to Taizé and to Continental Roman Catholic and Lutheran Communities, and there was involvement in local unity services and in Synodical government. She prevented the Community from turning in on itself and her vision enabled more people from outside to be touched by the Sisters' work. But without doubt her greatest work was her part in healing the breach between Clewer and Mendham and the resulting reaffiliation: that will be her abiding memorial.

On January 9th 1997 Sr Eudora, by now in her 96th year, suffered the first of a series of strokes and died peacefully on March 11th, the day after *Sisters of the Raj* finally went to the printers. I had hoped she would live to see the published book, which was launched in time for Commemoration Day and to which she had contributed so much. This included a chapter of her own memories of India taken from her memoirs written at the request of Mother Annys. Sr Eudora joined the noviciate in July 1931 and was professed in October 1933; within six weeks of her profession she was sent to India. At the time of her death she was the only remaining Sister to have worked in India, Barbados and America. After returning to Clewer at the end of World War II she had various responsibilities—in charge of the Training Home at Clewer; the retreat wing; the Salisbury Retreat House; parish Sister at St Andrew's Clewer; and finally from 1983–88, Assistant Superior. (My first sight of Sr Eudora was at the Clewer parish Harvest Supper when she was enthusiastically dancing the Gay Gordons!) After she became too frail for active work she had a ministry with individual retreatants. She could be formidable, but the years mellowed her and she retained her sense of humour throughout her long life. I remember one day shortly before her final illness when Sr Eudora came to see me on one of my research visits, and tapping the floor very firmly with her walking stick she suddenly said, "Some of them [ie the Sisters] say that I am a Victorian. Well, the old Queen died in the January and I was born in the May, so I am an Edwardian *not* a Victorian!" That said, we then got back to her favourite subject—India. In her last years she greatly enjoyed the open afternoons and Commemoration Day when she would 'hold court' amongst friends and acquaintances, particularly the clergy.

In spite of the number of deaths of older Sisters and some departures from the noviciate, the Sisters were extremely busy as the second half of the 1990s progressed. As well as involvement in much local work there was also work in the wider Church. For instance, over the past fifteen years Sr Pamela had been a member of the Association for Promoting Retreats, a member of the Executive Committee for several years, and from 1993–6 had been Chair of the Association. The coming of Mother Ann Verena and her four CJGS Sisters had also made its mark on Community life and they are frequently mentioned amongst the Sisters attending conferences, leading retreats, giving talks, visiting schools and meeting with local clergy. The death of Sr Katherine Mary CRJBS had temporarily brought to an end the work with the deaf and blind, but by the end of 1997 a new beginning had been made. Sr Doreen CSJB and Sr Angela Felicity CJGS had been going to the Slough deaf club with the Revd Louise Brown, Vicar of All Saints' Dedworth. Sr Angela Felicity was also attending signing and lip reading classes.

The Thames Valley Hospice celebrated its tenth anniversary in 1997. A close neighbour of the convent, there were strong links between the Hospice and the Community. Mother Jane Olive had been a volunteer worker for the past seven years, using her reflexology skills there. The Chapel of St John Baptist was the setting on November 29th 1997 for the blessing in the Eucharist of the marriage of David Dufour, a member of St Andrew's Clewer, and Prue Clench, formerly Director of the Thames Valley Hospice, who had latterly been living at the convent.

August 1997 saw a shocked nation mourning the death of Diana, Princess of Wales and a Requiem Mass was offered in the Convent Chapel on the day following her death. There were long-standing close ties between the Community and St George's Chapel, and this was reflected in the invitation by the Dean of Windsor (the Very Revd Patrick Mitchell) for Mother Jane Olive and some of the Sisters to take part in the Sung Requiem in the Chapel on the day of the funeral. Together with other local clergy, the Sisters helped to administer Holy Communion to a congregation numbering over 1,000.

Trans-Atlantic visits continued to be made between Clewer and Mendham. The autumn of 1997 saw Mother Jane Olive and Sr Pamela fly out for the installation of Sr Barbara Jean as Sister Superior in succession to Sr Suzanne Elizabeth, who had held the office since 1983. The formal election took place on October 1st and the installation next day. There was also a surprise party in Sr Suzanne Elizabeth's honour to thank her for her fourteen years' service. The visit to the USA had not been the first overseas visit for Sr Pamela during 1997. As she wryly commented, she might have thought, on entering the Community almost twenty-six years previously, that her travelling days were over, but far from it. As well as the autumn visit to Mendham, Sr Pamela had also visited the Holy Land earlier in 1997.

The St Albans and Oxford Ministry Course was having a high profile with the Community at this time, having three ordinands with convent connections—Sr Anne, Robert Langton (Spirituality Centre) and Prue Dufour. The Spirituality Centre was also being used as a venue for selection conferences for the Oxford Diocesan Ordained Local Ministry scheme. Meanwhile Sr Mary Stephen was approaching the end of a three-year Ignatian Spirituality Course which had taken her to London once a week. In addition, Sr Pamela was also doing a course on Spiritual Direction.

On September 21st 1998 another era came to an end with the death of Sr Gladys Mary. She came to the Community in July 1934 aged 26, and died in her 90th year. She was the last of the former lay Sisters; in 1946 the Community had undergone a major reform and the lay Sisters had been incorporated into the choir Sisters. She had an irrepressible sense of humour and many stories about her have passed into the communal memory of the Sisters.

The Community *Newsletter* for Easter 1998 announced that Sr Marjorie, who had been in Community since 1954, had reverted to her baptismal name, Margaret. At the time she joined the noviciate names were not repeated within a short space of time and the first Sr Margaret had only recently died (even though she was professed as far back as 1887!) Later in 1998 it was announced that Sr Margaret, as she was now called, was having a sabbatical. Sadly, the outcome of her reflection during a year away was to ask for release from the Community. At the end of 1999 she moved to accommodation provided by the Community but is still in touch with the Sisters and other friends made over many years.

By 1998 the writing on the wall was beginning to appear regarding the future of the Community. The buildings were becoming an increasing burden—the Chapel of St John Baptist, albeit a masterpiece of Victorian craftsmanship, was once more in dire need of repair. The exterior brick and stonework needed repointing and the work was proceeding. While an attempt was made to continue using the chapel while the work was being done, eventually it became necessary to use the Chapel of the Forerunner. Alongside the burden of maintaining the plant there was also the fact that the Community was growing older and becoming fewer. Immense workloads were being carried by fewer Sisters, together with the fact that the same expectations of what they could offer were being held by local clergy, organisations, and individuals. The *Newsletter* for autumn 1998 carried an article by the Chaplain, Fr Lister Tonge, in which he wrote about the way people expect Religious Communities to always stay the same, and the often unreasonable way in which people react when it is necessary to change. Clearly the article was a thinly veiled warning to those who were projecting negativities onto the Sisters. He concluded, "The three Communities of sisters now under this roof were each founded to meet particular needs … Because CSJB, CRJBS or CJGS have been special and important to us, we shall want to ensure that we do not burden the sisters with our expectations which might hold them back from fulfilling the developing role and mission God is entrusting to them as the new millennium dawns …"

In spite of all this speculation the Community maintained its everyday life, including more overseas visits. On December 9th 1998 Sr Edna Frances and Sr Anne flew to Bangladesh to spend a month with Mother Susila and the Christa Sevika Sangha Community. They were based at the convent at Jobarpar and spent Christmas there but also visited the Oxford Mission Brotherhood at Barisal, where they joined them for the feast of the Epiphany, their patronal festival, staying with the CSS Sisters who live and work there.

In autumn 1997 Sr Mary Stephen had visited Mendham and was especially impressed with Daytop, a charity founded in New York in the 1960s to help rehabilitate young drug users, and which from 1991 has occupied some of the former school buildings at the convent. Some of the Sisters help with the project. In February 1999 Sr Elizabeth Jane visited Mendham to represent the Mother House at Clewer for the celebrations of the 125th anniversary of the founding of the American House, originally in New York (see Chapter 9). By 1999 there were two novices and a Sister in first vows at Mendham and the Community was in good heart. But the Sisters at Clewer also had something to celebrate for on August 10th 1999 Sr Anne was professed in final vows, and on August 17th Mother Jane Olive was reinstalled for a further term of office. The Bishop of Reading, the Rt Revd Dominic Walker, presided on both occasions. Sr Laura Katherine and Sr Mary Neale came from Mendham for two weeks and were present at Sr Anne's profession.

Behind the scenes the heart-searching went on. It was clear that the only way forward was to move away from those vast buildings, and yet it was such a wrench. And there was the knowledge that the Founders and early Sisters had built and bequeathed those buildings to the Community in the expectation that the Sisters would remain there. But the Founders had lived at a time when the Community was growing so fast that the builders could barely keep pace with it. They would never have imagined that the Community would become so diminished in numbers, and they would have been mortified to think that these great buildings, once the flagship of the Oxford Movement, would become a millstone. But that was the awful truth—by the end of the 1990s, the upkeep of the Clewer buildings had ceased to be viable. And while visitors, retreatants, long-term friends, preservation groups and other interested parties mourned the thought of those buildings being abandoned, the fact remained that they did not have to live in them, nor maintain them. On a summer's day when the sun was shining and the gardens blooming, the convent buildings looked glorious. But in the dead of winter, with the early morning winds howling round the chapel turrets, as the elderly Sisters struggled along endless freezing cloisters, the writing on the wall was clear. "Please remember us as we go forward into a rather uncertain future," wrote Mother Jane Olive in the Community *Newsletter* for autumn 1999. "We have decided that we do need to move from our beautiful but very large building; this is not likely to happen for some time yet, but it will mean the closing of our present works. We are however, in good heart and believe that God still has work for us to do."

The first of the works to close was St Anne's House. In February 1998 Mrs Olwen Thompson had retired as manager, after working at the convent in various roles for twenty-two years. In April 1998 the Windsor and Maidenhead Unitary Authority replaced Berkshire County Council and this change meant that there would be less local authority funding for potential residents, thus reducing the number of places available. A further complication was that many more residents were in their 90s and needed more nursing care. In the Christmas 1999 Community *Newsletter* Mother Jane Olive announced with much regret the impending closure of St Anne's House as from March 31st 2000. The announcement by the Community that they would be moving and thus closing down the various works had meant that no new residents had been admitted. The resulting loss of income had forced an earlier closure than had been planned. All the remaining residents were rehoused, some in nearby Winton House, and others elsewhere.

Sr Esther Mary CRJBS celebrated the golden jubilee of her profession on September 22nd 1999. By this time she was aged 90 and had given up her active work which she had enjoyed until quite recently. Her reduced mobility had necessitated the use of a zimmer frame and, according to Mother Jane Olive, she got about with this at a fearsome speed! On the other hand, Sr Moira was also using a zimmer, but "goes at a more sedate pace!" October 11th had seen Sr Moira's diamond jubilee and she had enjoyed the day's celebrations especially as family and friends were present.

On December 5th 1999 Sr Pamela flew to the USA to spend a year with the American Sisters. During this time she was able to use her musical skills to help the Community in chapel and wrote much of their music; and her computer skills were used to set up a new website, having previously set up the one at Clewer. She was also able to take a chaplaincy course, and became a hospice chaplain for the Visiting Nurse Association of Northern New Jersey. After several extensions of her secondment Sr Pamela made a permanent transfer to Mendham in February 2005. There was a simple ceremony to celebrate her transfer at which Sr Anne and Fr Lister Tonge were present.

During the Spring of 1999 Tony Matthews, a playwright who lived in Windsor and had worked for the BBC, expressed an interest in dramatising part of *A Place in Life*. After careful thought, and in consultation with me, the Community agreed to the adaptation of the first part of the book dealing with Mariquita Tennant's establishment of the Clewer House of Mercy at 'The Limes', next to Clewer Church. I met with Tony Matthews several times and the script looked promising. The play (which had the rather unpromising title *Fallen Women*) was performed on September 28th and 29th 2000 in St Andrew's Clewer, using the talents of local people in the main parts. The Sisters had placed a good deal of trust in Tony Matthews, given the sensitivity of the subject matter, and everyone agreed that the result was well worth the element of risk involved. It was very moving to see the characters I had come to know so well through the Clewer archives come to life in this way.

1999 came to an end with the death on December 13th of Sr Letitia, aged 88 years. During World War II she had served with the ATS and always treasured her memories of those days. She was clothed as a novice in May 1953 and made her life profession in April 1958. She had been the Community sacristan for twenty-five years, a role she loved, and was well known by the clergy who came to celebrate the Eucharist. She had a very sweet smile and serene manner, under which lay a great sense of humour, which frequently saw the funny side of Community life and was translated into comic verse for the amusement of the Sisters.

Meanwhile, the firm decision to move was causing all sorts of repercussions, rumours and speculation, but in the Easter *Newsletter* of 2000 Mother Jane Olive was able to give some positive news. On January 25th the Community had purchased the Priory and Convent at Begbroke near Kidlington from the Roman Catholic Servite Order. It had housed the Servite Fathers in the 17th-century Priory and the enclosed Servite Sisters in the Convent (dating from 1975) next door. There was a certain irony in the fact that the Sisters were leaving behind a massive Victorian building for a smaller (though some might still say large) Cotswold stone manor house dating back to the Civil War period! There was much work to be done, so the move was not expected until sometime during 2001, but after all the necessary alterations the Sisters hoped to be able to accommodate up to eight visitors or private retreatants.

The purchase of the new accommodation before the Clewer convent was even on the market would inevitably strain their finances, but the Sisters hoped there would be some reasonable offers for the buildings even though their listed status would put constraints on future use. In May 2000 the convent was put on the market by Knight Frank and a glossy brochure was produced advertising this "exceptional residential opportunity in historic Windsor". It went on to list all the amenities: main Chapel; Chapel of the Forerunner; St Gabriel's Chapel; Oratory Chapel; five dining rooms; thirty-seven sitting rooms; library; 111 bedrooms; fifty bathrooms/cloakrooms; three kitchens; domestic offices; laundry room; garaging; store rooms; ancillary rooms together with extensive further accommodation; 86,600 sq ft gross internal area in about 9.3 acres. There was also extensive coverage in the national broadsheet newspapers and the local newspapers, of which there will be more later.

Now followed a stressful and distressing time for the Sisters as they decided what to take with them and what to dispose of—the library had to be 'weeded', some of the archives to be deposited at the Berkshire Record Office, furniture valued, potential buyers shown round, press interviews to be given. They received a great deal of help from Derek Norman and Jim Prescott; also from Yvonne Mease at Begbroke, and from the Community bursar the Revd Peter Viney. One group at Clewer were already old hands at the moving process—Mother Ann Verena and the CJGS Sisters had already experienced a major move from West Ogwell and had thought they were making their last move. However, they took the process in their stride, prepared for yet another move and were a great support to the CSJB Sisters. Later, Mother Ann Verena was to write with characteristic humour, "I can remember looking round the Convent and fresh from our recent move, recognised what a vast undertaking it would be to move from Clewer ... and praying 'O Lord don't let me be here if they ever move'. Fortunately God ignored that prayer ..."

21

MOVING ON

By the end of 2000 things were looking more hopeful and the Community was hoping to move by the following summer. Work at Begbroke had begun in August and the builders hoped to have completed their work by the end of May, but that remained to be seen. At Clewer, the sad task of winding down continued. By the end of August 2000 the residents of St John's Convent Home had all been rehoused, some to a residential home near Woodstock not far from Begbroke, and others in and around Windsor. The Clewer Spirituality Centre finally closed its doors at the end of March 2001 when nine of the Oblates met for their annual retreat. There was much thanksgiving for all that the Centre had meant to so many people and great regret at its passing.

Meanwhile at Mendham the Community was in good heart, having reached double figures, and the year 2000 was an eventful one: two novices had been clothed, Sr Laura Katherine had celebrated the 30th anniversary of her profession and on November 30th Sr Eleanor Francis had made her Profession in First Vows. Even though the move from Clewer to Begbroke was imminent, there were a number of comings and goings between Clewer and Mendham, as Sisters made their last visits to Clewer and also visited the new house. Sr Anne made a three-week visit to Mendham in May, which incorporated a short stay in New York and a visit to Sr Barbara Jean's home-town of Philadelphia. Whilst staying overnight in the Sisters' log cabin, Sr Anne was awakened by a bear, outside but very close to the cabin. (This is probably the closest encounter with a bear since an un-named Clewer Sister, sometime in the 1880s or 1890s, while ascending the stairs at the Presidency General Hospital in Calcutta was alerted to the fact that a bear was following immediately behind her!) Also, Sr Pamela came to visit her family and the sisters at Clewer in May, returning to Mendham in mid-June.

But in the midst of all the stress of moving and pain of parting good things were happening too. On September 30th 2000 Sr Anne was ordained deacon in Christ Church Cathedral, Oxford. Of the ten candidates, four came from Windsor, and in addition to Sr Anne these were Robert Langton, Prue Dufour and John Quick. (Sadly, Prue Dufour died from a brain tumour in

August 2004, having moved to a parish in the Diocese of Bath and Wells. A memorial service was held at Bath Abbey to commemorate her life and work, which had included the founding, some years earlier, of Dorothy House Hospice for the terminally ill near Bradford on Avon. Some of the Sisters were able to attend the memorial service.) Sr Anne, in addition to exercising her ministry within the Community, was also licensed to the ecumenical parish of Blackbird Leys near Oxford, and she began there on October 5th.

A letter from Sr Barbara Jean in the Christmas 2000 Mendham *Newsletter* provides a fitting summary of the Community ethos for the new Millennium: "Our Community, like a parish or a family, has changed much in the last 148 years. We have had our moments of birth, death, and resurrection. Our life has changed with each new generation, and is changing now as we receive new persons into our midst. Our work has also changed, as we respond to God's call to us today and use the gifts of those who come. Our understanding of the Gospel has changed, as we mature in our faith. The process of change can be painful, as in any birth, [but] the present builds on the past and leads to a future of vision and hope."

2001 marked the centenary of Canon Carter's death and the 150th anniversary of Harriet Monsell's clothing as a Sister of Mercy. On May 4th I gave the Carter Centenary Lecture in St Andrew's Church at the invitation of the Clewer Group. Canon Carter had recently been included in the Oxford Diocesan Calendar, his day being October 29th (the day of his death, October 28th, was already the feast of St Simon & St Jude, Apostles). Mother Harriet had already been included in *Celebrating Common Prayer*, an adaptation of the Franciscan Office Book, and is now commemorated in *Common Worship: Daily Prayer* with the designated feast day March 26th (March 25th, the date of her death, being also the Feast of the Annunciation). On May 20th 2001 I was invited by the Sisters to preside and preach at their Community Eucharist in the Chapel of the Forerunner. This was just a few days before Ascension Day and so we were able to celebrate the 150th anniversary of Mother Harriet's clothing, and what may now be seen as the starting point of the Community (although this has traditionally been observed as Mother Harriet's profession on November 30th 1852).

The 150th anniversary of the Community of St John Baptist was also observed in Mendham amidst great rejoicing, and special events were shared with Associates and friends from far and wide. At this time Sr Barbara Jean wrote, "Our present mission is the same life of prayer and spiritual nurture through hospitality, retreat giving, spiritual direction, diocesan, parish and chaplaincy work, and other ministries to which we are called … We ask your special help this year, so that the Community's outreach to retreatants, persons in need, parishes where we serve, Daytop, and Sr Jane's mission in Africa can continue. Our vision for the future is similar to that of 150 years ago, but relevant to the needs of today. We hope you will share this vision with us, so that together we can carry the good news of the resurrection to God's people." Sr Jane's mission referred to by Sr Barbara Jean was the Good Shepherd Home in the Cameroon. This home for HIV/AIDS orphans had been founded by Sr Jane Mankaa who had stayed with the CSJB Sisters at Mendham while undertaking a period of study. A strong link was thus forged between Sr Jane and the American Sisters, with Sr Mary Lynne making an annual visit.

The Community *Newsletter* for Easter 2001 bore news of the exchange of contracts with the purchaser of the convent buildings at Clewer early in February, and the completion of the sale a month later. This was good news for the Community given the limitations of the buildings. The purchaser hoped to convert the main buildings into apartments, and this in itself proved to be controversial. In the summer *Newsletter* Mother Jane Olive gave the next instalment in this stressful saga. Apparently a local newspaper had reported the convent sale in such a way as to lead local residents to believe that the development would cause difficulties in Hatch Lane due to increased traffic. Therefore the developer had set up an exhibition showing what the convent would look like, and he invited local residents to view the plans and to look over the convent. Although the convent no longer belonged to the Sisters they were still living there pending the completion of work at Begbroke. Over the space of two days 600 people passed through the convent; many were old friends of the Sisters, but many others had simply come to look.

On March 25th 2001 at Mendham, Sr Margaret Helena celebrated the sixty-fifth anniversary of her profession amid much rejoicing. Many old and new friends came to a festive tea party followed by Solemn Vespers in the main chapel. Thanks to the generosity of an Associate, a wheelchair lift had been installed, thus making the main chapel completely accessible.

September 11th 2001 would be a day that would burn itself into world history as the day when everything changed, the day that some commentators would claim that the 21st century really began. The destruction of the twin towers of the World Trade Center in New York and at other sites by terrorists shocked the world and the Sisters at Mendham were caught up in the maelstrom. At the time of the attack Sr Mary Lynne was sitting in a plane at Newark airport awaiting take-off for Portland, Oregon, where she was to attend an Associates' meeting. She had a direct view of the two planes crashing into the towers. Her flight was immediately cancelled and she returned to the convent by taxi. Writing in the Mendham *Newsletter* of Christmas 2001, Sr Barbara Jean described the challenge to faith and all former values that the attacks had brought about. Sisters Mary Neale, Eleanor Francis and Shane Margaret subsequently volunteered to help pastorally at Ground Zero. They worked in the respite centres set up for the workers toiling twenty-four hours a day to clear the site, providing food, rest, a place for prayer, listening and showing the presence of God in the midst of all the desolation. The Sisters found this work profoundly moving: "I have received much more than I have given," wrote Sr Shane Margaret in the Christmas 2001 *Newsletter*. "God lives in the rubble there, binding and comforting those who continue to grieve and those doing the dangerous and tragic work of finding victims and clearing a wasteland."

Frustration was the order of the day at Clewer as the summer moved towards autumn and the removal date had to be cancelled twice because the Begbroke property was still not ready. The Sisters were finally able to move on September 8th 2001, even though the builders were still at work. Over the space of five days, sixteen large furniture vans plied between Clewer and Begbroke. There was an immense sense of relief even though some Sisters missed the familiar surroundings. And the Sisters were already looking forward to receiving up to eight resident visitors from Christmas onwards. However, two Sisters did not move to Begbroke. Sr Veronica Joan had been struggling with poor health for some years and in autumn 2001 she was released from her vows on health grounds. And Sr Esther Mary CRJBS, last of her Community, now in need of full residential care, moved instead to the Sisters' Infirmary at St Peter's Convent, Woking.

The first major event following the move was Sr Anne's priestly ordination on Sunday September 30th 2001 by the Bishop of Dorchester, the Rt Revd

Colin Fletcher, in St Mary's Kidlington. Amongst the clergy who laid hands on Sr Anne were Fr Lister Tonge, Chaplain, and Sr Barbara Jean. Following a celebratory lunch at Begbroke Priory, Sr Anne presided at her first Eucharist in the Priory chapel. This was also the very first Eucharist the Community had celebrated in the main chapel as it had not been ready for use until that day. A few days later the Bishop of Oxford, the Rt Revd Richard Harries, came to bless the new house for the use of the Sisters—a new beginning for the Priory and a new beginning for the CSJB and CJGS. But new beginnings do not always mean an end to trouble, as the Sisters discovered when they came into the main chapel on St Stephen's Day (December 26th). There they discovered a flood due to one of the new radiator pipes bursting, thus ruining the wooden floor and carpet tiles. But they hoped to be back in chapel by Easter.

The Sisters were very quickly immersed in their new environment, taking delight in the new garden, making new friends in addition to welcoming old ones, and undertaking new work outside the convent. Fr Lister Tonge, in an article in the Community *Newsletter* of Easter 2002, remarked, "We are ceasing to regard the previous dwelling as 'home' however long it held that meaning for us in the past. For the past is past and a new world of opportunities is opening before us … Here is light, colour, beautiful Cotswold stone, lots of windows, a sense of a home inhabited rather than an institution hardly inhabited any longer. Yes, even our old friends and supporters are increasingly able to let go of Clewer as we are learning to do." And indeed there was a new look to the Sisters as well as a new house to live in. The Sisters in England had put aside the black habit in favour of something new and simpler. Fr Lister wrote, "Above all, people are saying that the sisters have changed. Well, yes, they have: into their new blue gear. More than that though, they have changed and are continuing to change precisely because they are becoming increasingly able to let go of Clewer …" At Mendham the Sisters also have a new look in that they have retained the CSJB black habit though without veils.

All this was of course completely in the spirit of Mother Harriet who had urged her Sisters not to let the sparkle go out of the Community. And as Sr Mary Stephen wrote in the summer 2002 *Newsletter*, "… I believe to have stayed [at Clewer] would have been suicide for CSJB … We continue to change. We continue to grow. May we continue to be open to the life and light of Christ, and to share that life with others. It's what Mother Harriet and our early community did, and if we don't do it ourselves, we will be truly dead … The Eucharist often ends with the instruction, 'Let us go in peace to love and serve the Lord.' I believe we have come to Begbroke, not to retire, but to do exactly that."

In practical terms loving and serving the Lord meant beginning to host groups of up to twelve people; taking a small number of guests; Sr Anne's continuing ministry at Blackbird Leys; attending conferences; and being a presence within the village of Begbroke which sometimes included attending the parish church. Sr Mary Stephen, in addition to her work as a spiritual director, had just been recommended for ordination training on the St Albans & Oxford Ministry Course commencing in September 2002. Sr Monica had celebrated her 80th birthday in December 2001 and a few months later laid down the office of Oblates' Sister after twenty years. Sr Anne now took over this responsibility.

The Sisters continued their 150th anniversary celebrations into 2002, the Bishop of Oxford having visited in April and presided at the Eucharist. On June 19th the first Commemoration Day at Begbroke was celebrated with great joy and clouds of incense which set off the smoke alarms! The Bishop of Dorchester, the Rt Revd Colin Fletcher, preached and afterwards lunch was served in a marquee on the lawn.

*

On October 3rd Sr Barbara Jean was re-elected for another term of office as Sister Superior at Mendham. In November Mother Jane Olive and Mother Ann Verena visited Mendham in order to be with the Sisters as they celebrated the 150th anniversary of Mother Harriet's profession. They were able to participate in a Conference for Religious Communities called 'Building Foundations'. This was hosted at Mendham and a number of American Communities were represented, some of which had originated in England. On St Andrew's Day (November 30th) there was a Sung Eucharist in the large crypt chapel, and in addition to four bishops, there was a large number of priests including Fr Lister Tonge, and many guests.

This was the culmination of a busy year of celebrations at Mendham; earlier the Sisters had held an open day called 'Monastery in May'. Many people had responded to the invitation and this became a regular event.

Also, the American Sisters were renewing their efforts to restore the convent buildings. An appeal had been launched in 1992 and again in 1995 to raise funds to renovate the buildings to meet current fire regulations. Now the appeal was being relaunched because the Community had doubled in the previous six years, thanks partly to the 'Search' programme held at regular intervals for women wanting to explore the possibility of a Religious Vocation. The running expenses had consequently increased, but this was an extremely happy reason for launching an appeal, coming as it did when so many Communities were decreasing in numbers.

2003 witnessed the ending of an era in two ways. Godfrey Carter, great grandson of Canon Carter, died suddenly on July 28th. He had been in regular touch with the Community since the publication of *A Joyous Service* and was very proud of his connections both with Canon Carter and with the CSJB. He had given a copper beech tree to the Community to be planted at Begbroke; there had been an earlier one at Clewer many years ago in Canon Carter's time, but this had been damaged by a storm. Mr Carter had hoped to be at Begbroke for the planting of the new tree but died before this was carried out. His son took over the project, and the tree was planted by the Bishop of Dorchester on September 17th. About fifteen members of the Carter family were present as well as the Community, and all took a turn at the shovel. Tea followed, bringing a historic occasion to its conclusion. (It was Godfrey Carter who, some years earlier, had recalled that within his family large spiders had earned the generic name of 'Clewers' because of their profusion in the convent buildings!)

A few weeks later, on October 30th 2003, Sr Margaret Helena had died at Mendham a week before her 99th birthday. She had entered the noviciate in January 1934 and was professed in March 1936, but her first links with the Community dated from 1928 when she visited the Sisters at St Helen's Hall, the diocesan school for girls which they ran at Portland, Oregon. Having joined the Community and after serving her noviciate, she returned to Oregon to teach there. The Sisters left Oregon in 1944 and St Helen's Hall became part of the Oregon Episcopal School, but Sr Margaret Helena kept in touch and a branch of CSJB Associates was formed which continues to meet there. She was Mother Superior from 1949 until 1979 and it was during her time as Mother that negotiations opened with Clewer, then under the leadership of Mother Annys. The consequent reaffiliation took effect from February 1974, the centenary of the American House. After resigning as Mother Superior, Sr Margaret Helena remained a source of strength and wisdom to the Community. The Oregon Associates held a celebratory Eucharist at the Oregon Episcopal School on November 4th to give thanks for Sr Margaret Helena's life and work. A plaque was unveiled, and a copy given to Mendham for St Michael's Chapel. Sr Suzanne Elizabeth and Sr Mary Lynne flew out to Oregon for the occasion.

The Sisters had not been at Begbroke very long before they began to feel the need of a larger space for hosting groups than that afforded by the present arrangements. They could take up to twelve people in a group but more requests were being made from larger groups for quiet days, as well as from individual applicants. So it was decided during 2003 to apply for planning permission to extend the visitors' dining and sitting rooms. The work took several months and involved some upheaval and temporary curtailing of hospitality. However, the result was worth the effort and the extension, which was in use by 2004, was appropriately named the Harriet Monsell Centre. This proved to be a boon to the Community and was soon in regular use by groups including the Diocesan training group STEM (Stewardship, Training, Education and Ministry). It was also used by a group training to be spiritual directors; for parish quiet days; and during 2006 the first 'Drop in Days' were held since the Community left Clewer.

Sr Jane Patricia, an American Sister, died on January 26th 2004 aged 93. She had been professed in the CSJB in 1941, and taught Latin and music at St John Baptist School, where she inspired, challenged and encouraged a generation of students. In 1980 she left the Community to live with her sister and cousin in Amherst, Massachusetts, but she continued to wear a habit styled on that of the CSJB, though with a different cross. She was an academic, having gained her Master's and Doctoral degrees while in Community. In later years she would spend part of every summer in England, basing herself at Clewer from whence she would visit European religious communities and academic libraries. Her speciality was the translation of the works of Peter Abelard from medieval Latin into English. When in England she would hire a car, continuing to do so until she was 90. At the age of 93 she was admitted to a nursing home, having broken her hip, and she died peacefully there. Her funeral at Grace Church, Amherst was attended by about seventy-five people including several Sisters from Mendham.

July 2004 saw Mother Jane Olive reach the end of her term as Mother Superior, and the decision was made to have a Leadership Team rather than have the weight of leadership fall upon a single pair of shoulders. This was a pioneering decision for an English Community, though not unique in the wider Church. (In 2001 the Community of the Holy Spirit, New York, had introduced a Community Council consisting of three Sisters to lead their Community.) The Leadership Team at Begbroke consisted of Sr Anne and Sr Mary Stephen, with Sr Ann Verena CJGS as a co-opted member. After serving twelve years as Mother Superior, Sr Jane Olive took a well earned sabbatical month at St Deiniol's Library near Chester, and after she returned to Begbroke, continued her ministry as the visitors' Sister. Both Sr Zoë and Sr Mary Stephen were busy with courses of study in 2004. Sr Zoë, in addition to her duties as Community infirmarian and librarian, was studying with the Open University, though pressure of other duties resulted in her eventual withdrawal from the course. Sr Mary Stephen was preparing for ordination with the St Albans & Oxford Ministry Course and it was amid great rejoicing that she was ordained deacon on Saturday September 24th 2005 in Christ Church Cathedral, Oxford. She was licensed to serve her curacy in the nearby parishes of Hanborough and Freeland. Sr Ann Verena, as well as her work on the Leadership Team, was a local vocations advisor and also had a ministry at Bullingdon Prison. Sr Anne, meanwhile, had withdrawn from her ministry at the Church of the Holy Family, Blackbird Leys, in April 2004, and in July 2005 began a ministry among the homeless in Oxford. This was a new appointment under the auspices of Churches Together in Central Oxford.

On November 24th 2005 Mariquita Tennant was at long last honoured in her own adopted town by a blue plaque placed at 'The Limes', where she began her great work of rescue and rehabilitation. In a ceremony attended by members of the Windsor and Eton Society, the Windsor Local History Group, the Clewer Group, Friends of the Royal Borough Collection, and the then owner of 'The Limes', the Mayor of Windsor, Councillor Eric Wiles, said of Mariquita Tennant, "… she was a fierce and fearless worker on behalf of very vulnerable women and, despite her own ill health, established a caring climate in Windsor that was a foundation for others to build on in future years." The plaque was placed on the side of the house facing St Andrew's Church to ensure that the public would have the best possible view.

MARIQUITA TENNANT
1811–1860
Lived here and started her
work of helping the
impoverished
women of Windsor

One advantage of the Sisters' living at Begbroke was the close proximity to other Religious Communities, and new friendships were being forged with the Poor Clares at Freeland, the Benedictines at Burford, the Carmelites at Fairacres in Oxford, the Wantage Sisters and the All Saints' Sisters in Oxford. (The Benedictines have now moved from Burford Priory to Mucknell Abbey in Worcestershire.) And there was also the growing friendship with the parish of St Michael Begbroke. In 2006 the Sisters kept the marquee, hired for Commemoration Day, for a few days longer so that the village could use it for a Strawberry Tea in aid of the parish church. Clearly, the arrival of the Sisters had made an impact on the village and much good had come of it.

Sr Florence CJGS kept the diamond jubilee of her profession on July 31st 2006 with a tea party and special cake. The following week there was a special Mass at which the Rt Revd Dominic Walker, Bishop of Monmouth, presided, followed by a buffet lunch. Sr Florence, along with Sr Doreen CSJB, continued to maintain close links with the deaf by attending regular services at St Ebbe's Oxford. In October 2006 Sr Kathleen Frideswide CJGS kept her 90th birthday with a celebratory tea party.

There were two deaths in 2006. The first marked the completion of a Community, and the second marked the ending of a chapter of CSJB history. Firstly, Sr Esther Mary CRJBS died aged 96 on January 5th. She was the last Sister of the Community of the Reparation to Jesus in the Blessed Sacrament. Before joining the Community she had been a Church Army Sister, during which time she met Florence, who became a life-long friend, and who later joined the Community of All Hallows at Ditchingham and died in 2004. Esther Mary was received as a novice in the Community of St Mary the Virgin at Wantage but transferred to the CRJBS and made her life profession in 1949. She came to Clewer with her Community in 1980. On the Feast of Corpus Christi (June 15th) 2006, a Eucharist and celebration lunch was held at Begbroke to give thanks for Sr Esther Mary and the work of the

CRJBS. Friends, Associates of CRJBS, and relatives of Sr Esther Mary and of Mother Eunice their last Superior were invited. And then on All Souls' Day 2006 Sr Anne and the Revd Peter Viney went to Southwark Cathedral and presented the CRJBS funeral pall to the Cathedral at the Requiem Mass. This seemed a fitting way to conclude the ministry of a Community which had served the Southwark Diocese for so long and so well. The CRJBS memorial plaques, following the addition of Sr Esther Mary's name, were later taken to Southwark Cathedral.

The second death in 2006 was that of Sr Moira CSJB on Shrove Tuesday (February 28th), aged 94. She died in St Luke's Wing of St Katherine's House, Wantage, having been too poorly in her last months to remain at Begbroke. Moira, aged 16, had been sent by her aunt to the London Diocesan House of Mercy at Highgate, run by the Clewer Sisters. This was not because of any bad conduct (unlike many of the other girls) but because her aunt could not cope with caring for all her deceased sister's children. Moira was very keen to train as a nurse but her aunt had other ideas—Moira was to work in her father's floristry shop, a prospect that did not appeal to her at all. Although Moira settled down very well at the House of Mercy, she had been completely unaware of the nature and purpose of the Home. Later she would recall her sense of being punished unjustly by her aunt and the disadvantage she felt at not knowing that it was a penitentiary. Contrary to expectations Moira loved the life there and asked to join the Order of Magdalens. She was admitted as a postulant Magdalen on October 31st 1933 and consecrated on October 11th 1939. She continued to serve at Highgate until it closed in June 1940, after which she was sent to the House of Mercy at Great Maplestead. The Community withdrew from Great Maplestead at the end of 1943 but Moira Magdalen had already moved to Clewer in January 1943. When the CSJB reformed and the Magdalens became the Society of St John the Forerunner, Moira was transferred to the SSJF. But during the next few years she began to feel called to the CSJB and against all odds was accepted. She was clothed as a CSJB novice in August 1959 and was professed in life vows on October 17th 1960. Sr Moira was a sweet-natured, gentle person who will be remembered with affection.

The crowning event of 2006 was undoubtedly on Sunday September 24th when Sr Mary Stephen was ordained to the priesthood by the Rt Revd Colin Fletcher in Dorchester Abbey. She presided at her first Eucharist in the

Priory chapel at 5.00 pm on the same day. Sr Barbara Jean, Sr Mary Lynne and Sr Pamela came from Mendham for the ordination.

Back in the USA, the Sisters were as busy as ever and twelve in number at the end of 2006. Much work had been done on the convent and its grounds by volunteer labour. The work of the CSJB Development Board had resulted in State grant aid for improvements to the convent and St Marguerite's Retreat House, and historic designation for the buildings. This would help offload the stressful business of fundraising to maintain the buildings, and enable the Sisters to engage with their mission and ministry. A wide variety of ministries was undertaken by the Sisters including leading retreats and pilgrimages, assisting at Daytop, the centre for young people recovering from drug and alcohol dependency, working in a shelter for the homeless, hospice chaplaincy, helping repair homes for those in need, parish ministry, and supporting the Good Shepherd Home in the Cameroon, West Africa. Also, at the end of 2006 Sr Shane Margaret was in her second year of seminary. On December 5th 2006 Sr Eleanor Francis was blessed as Assistant Superior, just a few weeks after being accepted for candidacy for ordination in the Diocese of Newark.

2007 saw a new beginning for the Diocese of Oxford when the Rt Revd John Pritchard was installed as Bishop of Oxford, Bishop Richard Harries having retired. Sisters Ann Verena and Mary Stephen attended the Installation service in Christ Church Cathedral on June 8th. On June 10th Sr Anne attended the Eucharist for the Oxford clergy in the cathedral, at which the new bishop presided and preached.

However, the year 2007 was to be a time of sadness for the Sisters at Begbroke. In July Sr Edna Frances moved to St Mary's Convent and Nursing Home at Chiswick, run by the Society of St Margaret. She had been well cared for in a local nursing home at Cassington but missed the ethos of community life and especially the daily Eucharist. So the decision was made that she would move to Chiswick where she would be spiritually nourished as well as physically cared for. But her departure was a loss, for she had contributed hugely to the life of the Community and had been the Mother Superior during an earlier period of discernment about the future of the Community.

Sr Zoë's health had been a cause for concern for some months, but her death at the beginning of October 2007 came as a great shock. She had been in hospital for just five days before she died and had been visited by family, friends and Community. Writing in the Christmas 2007 issue of the CSJB *Newsletter*, Sr Mary Stephen described Sr Zoë as "part of the backbone of our life", and went on to describe her illness and death as having overshadowed everything else over the past few months.

Sr Zoë had joined the Community in November 1965 and was clothed as a novice on March 29th 1966 and professed in life vows on March 31st 1971. A Yorkshirewoman by birth, she was a practical, down-to-earth person, having qualified as a State Registered Nurse and State Registered Midwife. Whilst still in first vows Sr Zoë worked at the retreat house in Salisbury which was run by the Community, Sr Eudora being in charge at that time. Once in life vows, and by now back at Clewer, Sr Zoë assumed a number of roles, some of which she would retain until her final illness. Firstly, she was assistant infirmarian, working under the formidable Sr Evelyn Joan, whom she succeeded as infirmarian and remained so for the rest of her life. After the arrival of the CJGS Sisters in 1996, Sr Zoë shared the role of infirmarian with Mother Ann Verena who later wrote, "Zoë excelled at diagnosis. Through the work over the next eleven years we came to trust and support each other, especially through the hours we spent in casualty." She was also in charge of St John's Convent Home at Clewer, caring patiently for the eight residents whose special needs she understood perfectly. She knew exactly when firmness was required, not only with the residents but also with the Social Services who in later years oversaw the work.

As community librarian Sr Zoë continued to build up a valuable resource, primarily for Community use, but also for serious students such as ordinands. Weeding such a large collection for the move to Begbroke was a great wrench for someone who had worked very hard to incorporate the library of the CJGS into that at Clewer. Sr Zoë kept abreast of issues that were in the news, especially those touching on medical ethics surrounding the beginning and end of life, her nursing and midwifery training standing her in good stead. (As an ordinand, I benefitted from conversations with her when wrestling with these issues for essays.)

Sr Zoë was one of a small number in the Community who had a conscientious objection to women priests. Soon after the General Synod's decision in 1992 to ordain women as priests, the Community had discussed the situation. Sr Zoë, while expressing her concern, indicated that she would accept whatever decision the Community made. This gracious gesture, in which other Sisters also shared, allowed the eventual ordination of Sr Anne in 2001, followed by Sr Mary Stephen in 2006.

New work had begun in New York in 2007. Sr Deborah Francis and Sr Laura Katherine had been invited to base themselves at St Mary the Virgin New York, where they were provided with a flat adjoining the church premises. This invitation was more than welcome because the Community had originally worked in New York, and this was seen not merely as a return to their original roots but as a new beginning. In addition to joining in the worshipping life of St Mary's, the two Sisters have become fully involved in deepening the spiritual life of the parish through workshops, spiritual direction and classes and through parish visiting. Also, on the more practical side, the Sisters have worked alongside St Mary's Guild which cares for the altars.

Another milestone in the life of the Sisters at Mendham was the life profession of Sr Linda Clare on June 10th 2007. The Rt Revd Herbert Donovan, the Episcopal Visitor to the Community, received her vows and presided at the Eucharist, and Fr Gerald MacIntyre SJ preached. The main chapel was packed and there was a joyful celebration afterwards.

Part of the ethos of the Community of St John Baptist has been to show forth the love of Christ to those most in need. In Victorian times this was expressed through the various Houses of Mercy, orphanages, schools, convalescent hospitals and parish mission work. The 20th and 21st centuries have seen the abandonment of outdated ways and the embracing of new challenges. So it should come as no surprise to read in the Mendham *Newsletter* of Fall 2007 Sr Lura Grace's account of her work amongst the street poor in New York. "One day a week I take the train into New York City, [and] the subway to Wall Street. In less than two hours I morph from comfortable urban Sister to outreach volunteer for the John Heuss House, a 24/7 drop-in center for homeless mentally ill and medically fragile single adults run by Trinity Church Wall Street. One of my 'jobs' is to comb the streets of lower Manhatten ... to alert the chronically homeless that critical support services are available—all they have to do is come with me to the shelter. Food, coffee, a shower, clean clothes, detox ... My litany of help increases, as does my desperation. 'I don't want you to die on the streets,' I plead ... For two months I've patiently tolerated William's spitting at me and his tirades of verbal abuse … Will William ever follow me 'home' to John Heuss House? I doubt it. Eighteen years of medical and mental self-abuse, slum dwelling, hard drugs and gin have taken their toll on this 68-year-old diabetic schizophrenic. I huddle with him in the grimy New York City alley … and thank God that he is even still alive. 'God loves you, William,' I whisper, 'and so do I.'"

BUILDING FOR THE FUTURE

The convent buildings at Mendham were showing their age. Although not as vast as the buildings at Clewer, they had for some years begun to pose a problem because building regulations had changed, health and safety measures were much more stringent, and if the Sisters were to continue using the buildings to the full for their various ministries then something needed to be done. So it was that the Capital Campaign was launched in 2006–7. Unlike in the UK, there are various forms of State funding available and the Development Board had begun to explore the possibilities. An early and very welcome grant of $175,000 was given by the Morris County Board of Chosen Freeholders to assist with the first project, namely an upgrade of the convent heating system. A further grant of $50,000 had been given towards the construction of a new wheelchair-friendly access and handicapped-access bathroom in St Marguerite's Retreat House. The Capital Campaign was planned as a long-term project but the Sisters, far from feeling daunted by it, were immensely encouraged by the amount of support shown.

The CSJB *Newsletter* for Easter 2008 contained a challenging reflection by Fr Lister Tonge called "Religious Life: on dying well". This highlighted the fact that most Anglican Communities had reached a point of no return where, in many cases, no novices had been received for several years, and where in some cases the Community was struggling to maintain large, cold, cumbersome buildings that were no longer appropriate for the dwindling numbers. Readers of this reflection might well have wondered where it was leading. For the Sisters had already broken free of the great mother house at Clewer and had found new life and ministry at Begbroke. So was this not a case of preaching to the converted? Or was this a preparatory 'shot across the bows' in preparation for something even more challenging? Fr Lister concluded his reflection with the words, "At Begbroke, ears and eyes are open and alert, attentive and full of hope that the God who has called us is faithful and that we need not struggle against letting him have his way." But there was a clue to the conundrum elsewhere in the same *Newsletter*. "Our Commemoration Day celebrations this year will be on June 24th, St

John Baptist's Day. We're particularly pleased that the Revd Canon Martyn Percy has agreed to be our guest preacher. Martyn is the Principal of Ripon College, Cuddesdon … We are developing close links with the college and Lister, our Chaplain, is also Chaplain to the students …" By the time of the publication of the *Newsletter* for Christmas 2008 Sr Anne was able to report: "During the weeks running up to Advent there have been numerous meetings connected with the proposed move to live on the Ripon College Cuddesdon site, but slowly we are making progress on different aspects." Over the coming months more would be revealed.

April and May 2008 saw two milestones for Sr Sheila, the great-great-niece of Mother Harriet. On April 29th Community and friends celebrated the golden jubilee of Sr Sheila's profession (counting from her first vows in 1958). There was a mid-day Eucharist and special lunch, and in the afternoon local friends joined the gathering for a tea party. And then on May 27th there was another special celebration to mark her 90th birthday. A large number of O'Briens were present including Amaris, the youngest.

Sr Anne made a brief visit to Mendham in June 2008 for Sr Eleanor Francis' ordination as deacon, and Fr Lister Tonge was present at Sr Eleanor Francis' ordination to the priesthood in December 2008. Sr Suzanne Elizabeth came from Mendham to Begbroke for two months during the summer of 2008 to assist in the care of the older Sisters so that other Sisters could have some holiday. This was the fourth year that Sr Suzanne Elizabeth had made this extended visit. A new innovation was introduced in 2008/9 in the form of three-month sabbaticals for each of the Leadership Team. Sr Mary Stephen took hers starting in September 2008, followed by Sr Anne early in 2009 and concluding with Sr Ann Verena in the early summer.

Sr Anne began her sabbatical with a visit to the Good Shepherd Home in the Cameroon founded by Sr Jane Mankaa. She was able to spend several weeks with Sr Jane, during which time she celebrated the Eucharist in the chapel and shared with the chaplain in the baptism of twenty-seven of the children. She was also able to visit another home where the children suffer from epilepsy and as a result of this are driven from their homes and villages out of a superstitious fear of demonic possession. These children are rescued, put on appropriate medication and given an upbringing in a caring environment.

The final part of Sr Anne's sabbatical was spent in India and Bangladesh.

This was her first visit to India and a return to Bangladesh after eleven years. During the visit to Calcutta (now renamed Kolkata by the Indian Government), Sr Anne stayed at the Oxford Mission at Behala, a place I had visited in 1995. Sadly, Br Amit Biswas, who had shown Joyce Sampson and myself around the Oxford Mission compound, had died. Sr Anne writes, "My first conscious thought on waking on the first morning was where can the singing be coming from …? It was a hymn, sung in English and I discovered at breakfast when I met Fr Ranjeet Banerji that it was the hostel boys at morning prayer held at 6.30 am in the chapel just across the path from my room … After breakfast Fr Ranjeet showed me round the whole compound which was even more extensive than I had imagined. We visited the schools where the children were all having their end of term exams and the older ones the public exams to determine whether they could go on to Secondary school. This meant I was not able to stay long in the class rooms, but they did all take a minute or two to greet me and the smaller ones sang a song."

The Oxford Mission Administrator, Arijeet Roy, had been looking forward to Sr Anne's visit, but had died at the end of December. Another death since my own visit had been that of Sr Florence of the Oxford Mission Sisters of the Epiphany, but Sr Anne was able to see her cottage and the flourishing work of the College of Advanced Nursing on the same site, which was sponsored by the Diocese of Kolkata. The College was run by Mrs Reena Bose, former head of the Nursing School attached to the Seth Sukhlal Karnani Memorial Hospital, formerly the Presidency General Hospital and still commonly known as the 'PG'. Mrs Bose arranged for Sr Anne to visit the hospital and the School of Nursing, still in the same building where the Sisters began the work. Sr Anne then visited a small care home for the elderly, an orphanage, and a hospice for men and women in the advanced stages of AIDS.

A visit to the new Bishop of Kolkata, the Rt Revd Ashoke Biswas, who praised the work of the schools formerly run by the Clewer Sisters, proved very productive in that he arranged for Sr Anne to visit St John's Diocesan Higher Secondary School for Girls, the Pratt Memorial School and to visit Darjeeling. Upon arriving at St John's School Sr Anne discovered that the girls had just left for their holiday, but Mrs Chrestien, the Lady Principal, and the staff had stayed to welcome her. It was at St John's School that

Joyce Sampson and I were given such a wonderful welcome by staff and students in 1995 (see chapter 31 of *Sisters of the Raj*). Upon her arrival Sr Anne found the staff gathered at the school entrance, where they welcomed her with floral garlands. New buildings have been added to those already in existence in 1995 and two have been named after Clewer Sisters. There is the Sr Hilda Frances block and the Sr Eudora block, as well as the Rosita Chrestien block and the Angelina block, the latter named after the founder of the school, Angelina Hoare. How thrilled Sr Eudora would have been to know that she is still remembered in this way. In addition, there is in the school a large framed photograph of Sr Eudora and Mrs Chrestien, taken on the latter's visit to Clewer in October 1995.

Sr Anne was also warmly welcomed when she visited the Pratt Memorial School a couple of days later. "Another grand tour of the buildings, the main block of which had barely changed since it was first built—so there I was nearly seventy years on going up the same staircase as the Sisters who, seventy years before that, had built up the school from its beginnings, and left behind a very firm foundation which enables it to maintain present day standards." A new addition to the school was a large kindergarten department with bright pictures on the walls. Sr Anne returned to the Pratt Memorial School the following week for the prize giving, which she greatly enjoyed.

A visit to the Presidency General Hospital began in the Canning Nurses' Home but was complicated by a huge media presence having been informed of Sr Anne's visit. This took away precious time and resulted in her not seeing as much as she would have liked to see. Even so, "I had a huge sense of the history of these buildings, the extent of the Sisters' work, and the heat (and smells outside the hospital) that they had to cope with."

Sr Anne also succeeded where Joyce and I failed in finding the site of the Sisters' graves in the Bhowanipore Cemetery (we had gone to the wrong cemetery). Alas, the ground has been reused and the headstones replaced after Independence, but "it was well cared for in a natural way with lots of flowers and butterflies; a place of peace for the Sisters who had given their lives to the Indian work."

A brief visit to St James' church near the Pratt Memorial School—very English and Victorian—found the helpers there making palm crosses for the next day. The priest then took Sr Anne to St Stephen's church, where she was to preach next day to a congregation of mostly Anglo-Indians, plus a small number of Indians, in a service as English as it could be, even using the *English Hymnal*. (Joyce Sampson and I had a similar experience of worship in 1995 when we attended Calcutta Cathedral.)

The last few days of Sr Anne's Indian visit were spent in Darjeeling, where she was the guest of the Warden of St Paul's School, which is still a leading boys' school. A visit to the former St Michael's School, now a Government College known as the Indira Gandhi National Open University, was arranged. A tour inside showed the former chapel in good repair, now forming part of an extensive library. Degrees are awarded from the University of Delhi and there are also a number of research students.

A few days revisiting Sr Susila and the Sisters of the Christa Sevika Sangha in Bangladesh rekindled memories of Sr Anne's previous visit and brought her sabbatical to an end.

Writing in the *Newsletter* for Easter 2009, Sr Mary Stephen noted, "Our links with Cuddesdon grow closer. We've been to a number of meetings about the planned expansion, and sisters who wish have the chance to meet once a month with Martyn Percy, the Principal, and others from the college for tea and an informal exchange of information. I've been privileged to take part for the first time in the annual Retreat in Daily Life at the College, as a guide to some of those taking part ..." Further light was shed on the Sisters' plans in the Ripon College, Cuddesdon *Newsletter* for 2009. An article bearing the title "Relocation, Relocation, Relocation" stated that "The move to Cuddesdon of the Sisters of Begbroke Priory is a remarkable venture for a group of women who thought they had moved for the last time when they came up from Clewer, Windsor in 2001. They have loved their Oxfordshire home ... but they know there are adventures awaiting them ... There is also a great sense of energy and excitement amongst the Sisters about their future prospects. Sr Monica admits that she was thrilled when she first heard of the idea. Sr Jane Olive had already master-minded the move from Clewer and found herself wondering, 'What's this all about? Let's see what it means.' She has come to see that God is in it. Sr Ann Verena is looking forward to the mental stimulus of lectures and getting her hands on the library ... Having young people around—and especially children—will be a delight to these aunts and great aunts ... Sr Anne and Sr Mary Stephen are both priests and are fascinated to see how their ministry will evolve. Sr Doreen and Sr Elizabeth Jane both love being amongst people and, like

Sr Florence, will soon have names learned and new friendships established … What the Sisters are clear about is that they hope to contribute to the life and future of the College from their wealth of human experience and, especially from their life of vowed commitment and prayer." And then there was a clue to the great contribution that the Sisters planned to make: "The Sisters hope that the planned new chapel will be a magnet to draw people to a life of regular prayer … This is perhaps the greatest legacy the Sisters can bequeath from their Community histories and their individual experience to the Church of the future. As one of their enthusiastic supporters said of the move, 'it will put their DNA into the College.'"

An Appeal had been launched by the College in 2008 with the Revd Stephen Fielding as Appeal Director. He had a background as a banking lawyer and had also trained for the priesthood on the Oxford Ministry Course at Cuddesdon and served as a Non-Stipendiary Priest in the diocese of St Albans. Writing in the Cuddesdon *Newsletter* of 2009, he described his vision for the College in 2013 as having a new chapel in the heart of the site; a Community of Sisters living on the campus, joining in the life of prayer and providing spiritual direction and counselling. As well as contributing to the funding for the new chapel, the Sisters would also be building accommodation for themselves. The decision was made to hold a competition for the design for the new chapel. There were 127 entries and the Sisters shortlisted five architects from this number. The final judging took place on September 7th 2009 and the winning submission came from Niall McLaughlin Architects. The winning design was an elliptical chapel with two focal points, the altar and the lectern. The artist's impression of the interior shows a soaring, high building that somehow evokes the memory of the high vaulted Clewer chapel, but with all the emphasis being on lightness.

The Cuddesdon *Newsletter* for 2010 carried a two-page spread devoted to the Development Appeal. This included a Vision Statement with sections relating to the Sisters: "A Vision that will include a Community of Sisters here with us from 2011, praying with and for the College, a spiritual presence modelling Christian community and providing spiritual counselling and direction. A Vision that includes a new chapel of outstanding design, providing a place of worship for all the community here—the Sisters as well as the … ordinands … To realise such a vision needs capital and investment. The Sisters and others have already pledged a significant part of the capital required, and we are immensely grateful for their generosity … To complete the work on the Chapel, we need upwards of £0.5 million … The application for planning permission on our new buildings has just been submitted."

The same *Newsletter* carried a message from Sr Ann Verena: "The prospect of moving to Cuddesdon is exciting and challenging … We are an active community and between us have much experience to share in our new situation. We have experience in accompanying others on their spiritual journey, in leading Quiet Days and Retreats of various kinds and also in offering hospitality. Our two ordained sisters have considerable experience in parish life, its rewards and its problems, and also in working with people outside the church. One sister is a Vocations Adviser. We hope that the new convent in the grounds of the College can be a place where others may come when they need quiet space and time for reflection in peaceful surroundings, and also where people will feel welcome and at ease as they seek to discern the will of the Lord in their lives."

Several Sisters from Begbroke would not be making the move to Cuddesdon because they needed the extra care that only a Nursing Home could give them. During the course of 2009 Sr Evelyn Theresa CJGS and Sr Doreen CSJB both went into residential care in Longlands Nursing Home at Cassington, just a short distance from Begbroke. And early in 2010 Sr Kathleen CJGS went to live at St John's Home, Oxford.

Sr Evelyn Theresa CJGS died in January 2010, shortly after her 89th birthday on Christmas Eve. Earlier in life she had trained as a teacher before becoming a novice with the Companions of Jesus the Good Shepherd. She made her final vows in 1960 and spent much of her life in what became Guyana. During a very difficult time politically, Sr Evelyn Theresa, as head of the Community School, took great risks to safeguard her pupils. After returning to England she taught for a time at St Gabriel's School, Newbury, before moving back to the Mother House at West Ogwell. After a time as Community Bursar, she became the Mother Superior until 1996, when the Community moved to Clewer and Sr Ann Verena became the Mother. She loved company and was equally glad to tell stories of her own varied life as well as hearing about other people.

Towards the end of 2009 the decision was made by the Community Chapter to dispense with a shared Leadership Team and instead to elect a

Community Leader. But this was not a reversal to old ways of leadership—on November 5th Sr Ann Verena CJGS was elected not as the Revd Mother Superior, but as Community Leader of CSJB. She was installed as Leader on November 26th by the Bishop of Oxford, the Rt Revd John Pritchard. Writing in the *Newsletter* for Christmas 2009, Sr Mary Stephen explained the significance of the change. "You'll notice that she is very definitely our leader—not the Reverend Mother Superior. And for the first time, she is a member of another community: Ann Verena is already the leader of the Companions of Jesus the Good Shepherd, who have lived alongside us since 1996." Over the years since the move to Begbroke both Communities had increasingly become known as 'the Begbroke Sisters' with no distinction between the two Communities. In the same *Newsletter* Fr Lister Tonge wrote, "The Leadership Team was a natural development, even though it seemed strange at first, and never quite won everyone's heart as a way of proceeding. What it did do was to cement further the relationship between CSJB and CJGS so that they feel, in ways few of us might have ever predicted, to be 'one family'. The 'us and them' feelings—inevitable at first—have virtually evaporated. Sr Ann Verena's election to lead CSJB is another step on this journey of common life, vision and ministry to which God has called the Sisters and through which God continues to make great use of talents and energies and even … eccentricities … Two small communities working to ensure life before death is what God has planned at this stage … It is all cause for marvel and rejoicing … and a good deal of thanks."

Meanwhile, the Sisters at Mendham had not been standing still! New ways of prayer had been explored for some years, for example the labyrinth, installed in the garden in the millennium year, continued to be a fertile means of prayer and meditation. Days devoted to the 'Labyrinth Walk' continued to be popular and were held several times a year. The making and selling of prayer beads (similar to the rosary) in the 'Nun Better' shop was providing many people with a practical as well as a spiritual way into prayer. These proved to be an effective way of prayer ministry to members of the armed forces serving in Iraq and Afghanistan. A soldier had been given one and had then asked for more at the request of his fellow soldiers. The Sisters were also producing prayer shawls. When a shawl was completed the Sisters would lay hands upon it and pray for the recipient and their particular needs. This was proving to be a really tangible way of ministering prayerfully to the sick and dying. As Sr Suzanne Elizabeth wrote in the Mendham *Newsletter* for Spring 2009, "Most of the time each of us has no idea how we have touched someone's life, but how gratifying and encouraging it is to hear and see that we have indeed been a blessing. In return, we can feel so blessed far beyond our simple act of loving prayer. Let us 'take heart', and 'be blessed' in all we do and be …"

A new venture begun at Mendham in Spring 2009 was the cultivation of a community garden (to be called the Garden of Hope) in the grounds of the convent to grow vegetables for the Morris County Food Pantry to help needy families. A number of volunteers helped Sr Linda Clare with growing and harvesting the produce, which by July 2010 had yielded 310 pounds of various types of vegetables.

For those who wanted to explore prayer further afield, Sr Margo Elizabeth continued to lead her Celtic pilgrimages. In May 2009 she led a group to Ireland, visiting Dublin, the Wicklow Mountains and the Aran Islands, to name but a few places. And in September she set off with another group to Cornwall and Wiltshire, visiting Tintagel, Truro Cathedral, St Ives, Salisbury, Stonehenge, Glastonbury and Wells. Further pilgrimages were being planned for 2010 to Ireland in May and Scotland in September, and for 2011 to Ireland in May and Wales and the north of England in September.

On February 11th 2009 Sr Deborah Francis travelled from Mendham to Richmond in South Africa on a mission trip with Dr Michael McNett, a member of the church of St Mary the Virgin New York. Dr McNett and his team were involved in a project to transform a former Afrikaner property into a multi-purpose community centre. Aided by a grant from Rotary International, the building had become home to a soup kitchen, an HIV clinic, a soccer programme and a community hall. The Grass Roots Soccer programme targeted children and young people and as well as the soccer, aimed to teach them how to avoid HIV/AIDS. The soup kitchen gave a meal to around 300 children a day. The Hope for Richmond project had provided medical supplies for the clinic and hospital, as well as teaching about HIV/AIDS prevention. Richmond, while having overcome many problems since the abolition of apartheid, was still suffering deep divisions between the white town and the African township, but Sr Deborah Francis was deeply touched by the vibrant faith of those whom she met, and she left with a strong feeling of hope. "I was inspired by the courage and perseverance of these people as they surmount the deep divides in their town and township … They gave me hope that we in America, who have so much in material goods, education and opportunity, can also overcome our own divisions and inequalities."

Sr Shane Margaret was ordained deacon on June 6th 2009 at Trinity and St Philip's Cathedral. And on December 12th she was ordained to the priesthood at St David's church, Kinnelon, where she had served as a seminarian and as a deacon. Sr Shane Margaret would be living away from the convent while exploring full-time parish ministry, and early in 2010 she became Priest-in-Charge of St Luke's Haworth, New Jersey.

In July 2009 Sr Eleanor Francis and Sr Suzanne Elizabeth travelled to California to attend the General Convention of the Episcopal Church (the US equivalent to the Church of England's General Synod). Both found the experience inspiring.

"The Community of St John Baptist has experienced many cycles in its 150-year history," wrote Sr Barbara Jean in the *Newsletter* for Fall 2009. "Some have come unexpectedly and some were planned carefully. We are about to experience another one. I have come to the end of my term as Superior, and … there will be an election for a new Superior." The election was held on December 15th and Sr Eleanor Francis was elected as the new Sister Superior. She was installed in her new role by the Rt Revd Herbert Donovan, the Community Visitor, at a private ceremony on January 5th. Sr Eleanor Francis joined the CSJB in 1998 and had been Assistant Superior for three years. In 2008 she was ordained to the priesthood and had worked in three local parishes as well as giving spiritual direction and having an involvement in interfaith activities for many years. Sr Lura Grace was appointed Assistant Superior in addition to her work for the homeless and her three-year course on spiritual direction. Sr Barbara Jean was appointed Novice Director, which included working with those attending the Search Programme (for those who were exploring the possibility of a Religious Vocation). She also continued to serve on the Board of Daytop and as a priest within the community and in local parishes when needed.

Just before stepping down as Sister Superior, Sr Barbara Jean made her first visit to the Good Shepherd Home in the Cameroon. Whilst she was there the two postulants and one novice took the next steps in the Religious Life, becoming two novices and a sister in first vows. Sr Barbara Jean found the visit a humbling and eye-opening experience. By this time Sr Jane had the care of 100 children, all from deprived backgrounds.

The other members of the Mendham Community were equally occupied during 2009–10. Sr Suzanne Elizabeth continued as a member of the board of the House of the Good Shepherd, a home for the elderly. In addition she had various roles in the field of church needlework, altar guilds and related fields, as well as spending two months each summer at Begbroke caring for the elderly members of the Community.

Sr Laura Katherine and Sr Deborah Francis, as already noted, were residing at St Mary the Virgin New York, where they do parish work, offer spiritual direction, and lead workshops and classes, as well as sacristy work.

Sr Pamela was still very involved with the Capital Campaign fundraising and planning the various stages of the restoration project to bring the buildings at Mendham up to the exacting standards required in the 21st century. She continued in her ministry as Guest Sister, and in addition kept the website up to date and was on the chapel team. Sr Pamela had also been instrumental in arranging an icon exhibition with Associate Tim Carr. Under the title 'The Glory of Orthodoxy' this was held in the main chapel from May 22nd–23rd 2010. Forty-three icons dating from the 17th to 20th centuries were exhibited, and the curator of the collection, Dr Corrado J Altomare, conducted lectures. Also, there was an exhibition catalogue describing each icon in detail. Orthodox Vespers was sung in English, led by Fr Thomas Edwards and the choir of St Gregory Palamas Church. The exhibition was arranged in aid of the Capital Campaign, which needed extra funds to augment the grants already given, and to move the restoration programme onwards.

Sr Mary Lynne continued to make jewellery as a popular line in the 'Nun Better' shop, in addition to the prayer beads already mentioned, and she also led prayer bead workshops. She was also on the Good Shepherd Home Advisory Board supporting Sr Jane's work in the Cameroon, and visits for two months each year. By 2010 Sr Jane Mankaa's work with orphans had expanded to several locations, caring for about 100 children. The work was guided by an Advisory Board in both the Cameroon and America. Sr Mary Lynne's visits provided Sr Jane and her fellow Sisters and helpers with much needed encouragement and practical help.

Sr Margo Elizabeth's ministry as a spiritual director had brought many new groups to St Marguerite's Retreat House, as well as being a spiritual director to individuals. Her Celtic pilgrimages have already been mentioned. She was also the author of *Sometimes a Star*. The book was written "as a way of bridging the gap between many of the books being written on Celtic spirituality, and what Sr Margo Elizabeth herself was seeing while in Ireland. The result is an exploration of what 'real people' are currently thinking and feeling about faith in Ireland." The book consisted of a series of candid, absorbing conversations between the author and a variety of people: a retired steel worker; Tony Flannery, a Redemptorist priest and author; a student; a young journalist; a Church of Ireland member; a farmer; the founder of the Alpha movement; a former Religious who now does charity work for the travellers in Ireland; Liam Lawton, a priest and a composer and performer of spiritual music—and many others. The book sought to engage with the current questions and problems confronting Christians and faith seekers in the context of Ireland in the 21st century.

For several years Sr Linda Clare had been working closely with the architect Annabelle Radcliffe-Trenner on the restoration projects, and was in charge of property maintenance. She was also serving on the Mendham Interchurch Committee, and had charge of the Garden of Hope at the convent, already mentioned, which aims to provide fresh vegetables for the Morris County Food Pantry for the homeless and needy.

All these various activities by the Mendham Sisters were of course carried out in the context of the rhythm and pattern of prayer, the Eucharist, the daily office and their own prayer life.

Back in England, on January 28th 2010, Sr Monica moved to St Mary's Convent and Nursing Home, Chiswick, where Sr Edna Frances was also in residence. She had wanted to move there while still able to take an active part in the life there, but her departure left a large gap at Begbroke.

On August 21st 2010 Sr Sheila died in the ninety-third year of her life and the fifty-third year of profession. Her family lineage, as a descendent of Mother Harriet, gave her a special place within the Community history, and she was always extremely proud of that connection. She was born in May 1918, one of a family of two boys and two girls. It was through her aunt Geraldine, a niece of Mother Harriet, that she learned about the Community at Clewer and the O'Brien family connection. But she did not rush to join. Instead she led a varied life: attending secretarial college, being presented at Court in what was to be the last presentation of débutantes before the War, joining the ATS during the War and finally becoming a commissioned officer. Tuberculosis, often a killer in those days, struck her down in 1946, but she made a good recovery. Then she followed a career as a hospital almoner (now called a medical social worker). All this time Sheila had been on a varied spiritual journey ranging from Christian Scientist (with her mother) to Anglo-Catholic, through a time of loss of faith and then the return to faith aided by a priest from the Community of the Resurrection, Mirfield. Now came the call to the Religious Life, and having considered the Communities at Wantage and Woking it was to Clewer that she came as a postulant in April 1956. She was professed in first vows in April 1958 and made her life profession on May 11th 1961. Sr Sheila had many roles in the Community, including working in the kitchen when she was a novice, and Sister Secretary from 1961 until 1983 and again from 1990 until 1997. Also, at various times she was Community Librarian, visitors' sister, lodge Sister, Novice Guardian, and was also an active member of the Guild of Church Braillists. Sr Sheila had a great sense of humour and often kept the Community amused at recreation with her fund of humorous verses. Her family was her great pride and joy and she did extensive research into the various branches of the O'Brien family. About fifty O'Briens attended her 90th birthday party at Begbroke, much to her joy and delight.

The passing of Sr Sheila marked the end of an era, for with the exception of two short periods there had always been an O'Brien in the CSJB. These were the five years from the death of Mother Harriet in 1883 until the admission as a postulant of the Hon Louisa Anna Maria O'Brien in 1888. She became Sr Mary Louise CSJB and left the Community in March 1897 in order to join the Roman Catholic Church. The second period without an O'Brien in the Community was the seventeen years from the death in 1939 of Sr Amabel (the Hon. Alicia Amabel O'Brien) until the arrival of Sheila as a postulant in 1956. Sr Mary Louise and Sr Amabel were both daughters of Sir Lucius O'Brien, the 13th Baron Inchiquin, who was Mother Harriet's brother.

As the year 2010 progressed, the Sisters' plans to move to Ripon College, Cuddesdon were slowly making progress. In June Local Authority planning permission was granted for the new buildings, a cause for celebration. The Sisters were now able to work with the architects to refine the plans so that they could go out to tender before the end of the year. Hopefully building work would start in March 2011. With all this in mind, the last Commemoration Day at Begbroke was held in July 2010. Once more the process of weeding out surplus possessions began in preparation for the move. An Oblates' and Associates' Day was held on October 16th, preceded by a short retreat, and the ministry with guests was scheduled to end at Christmas. The really good news was that a buyer had been found for the Priory, although nothing had been signed, but it meant that an interim move would have to be made, something previously unforeseen. However, by the time the Christmas *Newsletter* was published (the first joint letter from the CSJB and the CJGS) there were clouds on the horizon. It had been hoped that contracts would soon be exchanged, but complications had arisen.

Meanwhile the Community life and work of the Sisters continued. Sr Jane Olive had been the visitors' Sister ever since the move to Begbroke in 2001 until the last visitors left at the end of 2010. Also at the end of 2010 Sr Anne gave up her work as Chaplain to the Homeless in Oxford after five and a half years. In the *Newsletter* for Christmas 2010, Sr Mary Stephen wrote of Sr Anne's ministry, "Anne has been working very much in the spirit of Mother Harriet and so many of the early sisters, in her ministry to those who are on the very edge of society, and has made a considerable difference to many lives." During 2011 Sr Mary Stephen became a Trustee of the Bible Reading Fellowship, in addition to ministry in Community and parish. And Sr Ann Verena CJGS was working with the Chaplaincy at Bullingdon Prison. The Sisters in residential care, Sr Monica and Sr Edna Frances at Chiswick, Sr Kathleen CJGS at St John's Home, Oxford, and Sr Doreen at Cassington, were all happily settled. In 2010 Sr Doreen celebrated the golden jubilee of her profession and was visited by the Sisters, and all enjoyed a celebratory cake.

If the death of Sr Sheila had marked the end of an era in the English Community of St John Baptist, then it may be true to say that the death of Mother Susila CSS marked the end of a connection with the Indian work. Sr Anne had visited Mother Susila towards the end of her sabbatical in 2009 and this was to be the last time they would meet. Mother Susila died peacefully after a long illness on May 18th 2011 in Jobarpar, Bangladesh. Taught by Sr Eudora at the Pratt Memorial School, Susila had never forgotten the Clewer Sisters. And it was a cause of mutual joy that she was able to visit

Clewer and talk of old times with Sr Eudora. From those far off days of the British Raj the seed of a religious vocation was sown, and it bore fruit through the Oxford Mission Sisterhood of the Epiphany and finally in the Christa Sevika Sangha (the Handmaids of Christ), which kept its fortieth anniversary in 2010. In many ways the work of the CSS reflected the early work of the CSJB—caring for the poor, the homeless, the rejects of society. But in other ways Mother Susila's ministry embraced up-to-the-minute technology. For instance, it was under her guidance that fifty deep tube wells were sunk over a number of years, so that the surrounding villages could have pure drinking water. She showed great courage in the face of threats from the invading Pakistani Army, during the War from which emerged the country of Bangladesh. Her courage saved many women and girls from rape and massacre, and she reached out in that predominantly Muslim country to all, irrespective of their religion or ethnicity. Hindus and Muslims as well as Christians found employment in her compound. Her Community, with the ongoing support of the Oxford Mission, will continue her work.

Nancy Leslie, a long-standing Oblate of the CSJB, died on July 6th 2011. She had been educated by the Clewer Sisters at St Michael's School, Darjeeling. Later she became an Associate and after thirty years, in 1993, she was admitted as an Oblate. Later, after the move to Begbroke, she reverted to being an Associate, but during the years at Clewer she would come and stay for an extended visit and would help in the lodge by receiving guests and answering the telephone.

As the year 2011 dawned the Sisters on both sides of the Atlantic were occupied with their buildings. At Mendham the Capital Campaign had been in progress for several years and much had been achieved, thanks to fundraising efforts by the Sisters and their supporters and substantial grant aid, the latter being on a 'match-funding' basis. Visitors were now benefitting from easier access to the buildings by means of ramps, and the heating in the convent was greatly improved. Also, extensive work had been carried out at St Marguerite's Retreat House, where the leaded glass was being renewed in the windows. The *Newsletter* for Spring 2011 brought news of Phase II of the Capital Campaign under the banner *Renewing our Ministry*. Sr Barbara Jean, writing as the Development Officer, stated, "We have not yet raised the full $500,000 to match our grant from the State. Therefore, we have set our goal for Phase II at $1,500,000." The projects planned for Phase II included a ramp along the south cloister leading to the front door; an internal barrier-free passage to the main chapel; the infilling of the underground tunnel linking the two wings of the convent, now deemed to be unsafe; electrical work; preservation and restoration work to the convent roofs and also to the retreat house roof; and restoration of the stucco on the exterior walls of the convent. By the time of the Fall *Newsletter* some of this work was under way. The convent was surrounded by scaffolding and many of the dormer windows had been removed for releading. Also, work on the roof had begun, though it would take several years to complete this part of the project. Further State grant aid had been given and this was a great source of encouragement for the Sisters. The support given through these grants may be seen not only as aid to restore historic buildings, but also an as an affirmation of the presence of the Sisters and the varied ministries exercised by them.

In a news bulletin dated May 2011, Sr Mary Stephen brought Associates and Friends up to date with the Sisters' plans. Firstly, the Sisters had made their interim move to 'Priory House' in the grounds of Begbroke Priory, but the sad news was that the sale of the Priory had fallen through due to various complications that had arisen towards the end of 2010. Begbroke Priory was once more on the market. This was a depressing prospect for the Sisters and was to be the prevailing situation throughout 2011. Meanwhile, at Cuddesdon things were moving forward. On June 20th 2011 Sr Jane Olive signed a provisional contract for the work to proceed and the building work began in July.

The Church Times of July 1st 2011 contained an illustration submitted by the architects Sadler Brown of the proposed new accommodation at Ripon College, Cuddesdon, to be named Harriet Monsell House. Constructed primarily of timber and glass, the new building would provide accommodation for the Sisters on the top two floors as well as extra facilities for the students, including a 100-seat lecture theatre. The bold design, whilst using modern construction methods, was also sympathetic to the Victorian gothic style of the older buildings. Thus the rooflines soar upwards at a steep angle and the upper windows are set into gables reminiscent not only of the original buildings on the site, designed by G E Street, but also of Henry Woodyer's buildings at Clewer. The building contractor Beard (Oxford) Ltd had made good progress with the foundations by October

2011 and was aiming to complete both the Bishop Edward King Chapel and Harriet Monsell House by August or September 2012. On November 2nd 2011 two new foundation stones were blessed by the Bishop of Oxford, the Rt Revd John Pritchard, and the Bishop of Gloucester, the Rt Revd Michael Perham. The foundation stones would later be incorporated into the buildings. They were carved with the Cuddesdon cross and the Lamb of God with banner, representing the coming together of the College and the Community of St John Baptist. The craftsman responsible for carving the stones was local master mason Bil [sic] Brown, whose work, spanning sixty-two years, included many gargoyles and grotesques for Oxford colleges, and also the gravestones of HM Queen Elizabeth the Queen Mother and Sir Winston Churchill. The naming of the two new buildings reflects the role of Bishop Edward King as Principal of the College from 1863–73 and Harriet Monsell as the Founder (with T T Carter) of the Community of St John Baptist.

2012 dawned with the news of the appointment of Fr Lister Tonge as Dean of Monmouth in the Church in Wales, with effect from April 1st 2012, remaining as non-residential Chaplain to the Sisters.

On May 22nd 2012 Sr Edna Frances died peacefully at St Mary's Convent and Nursing Home, Chiswick, after a short illness. She was in her 95th year and on March 19th had celebrated the golden jubilee of her profession. Her funeral took place in the chapel at St Mary's on June 7th, followed by burial in St Michael's churchyard, Begbroke.

Meanwhile, on Wednesday June 6th the 'topping out' ceremony had taken place at Ripon College, Cuddesdon. Many years previously, in 1926, Mother Evelyn had made the perilous ascent to place the cross on the roof of the oratory of the new Infirmary at Clewer. Now in 2012 the Sisters took part in the traditional ceremony when the final piece of the roof was put in place on the new buildings. The Revd Canon Professor Martyn Percy, Principal of Ripon College, conducted the 'topping out' ceremony, and as well as the Sisters, other guests included those involved in the design and construction of the buildings, plus students, staff and friends of the College. Prayer capsules were placed behind the foundation stones of the two new buildings and guests were invited to bring prayers to be included.

As summer moved into autumn and despite the very wet weather, the new buildings were moving towards completion. Begbroke Priory remained unsold, a stressful situation for the Sisters, but in August a new offer was made. As this book moved into the final stages before publication in November, all those involved with the building project were looking forward to entering the final stage. Harriet Monsell House was due for completion on September 24th, and the Sisters were looking forward to moving in during the early part of October. The Bishop of Gloucester, the Rt Revd Michael Perham was to give the first public lecture in the lecture theatre in Harriet Monsell House on November 3rd, and the Bishop Edward King Chapel was to be consecrated by the Bishop of Oxford, the Rt Revd John Pritchard at a later date.

Conclusion

The last years of the 20th century and the first decade of the 21st have seen the demise of several Religious Communities founded in the 19th century, and it would be easy to become depressed at the small numbers in CSJB and CJGS. But that would be to take a narrow view. No one knows what the future holds, but when Harriet Monsell was clothed as a Sister there was no Community, no convent and no Rule. The intervening years since the publication of *A Joyous Service* have seen the deaths of many Sisters, and other disappointments as novices and Sisters have come and gone. But there have been good things too, as challenges have been met, some novices have been professed, and new opportunities have arisen for mission. The monumental task of moving from Clewer after 148 years was liberating, unleashing new energy and resulting in new ways of being Community and fresh expressions of being Church. The very idea of a collaborative Leadership Team would have seemed impossible at Clewer, so bound up as it was in the old ways. And even though the Begbroke Community has now reverted to a single leader, the willingness to experiment, and then to rethink, shows an openness to change that could not have been countenanced at Clewer. Changes within the Church of England have brought the possibility and the reality of ordained ministry within the Community, something Mother Harriet would surely have welcomed. And the ever strengthening bonds between the American and English houses continue to be a source of encouragement and blessing to both, with the periodic visits of Sisters to and from Mendham and Begbroke.

The prospect of yet another move by the English Sisters—to

Cuddesdon—seemed at first to be utterly pointless, and yet there is the memory of Mother Harriet telling her Sisters not to let the sparkle go out of the Community. In those last years at Clewer the sparkle nearly went out, burdened as the Sisters were by a monolithic building, and also by the memory of what had gone before, which seemed to stifle any departure from the 'Clewer way' of doing things. So to even think about yet another move may signify a rekindling of the sparkle, of taking up the challenge, and of doing something so outrageously radical that the Holy Spirit must surely have been the prime mover. And who knows where it might lead? Whilst the English CSJB may no longer be in a position to receive novices due to the age of the remaining Sisters, and whilst it is also true that the students at Cuddesdon have responded to God's call to ordained ministry rather than to the vowed Religious Life, yet the presence of the Sisters will bring a new dimension into the life of the student body. Mother Harriet's words to the Sisters come to mind: "Do not plan out your life. Plans are God's not yours, leave them to him … We must just keep ourselves ready to answer God's call … for we cannot tell what he may do with us."

In these last years the Begbroke Sisters may be receiving one last call—to show the Religious Life to a new generation of church leaders who may never otherwise have any contact with it, and to be a spiritual resource which will widen and deepen their lives. The practicalities of the Cuddesdon project have brought unexpected complications, arising chiefly from the sale of the Priory. But now that the dream has at last become a reality then this final move may result in new and exciting things for the wider Church. "We cannot tell what God may do with us" is a word from Mother Harriet that still rings true however many or however few there are in the CSJB today. And rather than wait to die out, this final move will bring the English work of the CSJB to its conclusion in a positive way. As Sr Jane Olive has said, "It will be with all flags flying." The new Bishop Edward King Chapel, together with Harriet Monsell House, will be the Sisters' legacy to the church as a resource for the formation and nurture of those coming to explore their vocation to ministry in the church of the 21st century.

But even if the English work reaches its conclusion within the foreseeable future, the work in America goes sparkling on. New members still come, and while it is true that some go away, yet the life of prayer and work goes on. The Sisters continue to minister in many and varied ways to increasing numbers of people who long to hear the good news that God loves them. In the Mendham *Newsletter* for Spring 2011 Sr Barbara Jean wrote, "On April 30th 1913, the Community of St John Baptist gathered on a bare hilltop across the lawn from the newly-built St Marguerite's Home. There, they laid the cornerstone for their new convent. Our motto is carved on the stone in Latin (translated here), 'He must increase, I must decrease', a quote from John the Baptist. Always putting Christ first, we have sought for 100 years to follow his call in this place. As we prepare to celebrate this anniversary, let us work together to restore our center and build for the future." The Mendham Sisters now look forward to celebrating the centenary of their buildings on Saturday April 27th 2013.

Building for the future: by the American Sisters who are restoring their convent and neighbouring buildings in order to continue God's work there; and by the English Sisters whose buildings at Cuddesdon will eventually serve others as they prepare to fulfil different vocations and ministries. In these different ways the work of the Community of St John Baptist continues to give to God a joyous service.

APPENDICES

❧ APPENDIX 1 ❧

VISITORS OF THE CSJB (Bishops of Oxford)
Samuel Wilberforce (1852–69)
John Fielder Mackarness (1870–89)
William Stubbs (1889–1901)
Francis Paget (1901–11)
Charles Gore (1911–19)
Herbert Murray Burge (1919–25)
Thomas Banks Strong (1925–37)
Kenneth Escott Kirk (1937–55)
Harry James Carpenter (1955–70)
Kenneth John Woollcombe (1971–8)
Patrick Campbell Rodger (1978–86)
Richard Douglas Harries (1987–2007)
John Pritchard (2007–)

WARDENS OF CSJB
Thomas Thelluson Carter 1849
George Seignlay Cuthbert 1902
Bernard Moultrie 1912
Arthur East 1915
G H Tremenheere 1922
Philip Herbert Eliot, Bishop of Buckingham (Non-Resident) 1927
George Bernard Hardy 1945
Fr Thomson SSJE (N-R) 1957
James T Abell 1959
Gerald Triffitt SSJE (N-R) 1963
K G Symcox (N-R) 1966
F P Coleman 1968
Austin Masters SSM (N-R) 1979–1995
Fr Lister Tonge appointed Residential Chaplain 1996–2012 (N-R from April 2012)

MOTHERS SUPERIOR CSJB

M Harriet November 30th 1852
M Ellen November 18th 1875
M Jane Frances December 21st 1881
M Betha November 11th 1889
M Evelyn November 12th 1907
M Katherine Maud November 27th 1928
M Frances July 25th 1935
M Dorothy Frances July 7th 1939
M Annys September 15th 1958
M Edna Frances August 10th 1978
M Jane Olive August 1992–2004

Leadership team
Sr Anne, Sr Mary Stephen with Sr Ann Verena CJGS 2004–09
Community Leader
Sr Ann Verena CJGS elected Community Leader of CSJB 2009

INDIA (Sisters Superior)
Sr Lucy 1881
Sr Jane Frances 1889
Sr Margaret 1918
Sr Dorothy Frances 1931

Mothers Provincial of India:
M Dorothy Frances November 9th 1938
M Hilda Frances May 25th 1939

AMERICA (Mothers Superior, later Sisters Superior)
M Frances Constance 1881
M Gertrude Verena 1892
M Mary Angela 1903
M Florence Teresa 1915
M Alice Ursula 1942
M Waldine Lucia 1943
M Margaret Helena 1949

M Elizabeth Anne 1979
Sr Suzanne Elizabeth, Sister Superior 1983
Sr Barbara Jean 1997
Sr Eleanor Francis, elected Dec 15th 2009; installed Jan 5th 2010

✣ APPENDIX 2 ✣

SISTER EMMA AND HER SONGS

Sr Emma was born Eleanor Emma Waring at Lyme Regis in 1837. Her parents were Henry Franks Waring, a solicitor who became town clerk of Lyme Regis, and Catherine Mary Waring, formerly Rankin. The Rankin family had originated in Newcastle upon Tyne where they had been prominent Unitarians. The future Sr Emma had ten siblings (three brothers and seven sisters), of whom she was the eldest. Her family's reaction to her decision to become an Anglican nun is not recorded, but perhaps with all those daughters to marry off her father was not too perturbed! Following further education at Bedford College, she was admitted to the Community of St John Baptist, Clewer, on November 6th 1869 and was professed on February 7th 1872.

In January 1874 she, along with two other Sisters, set sail for New York to begin a new foundation for the Community following the earlier difficulties (see chapter 9). After a year she returned to Clewer and was sent to the mission district of Clewer St Stephen, where she had particular care for the boys attending the National School. It soon became apparent that there were some boys who were so poor and deprived that no one wanted to care for them. Except, that is, for Sr Emma, who found her main source of pastoral care in those ragged boys. Soon she had founded (and funded) St Augustine's Home and it was to be her lifelong work. That work is now well documented, but light is only just being shone on another important work of hers which lives on, whilst St Augustine's Home has long gone.

Thanks to the efforts of Matthew Edwards and Martin Graebe, two English folk song researchers, the story of the hidden work of Sr Emma in collecting and passing on a number of folk songs is now unfolding. Having had access to the archive material when the Sisters were still at Clewer I can say, with as much certainty as it is possible to have, that no one in the Community knew about Sr Emma and her folk songs. If anyone did know at the time, then no record was kept, possibly because it was outside the work of the Community. Also, there is the possibility that such an interest by a Sister would have met with disapproval and therefore be discouraged.

The end of the 19th century and beginning of the 20th was a fertile time in the history of English folk song. Thanks to the efforts of Cecil Sharp and Ralph Vaughan Williams, who travelled up and down the United Kingdom collecting folk songs and dances, much of our folk heritage was preserved at a time when it was in danger of being lost forever. Sr Emma is unusual in that most of Sharp's sources came from working-class backgrounds, whereas she was from a well educated, middle-class background. Matthew Edwards writes, "The songs are a wonderful and important collection of nursery songs, Northumbrian popular songs and some very good versions of old ballads. The songs from Sr Emma's great grandmother, according to a family tradition, had been learned in childhood from her own family nurse in Northumbria. This gives us a picture of songs and ballads being treasured by the women of the family for over 150 years." It seems that on February 27th and March 13th 1909, shortly before her death on March 22nd, Sr Emma, then aged 71, sang some songs to Cecil Sharp who noted them down. She had remembered them all her life and with the exception of two of them, they had never been written down before.

At the Vaughan Williams Library of the English Folk Song and Dance Society there is a handwritten annotation by Cecil Sharp to the song 'Giles Collins'. He writes, "She [Sr Emma] writes to me, 'I must have been certainly not over six years of age when my old nurse sang several of them, and my mother [sang] the others. My mother would have been then about 35 years of age, my nurse [? (one word)] 45. My mother learnt them from her grandmother Margaret whom I remember at that time as over 90—she had no music *written*, nor had my mother. The only ones I have seen in print are *We be soldiers three* and *Here's health to all these that we have*. All the rest are traditional. My own age is 71 the calculations are quite too difficult for me! But may be of use to you." Sharp continued, "Sister Emma was therefore born in 1837. At the age of 6 ie in 1843 her great grandmother was 90 so must have been born in 1753, and her mother who was in 1843 about 35 must have been born about 1808." No other letters or papers from Sr Emma relating to the songs have survived, but it is good to have this direct quotation from her, preserved by Cecil Sharp.

Yet another collector of folk songs was working on his collection at roughly the same time as Cecil Sharp. This was the Revd Sabine Baring-Gould, squire and parson of the tiny parish of Lew Trenchard in Devon. A high churchman, a hymn writer ('Onward Christian Soldiers'), a follower and historian of the Oxford Movement (*The Church Revival*), Baring-Gould had many interests and was a man of considerable influence. Folk song researcher Martin Graebe has a particular interest in Baring-Gould and has uncovered yet another connection with Sr Emma. A song in Baring-Gould's collection was found to be also in that of Sr Emma—it was the only other known version, and it begged the question, was there a connection? And indeed there was. Sr Emma's younger sister, Edith Seymour Waring, had also remembered the songs from her childhood and later in life she had given them to Sabine Baring-Gould. But the family tie was not immediately obvious because by this time she had married Sir Alfred Swaine Lethbridge and it was under the name of Lady Lethbridge that she had given the songs to him.

Altogether Sr Emma provided Cecil Sharp with twenty-five different songs and ballads shortly before her death. Perhaps she realised that those songs would die with her, and thanks to her prompt action they have now been preserved for posterity. It was with the publication of her version of 'Long Lankin' in *The Penguin Book of English Folk Songs*, edited by Ralph Vaughan Williams and A L Lloyd in 1959, that her name became known amongst folk song lovers and collectors. Matthew Edwards writes, "Some of her songs haven't been found anywhere else, while others are remarkably original versions which makes her an extremely valuable source. Many of the songs are children's songs which she may have used to entertain the boys in the Home. I'm not sure whether all of her songs can justly be described as 'entertaining' however; 'Long Lankin' in particular is notorious as 'the terror of countless nurseries' according to the ballad scholar Professor Francis Child. A few of the songs which she sang for Cecil Sharp have very distinctive origins in the North-East of England, such as *Dance to Thee Daddy*, *Bonny Pit Laddie*, and *Gang O'er the Burn My Canny Hinny*."

These are the titles of the songs Sharp collected from Sr Emma. The list is taken from the *Roud Index of Folk Songs* which is available online through the website of the **Vaughan Williams Memorial Library** at the English Folk Song and Dance Society, library@efdss.org

As I was Going to Banbury; Roud 2423
As She Was Keeping Her Flock; Roud 12842

Bessy Bingle ("Bessy Bingle had a little pig"); Roud 746
Bonny Pit Laddie; Roud 3487
The Carrion Crow; Roud 891
Dance to Thee Daddy; Roud 2439
"Dancing Thumbkin Dancing" Nursery Song; Roud 12837
The Derby Ram; Roud 126
Gang O'er the Burn My Canny Hinny; Roud 13282
Giles Collins; Roud 147; Child 42/Child 85
The Gypsy Laddie ("My lady came down in a silken gown"); Roud 1;
    Child 200
The Knight all out of Spain; Roud 8251
Lamkin/Long Lankin; Roud 6; Child 93
Last Night About Ten O'Clock; Roud 8167
Lord Thomas and Fair Ellinor/Eleanor; Roud 4; Child 73
The Mermaid; Roud 124; Child 289
My Dearie Will Ye Come Ben Ben; Roud 13283
Robin A Thrush; Roud 117; Child 277
"She was upstairs sewing her silk" Nursery Song; Roud 12838
Sir Hugh/Little Sir Hugh; Roud 73; Child 155
Three Little Tailors; Roud 2447
We Be Soldiers Three; Roud 8340
When First I Went to London Town; Roud 1640
Willie's Courtship; Roud 4740
Wraggle Taggle Gipsies O; Roud 1; Child 200 [This is a duplicate entry
    in the Roud Index of 'The Gypsy Laddie' above]
Young Henry; Roud 12839

So it is that an Anglican nun, who might otherwise have passed into obscurity with the passage of time, has given a legacy to all who value English folk song.

Note

Sr Emma was not the only member of her family to become a Clewer Sister. Her niece, Edith Alice Bellett, was the daughter of Sr Emma's younger sister Edith and her first husband George Bellett. After the death of George Bellett, his widow married Colonel Alfred (later Sir Alfred) Lethbridge. Edith

Alice Bellett joined the Community of St John Baptist, Clewer, on October 31st 1905 and was professed on April 23rd 1908. Lady Lethbridge was listed in the Community roll as her next of kin. In the 1911 Census Sr Edith Alice was listed as a Sister at St John the Baptist Home, Newport. She later went to the Community work in India three times between 1912 and 1931.

Another family member, Sr Emma and Lady Lethbridge's aunt, Emily Elizabeth Rankin, became Sister Mary Dorothea in St Dominic's Convent at Stone, Staffordshire. She had converted to Roman Catholicism from Unitarianism and she became mistress of music there.

✥ APPENDIX 3 ✥

AN AMERICAN IN CLEWER

Introduction

In June 1866 Helen Stuyvesant Folsom, together with her sister Margaret and a chaperone ("our faithful Janey"), visited the convent at Clewer. Her enthusiasm for all she saw there was recorded in a long letter to Sr Jane of the Community of St Mary at Peekskill, New York. I quoted a brief extract in the first edition of *A Joyous Service* and other short extracts in *A Place in Life*, but the letter is reproduced here almost in full for the first time. (A few brief omissions have been made where Miss Folsom mentioned in passing people or topics that cannot now be explained.) There are instances where Miss Folsom's enthusiasm for all she saw took off into flights of fancy, for instance, the Sisters 'gliding' along the silent cloisters. Those wonderful, but eventually hopelessly impractical, buildings at Clewer were at that time brand new works in progress, and the Sisters were full of youthful zeal and enthusiasm. And what would we all have given to have seen it then! Thanks to the words of Helen Folsom, who became the Foundress of the CSJB in America, we may catch a glimpse of those early days.

What Miss Folsom saw and described was the building as shown in the illustration on page 147, ie the earliest buildings, which became the central part of the convent after the later additions. When Miss Folsom wrote about the Chapel, she was referring to what later became known as the Chapel of the Forerunner, as the much larger Chapel of St John Baptist was not built until 1881. Any modern reader of this letter who knew the convent at Clewer in later years would instantly recognise exactly where Miss Folsom was describing, so unchanged were the buildings for 140 years afterwards. In particular, the desk at which Mother Harriet was sitting was the same one used by all the Mothers Superior until the move from Clewer in 2001. She was rather awe-struck by Mother Harriet and found Sr Ellen easier to talk to. Miss Folsom mentioned that Mother Harriet wore a gold cross, and this cross has always been a treasured part of the Community history. It was made from a gold nugget sent to Mother Harriet by her brother, William Smith O'Brien, when he was in Van Dieman's Land [Tasmania], having been transported there. In July 1848 he had led an abortive rebellion, for which he was tried for high treason and sentenced to be hanged, drawn and quartered. Following a Petition against such a barbaric sentence he was transported for life. In 1854 he was released on condition that he would never return to Ireland and he settled in Brussels. Following an unconditional pardon in 1856 he returned to Ireland and lived quietly, taking no further interest in politics.

Also, she mentioned 'the punishment room', and this may offend 21st-century readers, but it must be borne in mind that many of the women and girls at the House of Mercy came from violently dysfunctional backgrounds. Quarrels sometimes broke out and very occasionally violent attacks were made on each other and even on the Sisters. (I remember Sr Eudora showing me the marks on the wood panelling in the Sisters' refectory, which had formerly been the House of Mercy refectory. Those marks were made by the penitents' throwing dinner knives at each other. Fortunately they usually missed their target and stuck in the wood panelling!) The so-called punishment room was a last resort to allow tempers to cool. In all my years of research into the many and varied works of the Clewer Sisters I have never found evidence to suggest that the Sisters were in any way abusive towards those under their care, so this connotation should not be drawn. In reading Helen Folsom's letter we are time-travelling back to an era where different values were held, including different ideas about discipline and behaviour. Additional notes for clarification have been added in square brackets.

There is one final, sad point to be made. In the summer of 1867, just a year after their visit to Clewer, Helen Folsom's sister Margaret suffered a complete mental breakdown. She was 27 years old. In 1869 Helen and her brother George were named as legal guardians and executors for Margaret, who in the terminology of the time had been declared insane. Margaret Folsom died in 1925 aged 83, having spent fifty-six years in a private suite in the McLean Hospital for the Insane at Waverley, Massachusetts. Her sister Helen, who became the American Foundress of the CSJB, paid tribute to her by adding the name Margaret to her own at the time of her reception as a novice at Clewer.

London
June 18th 1866

My dear Sister Jane,

My long looked forward to visit to Clewer has at last come to pass, and you shall be the first person to have the benefit of it in writing.

On Thursday last I wrote a few lines to the Superior requesting some information with regard to the visiting hours on the following day, and stating that I was anxious to see the *House*, not only from personal interest, but partly on behalf of the New York House of Mercy. The answer did not reach us in season, but I had in the meantime grown very wise over 'Bradshaw' [the railway timetable] and determined to run the risk of being an unwelcome visitor, in consideration of our short stay in town. So at 10¼ [10.15] we started from the Paddington station, my sister and I, taking with us our faithful 'Janey' out of regard to *English propriety*. An hour's ride through a pleasantly wooded country brought us to the small town of Windsor, with its gray old Castle rising in the background. A fly was close at hand and almost before we knew it the half mile to Clewer was traversed and we were asking admittance at the gate which we were told belonged to the House of Mercy. I had my doubts on the subject when on passing through the garden to the porch I espied a number of curly heads at one of the windows, and a few words with the two Sisters who received us in the waiting-room confirmed us in the suspicion that this was the Orphanage [St John's Home]. The House of Mercy, they said, was quite near. They offered to show us over *their* House first, if we would like it, and as we had time enough before Sext we agreed to let them do so. 'Sister Harriet' [not to be confused with Mother Harriet] took us first into a schoolroom on the ground floor, where the owners of the curly heads above mentioned were busily engaged in conning their tasks under the supervision of a teacher or matron *not* in the attire of a Sister. They sang us a little song or hymn and then we continued our walk of inspection, during which we were shown several dormitories lined with small white beds, wardrobes filled with children's clothing in neatly arranged piles, the Refectory, and the Chapel where Matins and Evensong are said daily, in addition to the *Sisters' Hours*, at which the children are not present … On taking leave they advised to inquire for Sister Mary Virginia at the House of Mercy, she being one of

the two American Ladies staying there on probation [ie a novice. Sr Mary
Virginia was professed in July 1867].

After a few minutes walk along the road, we found ourselves at another
tall gate which, on our ringing, was opened by the portress, a small woman
in the habit of a lay-Sister. A covered passage extends from the gate to
the entrance-door, a distance of a few yards; a little to the right, forming a
tiny wing, was the Reception-room, but into this we were not shown, for a
Sister advanced at once to meet and greet us, saying that we were expected
and were to follow her at once to Sister Ellen's room. Janey was left in [the]
charge of the little portress while M and I walked with beating hearts thro'
the hall and the lovely Cloister, trying to imitate the softly gliding step of our
conductress and obeying her whispered injunction not to speak loud in the
passage. Presently she threw open a door and ushered us into the presence
of the Assistant Superior, 'Sister Ellen', whose gentle sweet face and kindly
reception put us at our ease in a moment. Her habit was a black dress plaited
at the neck in wide folds and fastened at the waist with a cord; a muslin cap
with two rows of fluting around the border, one row above the other, and
the one nearest the face adhering quite closely; a white collar at least a finger
and a half in depth and a thin silver Cross about three inches in length with
the Agnus Dei engraved within a circle in the centre, suspended from her
neck. The room in which she was sitting was very small, but ornamented
with a number of pretty pictures and knickknacks, and in a cushioned chair
nestled a downy ball of a kitten, her especial pet and favourite.

A knock at the door preceded the appearance of Sister Frances Constance
who was introduced as one of our countrywomen and who threw herself on
the floor at the feet of Sister Ellen finding no disengaged chair; remarking
in a merry way that that was the right place for *American Sisters*. Sister Mary
Virginia (Miss Seaver [sic]) came in too presently, and a very pleasant chat we
all had; it was pleasant to see the perfect understanding and affection which
seemed to exist between the three, and the total absence of all restraint,
save that of affectionate respect towards the elder Sister on the part of the
Novices. One or two messages were brought by other Sisters, each being
preceded at the door by a tap and a slight courtesy [curtsey] as she entered.
One of the messages was to summon us to the presence of the *Superior*
whither we were accompanied by Sister Frances [Frances Constance]. We
found her in a larger room furnished however in the same simple and tasteful

manner, seated before a secretary [desk] on which were numerous business-like papers, and above all a Cross, around the shaft of which clustered fresh flowers, springing from the earth around the base. Here we were received with more stateliness, but no less kindness, and were asked many questions about the Sisterhood of S. Mary and the American Church in general.

I thought the Superior evinced considerable knowledge of our Church affairs, besides much interest ... When she came to Clewer fourteen or fifteen years ago the House of Mercy consisted of a small building (of which no traces now exist) which had been abandoned first by the lady who founded it [Mariquita Tennant] and second by the lady who succeeded her [Elizabeth Cozens]. On her taking possession of it she styled herself the Superior and gathered around her two or three Sisters; from that small beginning have sprung the present noble buildings at Clewer, besides the many Houses in London and elsewhere under the care of the same Sisterhood, now numbering over *fifty* if we include Probationers [novices] as well as Confirmed Sisters [professed Sisters]. She laid great stress on Bishop Potter's [Horatio Potter, Bishop of New York] countenancing your labours, considering *that* a greater sign than anything else. She told us we should be under the charge of the American Sisters and that she trusted that I should gain from them whatever information I desired, and then we took our leave, fearful of engrossing too much of her valuable time. I afterwards learned that she was the Honorable Mrs Monsell, a widow without children when she formed the Sisterhood. She is a person of commanding presence whose dignity however is softened by great motherliness; she is called 'Mother' by all the other Sisters, and the Superior when spoken of by others. The Heads of the other Houses connected with Clewer are 'Sister Superiors'.

Sister Frances next conducted us to the garden, where we paced the broad walks for a few minutes chatting with her and Sister Mary [Mary Virginia], until the ringing of the Chapel bell summoned us to Sext. It proved to be a Litany service, intoned by the Superior, the other Sisters, visitors, and ourselves, responding, besides all the Penitents, who sat in chairs placed in rows of 8 on either side of the aisle; we observed their dresses differed slightly in the color of the calico and were told that they were divided into two classes, between which no communication was allowed excepting on one day of the year, the Festival of St John the Baptist. This arrangement is intended to prevent their forming too large a mass, a class of from 25 to 30 being quite large enough both for their own amusement and for the supervision of the Sisters at a time. On rainy days their recreation is spent in the Cloister [popularly known as the 'talking cloister'], but altho' there is a class at either end, they are not allowed to approach each other nor to exchange even a word. The Penitents wear plain white caps, covering their hair entirely [to prevent the spread of head lice], like night caps. Sext being ended, we were taken upstairs to see the dormitories, etc. We noticed that each room contained only about 5 or 6 beds; at the end of a long corridor we saw a tiny Oratory [distinguished by a cross built into the exterior brickwork—see page 147], to which the Penitents or Sisters have access for private devotion at any time and out of which opens another small room, the sitting room of the Sister in charge of the Dormitory work. We also saw the 'punishment room', the window of which is barred and in which there is nothing but a mattress rolled up in one corner on which the refractory individual can sit and meditate on her fault. The locking up lasts generally for several hours.

At 1 o'clock we were taken in to dinner in the Refectory [not the same refectory as that used by the Sisters latterly], and during the meal had an opportunity of seeing almost all of the Sisters together. There were two tables, one placed crosswise at the head of the other; at the former sat the Superior, with Sister Ellen on one side, and another Confirmed Sister on the other, there were places for two more adjoining them. At the other table sat 6 Novices or Probationers on one side, and opposite to them 5 Visitors besides M and myself. The Superior's dress was similar to that of the Confirmed Sisters, but her Cross was of gold instead of silver, and her cap of tarlatan fitting around her face with a full ruche, almost exactly like a widow's cap. The Probationers have a plain black cross also suspended to the neck, and a muslin cap with only one row of fluting around the edge. The Visitors wear any sort of black dress and a white cap with purple strings. They come for six months at a time.

The *Gray Sisters* also work 6 months out of the year, but undertake to do so for 3 successive years, and wear a gray habit. [Miss Folsom is confusing the Magdalens, who wore grey at the probationary stage, with the Second Order Sisters who wore blue habits, lived at the convent for part of the year and made a commitment for 3 years at a time. The Magdalens would not have eaten their meals in the Sisters' refectory.] There was one at the

table, but not a Clewer Sister; one of some Liverpool Order I believe …
The Superior said Grace before and after meat, all standing. The meal, for
Friday, consisted of a dish of cold sliced meat for the delicate ones, and
eight or ten good sized puddings, chiefly rice; potatoes, bread and ale or
wine for those needing it. The windows of the Refectory look out on the
garden, as indeed all the rooms do, the walls of all wainscoted half way up
with deal stained in imitation of oak, and most of the ceilings wainscoted
entirely. After dinner we were left in the 'Community Room' for a few
minutes while Sisters Mary [Mary Virginia] and Frances put on their bonnets;
this is a remarkably cheerful, pleasant apartment, with a piano at one end,
a book-case, a writing table in one corner, and a larger table in the centre
of the room, with drawers on all sides of it. Some very nice engravings
hung on the walls, and the windows afford one glimpses of the smooth
green lawn with gay flower beds here and there laid out with true English
taste.

It was now about a quarter before 2, and as my sister had an engagement
in town which obliged her to return by the 2.45 train, she had but half an
hour left for Clewer. I was to stay until a later train, as there was still much
which I wished to find out about the rules of the House, etc, for your
benefit … If I could have spared the time they w'ld have insisted upon my
spending the night there, but that was out of the question. Hearing that
we had already seen the Orphanage, the Sisters thought it might interest us
to see the invalids of St Andrew's Convalescent Home, of which you have
no doubt read in the *Church Review*. It will be completed in Nov and in the
meantime the patients are tended in a couple of cottages close by. Those
who occupy the front rooms can watch the progress of the new building
day by day, but their present quarters are so cosy, that the Sister in Charge
remarked that they were not at all anxious for the change, especially as
an increase of patients will deprive them of the undivided attention they
now receive. One cottage contained the men and the other women; some
of them looked more like incurables than convalescents, altho' none were
confined to their beds; all looked up in a bright grateful way on the entrance
of their especial Sister, which told us more than words could have done, of
the fruits of her ministrations among them. A neat red counterpane with a
small black cross tacked on near the top overspread each bed; and in one of
the cottages we were shown the small Oratory in which at least one service

a day is held and I think more. The Convalescents, especially the men, take great delight in perfecting themselves in the chants.

By this time the fly was ready and my sister took leave of our cicerones and with Jane drove to the Windsor station, while I accompanied them to the House, stopping on the way to inspect St Andrew's [Convalescent] Home. Here, however, their knowledge proved at fault, beyond the great ward they could identify nothing and we could only conjecture that such a portion w'ld be the Chapel, another the Refectory, and so on. It will be a commodious and substantial building of brick, irregular in outline and capable of being enlarged at any time by the addition of wings … Returning to the House of Mercy, Sister Mary Virginia suggested that we should sit down on one of the inviting benches under the trees … Their great object, subservient of course to the reformation of their [the Penitents'] characters, is to make good servants of them, two years is usually allotted for this work, but that time is generally exceeded. The two classes, the East class and the West class are instructed in different branches, one in laundry work and the other in dormitory [sewing etc] work. Sr Frances has the supervision of the former, with competent matrons under her to teach the actual labor, this class does all the washing of the House, besides that of the Eton foundation [Eton College] and of the Orphanage at Sloe [Slough], 5 miles distant. The Sister in charge of the Dormitory class does all the teaching herself, not I believe because it is required, but because she likes to do so. Besides these classes a few Penitents are taught to be waiters and a few others to be good pantry girls. Sewing occupies only the spare time and is chiefly taught to the Dormitory class, as they get through their work earlier in the day than the laundry class. As to reading, writing, etc Sister Mary said it would be impossible to find time for all that, even if it were desirable, but it is thought more important to fit them for thorough servants. She seemed to think that this system would not work so well in America, owing to the different qualifications necessary there …

Sister Mary gave me the routine of the day, but I am afraid I cannot remember it exactly. The first bell sounds at ¼ before 6 and all the Penitents must be down 5 minutes before half past. Matins is said at half past 6 at which they are all present. The Sisters say Prime afterwards, I believe, while the girls look over their lessons for the Bible-class which follows breakfast. At 8.30 the business of the day begins in the laundry and dormitories and lasts until 12, when Sext is said in Chapel. Dinner, recreation and work occupy the afternoon until 4.30, when they change their dress and appear in Chapel for Evensong at ¼ before 5. In the evening there is another short recreation (spent in a walk through the grounds), tea, a story read aloud, Compline and bed at 9.

There is a part of the House in which the most refractory ones are kept apart from the others, and there is another portion kept still more secluded, in which are the *lady-penitents*. The Sister (Sister Amy) who has charge of this department, takes her meals with them and rarely mixes with the others; these Penitents attend Chapel in the organ-gallery, behind a latticed screen. They do a great part of the Church-work, such as making surplices, altar-cloths, etc. A Penitent can never become a Sister, not even a lay-Sister, but if she gives herself to the work of the House for life and is accepted, she becomes a *Magdalen*, and has that name appended to her own … There are one or two in this House of Mercy. The lay-Sisters are of the rank of servants, and work for the House instead of for themselves in the world. The little portress is an example of these and a nice capable little body she seems to be, with a remarkably refined intelligent face … The habit is black and white, but differs somewhat from that of the Sisters proper. With regard to these latter, the time of probation is two years, but they cannot even then become Confirmed Sisters unless voted for by the other Sisters as well as by the Warden and Superior. Some have been known to wait seven years for admission.

The time of waiting for the *postulants* seems to vary. Sisters Mary and Frances became Novices after only one month. There are two very young Novices there at present, only about 17 or 18, but they cannot be voted for until they are at least 21. The Sisters, as a general thing, do not look very young and Sister Ellen, my favourite, seems to be quite advanced in life. [Here speaks a young woman: in fact most of the Sisters were young or early middle-aged, though Sr Ellen may have been an exception.] The office for the reception of postulants and novices is performed by Mr Carter, the Warden. Sisters are confirmed [professed] only by the Bishop of Oxford, their Visitor. It is generally done in their Chapel … The Superior is elected every 3 years, *re-elected* always in this case, but the Office is repeated every time with some slight omissions; it is a very solemn service, they say. The Book of Hours used in the Chapel is that used by all the English Sisterhoods, entitled 'Hours of the Church of England' [*The Day Hours of the Church of England*], or something like that … It is, however, rather complicated they say, and a new edition is being prepared, which will be a great improvement … At 3 the Chapel-bell rang and we postponed further conversation until after None, wending our way thro' the silent Cloister into the exquisite Chapel, whose very atmosphere seemed redolent with the fragrance of perfect beauty; one hardly wished to become conscious of details, delicate carving, rich tiles, soft-hued windows, one felt they were all there in lavish profusion, but all so perfectly harmonious, that it was impossible to do justice to one without including the whole. The Altar was vested in a green cloth embroidered with the emblems of the Evangelists, and on it were two tapers [candles], one on either side of the Cross. Two large candelabras stood in the Chancel, just below the Altar, and directly over the railing hung seven lamps of wrought brass, the centre one larger than the other six, all of them suspended from the ceiling by chains. The Superior and the Sisters nearest in rank to her occupied the stalls at the West end, while all the others, the Visitors and strangers occupied those on the North and South sides. Very calm and peaceful was that Hour of None, chanted forth in the low sweet voice of Sister Ellen and responded to by the band of Sisters with an earnest thrilling devotion, yet so rapidly that almost before I was aware of it, it was over, and we were passing out into the sunlight again.

Sister Mary Virginia and I resumed our seat under the trees and our pleasant chat, and she gave me the 'Rules for the Penitents' and the 'Rules for the Sisterhood' to look over, both of them in MSS. [The earliest extant printed edition of the Penitential Rule dates from 1873 and the Sisters' Rule was not printed until 1870.] Among the latter is a prohibition for any Sister to assume any other name than that given at her Baptism. [This was not always adhered to in later years. Also, Sisters sometimes added an extra name to distinguish them from other Sisters with the same baptismal name.] The Penitents' rules are read to them once a week. The Sisters also have a *Rule of Life*, which I was not permitted to see, and which is read alone among themselves periodically. [This would have been particular to each individual Sister.] They have seasons of *Silence*, for instance, no one is allowed to speak during breakfast-time on Friday, nor after 9 any night, at 10 they retire, and are required to be in bed at 11. The silence periods are quite frequent during Lent, and the three days occupied by a *Retreat* are marked in the same way.

At this time all the Sisterhood assemble and their work being entrusted to the care of the *Visitors*, they spend the three days in Meditation, Prayer and Silence, from Tuesday night until Saturday morning. The Hours are the same as usual, but the first one begins with the 'Veni Creator' and the Lord's Prayer, and after each of three [offices] every day the Priest who holds the Retreat delivers a 'Meditation'.

On the 3rd of July every year they celebrate the foundation of the House, last year the Corner-stone of St Andrew's Home [Convalescent Hospital] was laid on the same day by the Bishop of Oxford and the gathering was both large and interesting; the Bishop preached from the steps of the Stone Cross which rises in the centre of the Court, for the House is built around a large quadrangle. I believe I have not really described its external appearance as yet; it is built of red brick, in a simple but extremely pleasing style, with sufficient regularity to prevent any sameness, without being at all fantastic; the windows, sometimes of one light, sometimes of two, and again of three, but all latticed in diamond panes and arched in [a trefoil design] at the top. Several tall poplar trees on the lawn add greatly to the beauty of the scene, erecting their tall heads proudly as if conscious of the importance of the House entrusted to their guardianship.

And so the time slipped by only too fast and half past 4 came, when Sister Mary carried me to the Refectory for a cup of tea, which hospitality was shared by several other stranger-visitors, but not by the Sisters; immediately after she conducted me to Sister Ellen's room, in obedience to the wishes of the latter. I can hardly remember all the kind things she said, perhaps it was the manner more than the words which impressed me so very much, but one thing I have not forgotten, and that was a most cordial invitation to spend a couple of days there when I am next in England, to come on a Saturday, she said, and stay till Monday! She was sorry I could not stay that night, as the Superior had suggested in the telegraphic answer she had sent to my note, which telegram I had not received before starting.

On my mentioning the prospect of our visiting Holland soon, she [Sr Ellen] was much interested and asked if my Father was acquainted with her brother-in-law, the Count de Nyerett. [In the Clewer records listed as Conte de Zuylen de Nyvelte, at The Hague, 'a Romanist', ie a Roman Catholic.] I could not tell her, but on appealing to my Father afterwards I found that he was a great friend of his at The Hague, before his marriage to her [Sr Ellen's] sister. The Count is at present Prime Minister of Holland. While we were talking a parcel of letters and pamphlets done up for the mail was brought in and I helped to stamp them with a feeling of both pleasure and pride at being permitted to assist in the work of the Sisters, even in such a mere trifle as that was.

Then came the bell of Evensong, which was the signal for me to take leave of Sister Ellen, upon which I received from her a very warm farewell and 'God bless you', and following in the wake of the long procession of Penitents, resumed my stall-seat in the Chapel. The service was performed by two Curates, of whom there are three in charge of the Home, in addition to the Sub-Warden; there was no music as it was Friday, but the responses were intoned and very heartily. The Curates wore coloured stoles [this was very 'high' in the 1860s], but no vestments.

A Sisters' service followed Evensong, at which, on Friday, visitors are not permitted to be present. I therefore followed the train of Penitents as they left the Chapel and was met in the corridor by Sister Emily, the Sacristan, who informed me that she was to show me some of the Altar-cloths, etc, as specimens of the work done in the House. When we reached the room where they are kept, we were joined by Sister Mary Virginia and Sister Ellen, and the latter insisted upon the other returning to the Chapel while she showed me the work. I was very sorry to be the means of depriving her of the service, but she made light of it and said she wanted me particularly to see these things. She opened the doors of a large wardrobe the upper and lower parts of which were filled with drawers, while in the middle hung the Altar-cloths … There must have been 7 or 8, if not more cloths, one for every special season or great Festival. I saw a magnificent blue one most elaborately embroidered, and Sister Ellen tried to show me the red one, but not finding it easily, she opened some of the drawers where the smaller articles are kept. First there were the 'fair linen cloths', which had little if any work upon them, then a small square cloth, the name of which escapes me, on which the Chalice and Paten are placed on the Altar [corporal]; this is made of the finest cambric with a border of lace and work of the finest kind. Then the *Palls* which are also made of cambric and lace, and which are used to cover the Chalice with, while the Bread is being distributed, they are square, just large enough to cover a Chalice and have a piece of cardboard inside, to make them stiff. The *veils* are used to throw over the

Chalice and Paten after the Consecration, and are of silk and of cambric as well, both kinds embroidered very beautifully. The silk ones, however, are not used during the Celebration, but cover the Chalice and Paten when in the Vestry or on the Credence-table, and when carried thence to and from the Altar. I also saw the Credence-cloths which cover the Credence-table and a Bourse [Burse] in which the Priest lays the various small cloths etc after the Consecration; it is like a bag, open at one end and the sides stiff with enclosed cardboard and opens like a valve. Two drawers were marked with the words 'Maniples' and 'Purificators', the former Sister Ellen said, were for the wrists of the Priests, and the latter are the linen cloths employed by them in cleansing the Sacred Vessels on the Credence-table. Of all these exquisite things there are various sets, each to suit a particular Altar-cloth, so that on any Festival everything is in keeping.

Just as my admiring inspection was over, Sister Mary Virginia returned to claim me, the Service being ended and with another, and this time a final kind farewell from Sister Ellen, I accompanied Sister Mary to the garden for a few last words, the hour for my departure being close at hand. In speaking of the various duties of the Sisters, I believe I have forgotten to mention the charge of the Novices, which is allotted to Sister Elizabeth and on account of which she is called 'Mistress of the Novices'. It does not give her a higher rank in the Sisterhood, and the supervision is, I believe, not very strict, but whenever the Novices wish for advice or instruction, it is to her they apply. Sister Mary Virginia was very surprised to hear that there was no office of the sort in *your* Sisterhood, and asked how the Probationers learned to be Sisters; I told her I supposed the need had not yet arisen as the numbers were yet so small. I asked her what her plans and those of Sister Frances were with regard to starting a Boston Sisterhood; she said they had abandoned that idea, partly from the impression that the Church feeling in Boston is not sufficiently advanced, intimating also the probable lack of sympathy on the part of the Bishop and partly because they depend upon the assistance of Mr Doane [the Revd William Doane, later Bishop of Albany]; they say he is very eager on the subject and has promised to do everything in his power to help them. I suppose, therefore, that their work will be begun in his diocese, but they seem to think the *time* very far off; they intend to remain at Clewer until they are Confirmed Sisters [Professed], and of course cannot tell when that will be, it is always very uncertain.

Sister Frances is going home this summer or fall, on a visit; she has a Mother living, which Sister Mary has not; she has two months leave of absence and as one must be spent on the ocean, she will have but one for her visit; I begged her to spare you a few days, and said I c'ld answer for her receiving a warm welcome; she said she w'ld like to see your House of Mercy very much and had thought of calling there, but seemed to have entertained doubts about your caring to see her and was surprised that you had heard about her and Sister Mary [Sister Mary Virginia], and that you knew so much and cared so much about Clewer. Sister Ellen had expressed the same surprise and gratification previously. I think some vague idea of settling in New York must have crossed their minds at one time, for on my mentioning Dr Dix's [Revd Dr Morgan Dix, Rector of Trinity Parish, New York] opinion that there should be no other Sisterhood there than that of St Mary [Peekskill], they called Sister Ellen's attention to it pointedly and agreed with her in thinking him *quite right*. Sister Ellen remarked that great harm had been done in the English Church by the multiplicity of small Sisterhoods that had sprung up in all directions, or if not harm, it had interfered very much with the efficiency of their work. I promised to let Sister Frances know if I should hear of any available escort for her in *Sept* or *Oct* next … I was very much pleased with both of them [ie the two American Sisters]. Sister F [Frances Constance] is the younger and a little offhand, almost brusque in manner … Sister Mary Virginia is more staid, but very kind and genial, with a dash of Boston self-possession also.

And now my delightful visit was at an end; I cast a look around, hoping to impress the peaceful scene indelibly on my memory, and was dismissed at the great gate by Sister Mary with an affectionate kiss and an assurance that she had enjoyed my visit as much as I could have done. The portress walked with us to a stable close by, to order a fly and she would not leave me until she saw me inside and off to the station, she protested stoutly against a piece of silver which I pressed her to take and w'ld only accept it on condition of my allowing her to put it in the Alms-box. You may wonder at my not having seen Mr Carter, but he is at present in Switzerland. I saw his Church in the distance, but had no time to go there; the Sisters told me that it was remarkable only for its antiquity. They spoke of him with all the enthusiasm and affection I had expected. One substantial remembrance of my visit I carried away with me in the shape of 5 of the small Manuals of

Devotion for Sisters of Mercy, four of which are at present on their way across the ocean. I had an unexpected opportunity of sending a parcel in a box which my brother was sending to a friend in New York and I put them in. One is for you, another for Sister Agnes, one for Sister Sarah and the 4th for Cousin Edna. Sister Ellen was quite pleased at the idea of some more of them going to America, she said that Mr Doane had carried a few with him not long ago. [Cousin Edna was Edna Ela Baker, a cousin of Miss Folsom, who was a Novice in the Community of St Mary, Peekskill. She later joined the CSJB at Clewer and was professed on June 28th 1870. She transferred to the American CSJB in 1876 and died in 1896.]

My letter has grown to an unconscionable length, but I will not apologise, as I am sure you will not find anything about Clewer *too long*. But I find I have omitted one thing with which I will close. I refer to the very strong desire expressed by Sisters Mary and Frances, Sister Ellen and *the Superior*, that *you* should come over to England, and see Clewer for yourself. They could not see why you c'ld not find someone to take your place for a short time. I told them that they did not know how almost impossible it was to spare *you* for the House, overworked as the whole Sisterhood is even now, but they all thought that it ought to be managed in some way or other. Can it not be, dear Sister Jane? C'ld you not contrive to come over, say in August next and return with Sister Frances in Sept or Oct? How very nice that would be for you both! [In fact Sr Jane did visit Clewer accompanied by Novice Edna, Helen Folsom's cousin, who then stayed on as a novice at Clewer!] With kindest regards to Sister Agnes, believe me to be

Yours most sincerely,
Helen S. Folsom

Paris, June 23rd [1866]

FROM SLAVE OWNER TO CLEWER SISTER:
THE STORY OF JANE PEDDER

In the first edition of *A Joyous Service* and also in *A Place in Life* I referred to an early Sister, Jane Pedder, as an American. She joined the Community of St John Baptist on December 20th 1854 and was professed on December 12th 1856. But she may not have been American. In an early roll book kept by the Community, Sr Jane's next of kin was listed as her nephew, H C Pedder, c/o Messrs Arnold Constable & Co, New York. On the basis of this address I assumed she was American and had come to England to join the CSJB because at that time there were no American Religious Communities (the first was the Community of St Mary, Peekskill, New York, founded in 1865). In fact, her story is far more surprising than I could possibly have imagined.

Jane's parents were William Pedder and Jane Frances, née Wall. They were married in 1789 at St George's Anglican Church, Basseterre, St Kitts, in the West Indies. English by birth, the Pedders lived in St Kitts where they became sugar planters. There were at least six children, of whom Jane, born on September 19th 1803, was the only daughter. She was baptised at St George's Anglican Church, Basseterre, St Kitts, on October 11th 1804. The Pedders seem to have assumed a leading role in the civic life of St Kitts. William Pedder became Clerk to the St Kitts Legislative Council, and one of Jane's brothers, John Thomas Pedder, was a stipendiary magistrate. He was also Private Secretary to the Lieutenant Governor of St Kitts, Charles Thornton Cunningham. Another of her brothers, Robert Grimes Pedder, also had a number of equally distinguished roles in public life. In 1840 his name appeared on the Jury list in St Kitts and in 1856 he was appointed by HM the Queen to be a Member of the Executive Council of the British Virgin Islands. The following year he became a non-elective Member of the Legislative Council of the British Virgin Islands, and by 1862 he was Acting Judge and Member of the Executive Council in Jamaica. These roles were consistent with the lifestyle of the white English settlers who ran the colonial administration.

But there was a darker side. The white English sugar planters, including the Pedder family, owned slaves. Indeed the hard work of growing, harvesting and processing the sugar cane was done by slaves, who would have been brought to the West Indies from West Africa in the notorious slave ships. In 1807 the British Parliament passed the Abolition of the Slave Trade Act in order to suppress the transporting of slaves from West Africa to America and the West Indies, but there was still trafficking of slaves between the islands. The white sugar planters of St Kitts, Barbados and other West Indian islands continued to own slaves and the Pedders were no exception. In 1803 William Pedder leased an estate called Garvey's Plantation at Palmetto Point; two family members, Robert Grimes Pedder and John Thomas Pedder, had links to the Fancy Estate and the Kitts Stoddart Estate, respectively. All were sugar plantations. The extended Pedder family was huge and they lived not only in St Kitts but also in Nevis and Barbados, where their names were linked to the sugar plantations.

In 1817 the Slave Registration Act was passed, compelling slave owners to provide a triennial register of all their slaves. In the 1825 Triennial Return for St Kitts, Jane Pedder is listed as the owner of four slaves—a gift from her father. Perhaps this was a 21st birthday gift; of that we cannot be sure, but we can be sure that such a gift would have made Jane Pedder a wealthy woman. The value of a high quality slave was about £100, which translates into several thousand pounds in 2011. This begs the question, would she have known those four slaves personally? While it is possible that they may have been plantation workers and unknown to her, it is more likely that they would have been house servants, even personal servants to her. While not a member of the English aristocracy (unlike a number of Clewer Sisters), Jane Pedder was a member of what has become known as the 'plantocracy'—white English sugar planters who made their fortunes in the colonies. Slave ownership was something that pervaded very deeply into English society. Scratch the surface of many family trees and the ownership of slaves, or some association with the trans-Atlantic slave trade, was there.

Nothing definite is known about Jane Pedder's life between 1825, when her father gave her the four slaves, and 1854, when she was admitted to the Clewer Sisterhood. But it is highly likely that she lived the life of a lady of leisure and would most likely have been sheltered from knowledge of the worst things that could happen to slaves. Nor should we assume that just because some sugar planters sexually abused their slaves and also literally worked them to death, all owners did so. There is no incriminating evidence against the Pedders, but even so, the prevailing culture was that black slaves were deemed inferior to their white owners. Indeed the whole argument in support of imperialism and colonialism was based on the supposed superiority of the white races. In the post-colonial atmosphere of the 21st century the subjection of one race by another is rightly judged to be abhorrent.

The Slavery Abolition Act was passed by the British Parliament in August 1833 and came into effect a year later. Under the terms of this Act all slaves in the British colonies were to be emancipated and their owners were to receive compensation. There was a loophole in the Act which allowed slave owners to retain their slaves under an 'apprenticeship' system for a period of six years. In reality it meant six years of indentured labour which was slavery under a different name. It proved to be an unpopular system and was abolished in 1838. We do not know the amount of compensation received by the Pedders, or indeed the sum received by Jane Pedder, but it must have been considerable. In St Kitts and Barbados the total compensation received by the white planters was in the region of £20 million in 2011 terms. Jane Pedder would have been financially secure for the rest of her life.

On December 20th 1854 the 51-year-old Jane Pedder was received into the Community of St John Baptist, Clewer. She was the seventh Sister to be received and was professed on December 12th 1856 together with Sr Augusta. These two new Sisters would have been admitted and professed in the small chapel on the upper floor of the House of Mercy; the new chapel (known after 1940 as the Chapel of the Forerunner) was not completed until 1858. These really were the early, pioneering days of a Community that would eventually become one of the largest and fastest growing in the Church of England.

Many questions surround Jane Pedder's choice of life for which there are no answers, just speculation. There can be no doubt that she felt called by God to live a consecrated life of service, and she did so until her death many years later. We cannot know how she came to hear of Clewer—perhaps from a church contact at home. Nor indeed do we know when she first came to England. The Religious Life was just being revived in the English Church for the first time since the Reformation and it offered a means of living a life of mission, ministry and social care in an age where women had little choice between marriage or spinsterhood. Also, Jane Pedder may have felt a sympathy (perhaps unspoken) towards the abolitionist cause regarding slavery. Just because she owned four slaves does not necessarily mean she agreed with it. This is not to suggest that she became a Sister out of a penitential motive, but simply that she may have had her own thoughts and opinions about slavery that diverged from those of the 'plantocracy'.

Sr Jane did not spend the whole of her life at Clewer. In the 1861 Census she is recorded as in residence at the Manor House, Oxford (the Oxford Diocesan Penitentiary) which the Sisters had taken over in 1860. (The Census Return is inaccurate in that it records Sr Jane as being born in 1825 and therefore 36 years old—a typical example of the inaccuracy of Census enumerators.) At this time Sr Harriet was in charge, but in 1869 Sr Jane became the Sister Superior of the House until 1876. After that date Sr Harriet became Sr Superior again.

Sr Jane died at St Andrew's Hospital, Clewer, on July 12th 1885, nearly thirty years after her admission as a novice. The Community *Annals* for July 13th have an account of her death and funeral. It all seems very complicated, but this was the usual funerary ritual for Clewer Sisters in the 1880s. "Sister Jane departed. She had gone to the Hospital for the June Retreat and remained there. She passed away quite quietly in her sleep at 4.30 am. She had been unconscious for about two days before. It was thought probable she had had a slight stroke. The funeral was on Thursday 16th. Her body was brought over [to the convent] on the night before at 8.00 pm accompanied by four Professed Sisters and two Novices carrying the Celebration lights [candles], the Cross carried in front. The Warden [Canon Carter] and Choir met it at the West door. 'Light's abode' was sung going up the Chapel [this was the large Chapel of St John Baptist opened in October 1881] and the Litany of the Dead, the Sisters kneeling in the open space behind the clergy. The Watch was kept as usual. Sr Harriet Sarah and Sr Anna took the last [watch] until the Procession left the Chapel on Thursday am. Celebration [of the Eucharist] for the Departed at 7.00 am at High Altar and Choral [Eucharist] at 8.30 am. 'Dies Irae' was sung at the Offertory. Incense was used. The Warden celebrated and said the short Office [of the dead] directly after. The body was censed. Terce was said immediately after and when the Warden had breakfasted the first part of the Burial Service was said in Chapel. The coffin was nearly covered with crosses and wreathes, one entirely of white lilies. Mrs Coombe sent one from Oxford. The Sisters, about twenty, followed to the Churchyard. The Warden said the Burial office." So it was that Sr Jane was laid to rest in the churchyard of St Andrew's Clewer, a long way from St Kitts.

There is a postscript to Sr Jane's story concerning her nephew, Henry Charles Pedder of New York. It seems that he turned out to be something of a 'ne'er do well' although his by now elderly aunt may not have known about it. Henry Charles Pedder was born in 1840, the son of John Thomas Pedder. He married his wife Louisa in Barbados, but he was an ambitious man who sought to rise above his social class. He moved to New York where he became a confidential clerk for the dry goods store Arnold Constable and Company. In keeping with his social pretensions, in 1879 he commissioned a large mansion in a new suburban estate in Llewellyn Park at West Orange, New Jersey, just fifteen miles from New York. The architect was Henry Hudson Holly and the house was furnished by the New York firm of interior designers, Pottier and Stymus. He commissioned a library, which is still in the house and known as the H C Pedder library—the books were bound in matching bindings and dust wrappers and are still in pristine condition because they were never used. But they impressed his guests. The mansion was called Glenmont and survives to this day thanks to popular interest in its next owner.

Meanwhile, Henry Pedder had branched out into publishing. A chance meeting with the founder of a struggling monthly magazine called *The Manhattan* resulted in Pedder becoming a stockholder in the company. He soon changed the original character of the magazine and began to use it as an outlet for his own literary efforts. He poured money into the magazine, sometimes at the rate of $300 per page, for illustrated articles of his own, which few people read. Meanwhile his employers at Arnold Constable were led to believe that his wealth had come from a rich relative in the West Indies who had left him money. (Perhaps Aunt Jane had kindly made financial provision for him for when he came of age or married, when she left home to join her convent—but that is sheer speculation.)

In 1884 Henry Pedder, together with his wife, sailed for Europe for a holiday. He came to England and established a London agency for his magazine. One wonders whether he visited his now elderly aunt in her convent. But while he was away the bubble burst. At Arnold Constable a fellow clerk was found to have embezzled funds and upon further investigation it was discovered that it was only the tip of the iceberg. The truth came out when the man confessed that while he had taken a small amount, Henry Pedder had embezzled colossal amounts. Pedder was recalled to New York and the truth soon emerged. The company took possession of Glenmont, buying the house for just one dollar. *The Manhattan* went into receivership and publication ceased after the September issue.

As for Henry Pedder—he fled back to St Kitts, thereby evading prosecution. Later he returned to England and became the manager of a button factory in Derby, but he died in Bath. The Glenmont estate, consisting of 13.5 acres, was bought by Thomas Alva Edison in January 1886 for $125,000 as a wedding present for his new wife. He had gained a bargain as this was half the estimated value of the property. Now Glenmont is part of the 'Edison tour' where, in addition to touring the house, including the H C Pedder library, visitors may see the laboratories where Edison invented so many of the components of modern life which we now take for granted.

It is to be hoped that Sr Jane Pedder knew nothing of her nephew's fall from grace. But if she did know then perhaps her thirty years of ministering amongst the outcast and disgraced would have given her compassion for her fallen nephew.

THE COST OF ALL THE BUILDINGS IN CONNECTION WITH THE CLEWER HOUSE OF MERCY

A note on the undated, manuscript copy of this document states that it was drawn up by Sr Louise, CSJB.

House of Mercy, Clewer

The estate of 15 acres bought for	£ 2,500
Frackleton Field added in 1881	£ 600
The House built in 1855, cost including Old Chapel, Laundry & fittings & outside wall	£17,000
Magdalens' wing added in 1874	£ 5,158
Refectory wing added in 1875	£ 4,562
The New Chapel built in 1881 including stained glass windows	£33,000
New laundry built in 1888	£ 4,460
Kitchen wing & dining hall built in 1888	£ 3,794
An additional workroom over the entrance and ornamented gable in 1893	£ 1,432
A bell turret & bell & sacristy added to the chapel in 1900	£ 576
	£73,082

St John's Home

On the same estate, built in 1856	£ 3,500
The roof raised and additional rooms added in 1888	£ 500
A new wing built with large schoolroom in 1893	(cost not given)

St Andrew's Hospital

The estate upon which the Hospital, St Andrew's Cottage & Almshouses, and the Warden's Lodge have been built was bought in 1865 for	£ 2,800
Cost of building	£15,400
Chapel added in 1874 with dining hall & refectory	£ 4,397
Children's wing added in 1874	£ 6,022

A small Incurable ward added in 1888	(cost not given)
A ward altered for a Sisters' Infirmary in 1890	£ 1,453
An observation ward added in grounds later	(cost not given)
	£ 30,072

St Andrew's Cottage
Cost of building	£ 1,350

St Andrew's Almshouses [St Andrew's Cottages]
Cost of building	£ 2,100

Albion Place
6 cottages bought in 1894 cost	£ 1,150

St John's Lodge
Built in 1880 cost	£ 3,007

The Warden's Lodge
Cost of building	£ 2,790
Total cost of estate & buildings	£ 113,557

Notes

The buildings were completed by 1900, and the equivalent sterling sum in 2011 would be £10,728,865.36

Some of the buildings were paid for by benefactors such as Sr Elizabeth (see Appendix 6 for further details). Sr Elizabeth was not the only benefactor; other Sisters, including Mother Harriet, were generous too, but there is less evidence of the sums given, although it is known that Mother Harriet gave £1,000 towards building the permanent church of Clewer St Stephen. And there were lay benefactors too—many of the branch houses having been paid for by Associates and others. In the above list, St Andrew's Cottage was bought by the Ladies Charlotte & Louisa Greville and given to the Community. And the St Andrew's Almshouses were built by Sr Mary Ashpitel of the Second Order. St John's Lodge was built for Canon Carter after he ceased to be Rector of Clewer. The Council of the House of Mercy gave the land and the house itself was paid for by public subscription.

❧ APPENDIX 6 ❧

SISTER ELIZABETH'S FINANCIAL CONTRIBUTION TO
THE COMMUNITY OF ST JOHN BAPTIST

Introduction
I am indebted to Jill Owen for sharing her research concerning Sr Elizabeth Moreton, her family and her finances, which she has carried out on behalf of the National Trust, the custodians of Little Moreton Hall, Cheshire, Sr Elizabeth's ancestral home. Elizabeth Moreton joined the CSJB in October 1853. She was in her 22nd year and lived through five reigns (George IV, William IV, Victoria, Edward VII, and George V), dying in 1912 aged 91 years. Her immense generosity to the CSJB is well known but the full extent of her great wealth has only now come to light. In order to put these sums of money into a 21st century context, the equivalent sterling value in 2010 has been given in square brackets.

Who was Elizabeth Moreton?
Elizabeth Moreton was descended from a long line of Anglican Churchmen, notably Edward Moreton (c1599–1675) and his son, William Moreton (1640/1–1715), Bishop of Kildare and later of Meath in the Church of Ireland. William Moreton had inherited Moreton Hall (now known as Little Moreton Hall) from his father and he, in turn, left it to the son of his second marriage, Sir William Moreton, the last male heir (and who was not a clergyman). When Sir William died in 1716 he passed the Hall on to the Revd Richard Taylor (c1723–1783), the husband of his sister Annabella, on the condition that Taylor changed his surname to Moreton. There were three children from this marriage: William, Annabella and Sally. William (1759–1840) became William Moreton Moreton after his father had changed his name from Taylor. His sister Annabella died unmarried in 1787, and his younger sister Sally married the Revd Edward Frewen (1744–1831) in 1789.

William Moreton Moreton (1759–1840) was ordained, and he married twice. The first marriage was childless and ended with the death of his wife, Louisa, in 1811. He then married Elizabeth Hutton, the daughter of a clergyman, and there were four children. These were: William (1817–sometime between 1833 & 1843, as he is mentioned in his father's Will but his mother's reads as though he had predeceased her), Edward (1819–1831), Frances Annabella (1820–1892) and Elizabeth (1821–1912). In 1851 Frances Annabella married John Craigie, but it seems that they separated in 1855, although Frances continued to style herself Frances Annabella Moreton-Craigie, and her husband used the same surname. This marriage was childless and when she made her Will in 1857 she left her whole estate to her sister Elizabeth, who was by now a Sister at Clewer. When Frances died in 1892 her estate was valued at £129,611.0s7d [2010 equivalent £12,000,000]. Thus in 1892 an Anglican nun inherited Little Moreton Hall.

Elizabeth Moreton's money—where did it come from and how was it spent?

Her father, William Moreton Moreton (1759–1840) left Elizabeth £2,000 [2010 equivalent £150,000] and his properties in Westerham in Kent. She received this part of her inheritance on the death of her mother (also named Elizabeth), who had a life interest in the properties. Before he died her father sold one of the properties for £1,000 [£75,000] with the interest being paid first to her mother and on her death to Elizabeth. (The value of these properties is unknown.) Her mother died in 1849 and left the whole of her estate to Elizabeth as her sister, Frances, was well looked after in their father's will (the value of this estate is unknown).

As previously mentioned, Elizabeth joined the Community of St John Baptist in 1853. In 1856, shortly after her profession in November 1855, she gave the Community £3,000, £1,000 of which was to build the Chancel of the Chapel and for the Infirmary and Sisters' wing of the House of Mercy (£100 of this sum was to be laid out on the east window of the Chapel); £1,000 to build a home for the orphans under the care of the Sisterhood of St John Baptist; and £1,000 to be invested in a Community endowment fund, the interest to be paid yearly to the Sisters' account. [£3,000 was equivalent to £240,000 in 2010; £1,000 = £80,000; £100 = £8,000.] In 1871 her cousin Moreton John Edward Frewen died and left a life interest in his properties in Buckinghamshire to Elizabeth's sister Frances; this interest was to pass to Sr Elizabeth on Frances' death. He had properties in a number of counties and the value of his estate was under £180,000 [£16,000,000 in 2010].

In 1871 Elizabeth advised the Community that she would come into possession of her money in January 1872 and she wished, at present, not to use the capital, but wished to give £500 a year [£42,000] to St Andrew's Hospital to free the Community from anxiety about it.

By the early 1870s there were plans to extend the House of Mercy and Sr Elizabeth wanted to add to those buildings by building a wing on the north side to contain rooms for the Probationary and the Lady Penitents. She also wished to build a classroom, dormitories, chapter room and a small oratory for twelve or fourteen Magdalens or permanent penitents. She would give a yearly sum of £400 [£34,000] for their maintenance and would leave an endowment in her Will. Also, she wanted to enlarge the Sisters' Refectory which was now too small and make a suitable room over it for the novices and the novice mistress—and she wanted to enlarge the Chapel as much as it was capable of enlargement. As she wished to use interest and not capital to pay for this work it might not be possible to complete it all in one year; but it would be a good idea to have the whole scheme put on paper and then the building could be contracted for by degrees. She was able to give £2,000 [2010 equivalent £170,000] which would cover the building of the proposed wing on the north side of the House of Mercy. In June 1872 Sr Elizabeth stated that she wished to have accommodation for thirty-three penitents instead of the fourteen previously mentioned. If the plans were amended to allow this she would provide the extra monies. Henry Woodyer was the architect for all this work.

Between 1872 and 1885 she gave the following to:

House of Mercy	£ 4,000
St Andrew's Building	£ 250
House of Mercy	£ 418
For Chapel	£ 1,000
St Andrew's Hospital, Clewer	£ 5,000
Magdalens' and Chaplain's End	£ 17,000
Chapel	£ 3,000
New Hospital Folkestone	£ 1,000
New Dining Hall	£ 400
	£ 32,068

[2010 equivalents are £2,700,000 in 1872—£3,100,000 in 1885]

In 1892 Elizabeth was the sole beneficiary under her sister Frances' Will, the value of which was £129,611.0s7d [£12,000,000 in 2010]. Unfortunately we do not know what was included in this sum apart from Little Moreton Hall.

Between 1892 and 1911 she also gave the following to:

The Community Fund	£ 20,000
St Raphael's Home, Torquay*	£ 5,116
9 Rose St Soho Mission	£ 5,455
Newport Mission	£ 5,047
Working Girls' Home Nelson Square Blackfriars	£ 4,747
St Andrew's Hospital	£ 6,667
	£ 47,032

[2010 equivalents are £4,500,000 in 1892—£4,100,000 in 1911]

*This might not be St Raphael's Home, but St Barnabas' Home, Torquay, a short distance away, which Sr Elizabeth paid for in 1892. It was for the care of patients with advanced consumption. A lot of the monies were given in stocks and shares, primarily in Railway stock, which accounts for the odd amounts.

When Sr Elizabeth died in 1912 her estate was valued at £54,626 8s 6d [£4,727,917.08 in 2010]. She left the following bequests:

To her cousin Revd Charles Thomas Abraham she left her real estate wheresoever situated, except her house and land in Pau in France (inherited from her sister) which she left to Wilfred Leslie Waldegrave Brodie. (Value of these properties is unknown.) This bequest included Little Moreton Hall.

George Aubrey William Thorold	£ 500	[£ 43,275]
Charles Thomas Abraham	£ 5,000	[£432,750]
Melanesian Mission*	£ 5,000	[£432,750]
The Rode Trust**	£ 3,000	[£259,650]

*The Revd George Augustus Selwyn, curate of Windsor, had worked tirelessly to relieve the suffering of the poor in Windsor. In 1841 Selwyn became the first Bishop of New Zealand and in 1848 he visited the islands of Melanesia, hoping to establish a mission there. Following this visit five Melanesians were brought for training at St John's College, Auckland, and this is reckoned as the beginning of the Melanesian Mission. In 1854, Melanesia became a separate diocese from New Zealand. In 1870 Selwyn returned to England having been appointed Bishop of Lichfield. He died in 1878. Charles Thomas Abraham, who inherited Little Moreton Hall from Sr Elizabeth, was the son of Bishop Selwyn's great friend and fellow worker, Charles John Abraham, Bishop of Wellington.

**Little Moreton Hall is in the parish of All Saints' Odd Rode, and in 1875 a chapel of ease at Mow Cop was built and dedicated to St Luke. Under the terms of her Will Sr Elizabeth set up the Rode Trust and bequeathed £3,000 [2010 equivalent £259,650] to be invested, and the income from the capital to be used for the stipend of the curate of St Luke's church. She also directed that if at any future time St Luke's became a separate parish, the Trustees might direct the income towards the endowment of the incumbent's stipend, or to augment it. The Rode Trust still exists at the time of writing and continues to provide an income.

One half of the residue was to be left to the Universities' Mission to Central Africa and the other half to Clewer House of Mercy, which meant that they each received a legacy of £10,634.1s5d [2010 equivalent £920,378.83].

In addition to these lump sums she also gave in her lifetime over twenty-five small amounts which total another £4,477 [£387,484.35]. The grand total was a massive £97,246 [2010 equivalent £8,416,641.30].

Although Elizabeth Moreton had been a Religious Sister since 1853 she did not forget Little Moreton Hall. After she inherited it from her sister in 1892 she spent a considerable amount of money (the exact amount is unknown) in restoring the ancient building. The chapel was in danger of structural collapse and it was saved at her instigation by underpinning the walls and foundations as well as by the replacement of some windows in oak. She also replaced the altar and refurnished the chapel for worship. The entrance gateway and lower porch room were underpinned, and oak uprights were bolted to the walls of the upper storey to prevent further bulging outward. A new floor was put in the withdrawing room as well as repairs to the windows and panelling. The north wall of the great hall was completely restored as well as the doorway and staircase. In the south range the timber framing was repaired and the chimneys and fireplaces rebuilt. Stay rods were inserted in the long gallery to prevent further bulging. Sr Elizabeth visited the restored house on September 5th 1893 and was pleased with the restoration, especially of the chapel, which had been described as "in a dilapidated and ruinous state". A service of rededication was held on October 17th 1893 at which the Revd J M Egerton, Rector of Odd Rode, officiated and the parish church choir of sixteen men sang. Sr Elizabeth was not present at this service but it was attended by about sixty people, who were admitted by ticket. The collection brought in £4 9s 1d [£266.76]. No doubt Sr Elizabeth would be delighted to know that a short service is still held in the chapel on most Sundays when the Hall is open to the public.

Why didn't she have to give all her money to the Community when she entered it?

In order to avoid some of the controversy surrounding the question of Sisters' making a vow of poverty, the Clewer Sisters were not obliged to give up their personal wealth upon joining the Community (see chapter 14 of *A Place in Life*). The Community Rule stated that before being professed, a novice had to declare her possessions and to make arrangements with the Warden and Superior for its disposal. She could keep her capital, but the annual proceeds had to be given either to the Community Fund or an external source which she wanted to help. She was no longer able to spend anything on herself. She could also receive legacies and other bequests; however, the disposal of such property was made with the agreement of the Warden and Superior. Also, if she wished to bequeath any property to the Community she had to satisfy the Visitor (the Diocesan Bishop) that she had informed her next of kin and that they had no objection.

What is the Community Fund?

The Community Fund paid for the Sisters' needs. Sisters who were able were expected to contribute £50 to the fund each year. This sum could be increased if the Sister so desired. From the records examined it seems that between 1855 and 1885 Sr Elizabeth gave to the Community Fund a further £23,350.8s10d [2010 equivalent £1,900,000–£2,200,000]. But as the records could only be traced up to 1885, the sum was in fact far greater. It appears that Sr Elizabeth gave the Community at least £120,596 [2010 equivalent £10,437,583.80].

From the available records it appears that Sr Elizabeth was by far the greatest benefactor to the Community. As she also left bequests in her Will to two other charities it is likely that she may also have given money to these during her lifetime. We will never know for sure just how much money Sr Elizabeth had or how it was spent except to say it was 'a great deal of money'.

Note

Two websites have been used to calculate the 2010 Sterling equivalents to the sums mentioned. The first is to be found at www.thisismoney.co.uk and gives equivalents since 1900. The other site is safalra.com and gives equivalents since 1750, based on the Retail Prices Index (RPI) Inflation measure. The historic data on the safalra website was taken from the 2004 paper "Consumer price inflation since 1750", ISSN 0013-0400, *Economic Trends* No 604, pp38–46.

Information regarding Sr Elizabeth's finances is held at the Berkshire Record Office together with other archive material relating to the CSJB.

Information on William Moreton (1640–1715) has been taken from the *Oxford Dictionary of National Biography* (Oxford 2004).

WHAT BECAME OF THE BUILDINGS?

The Community of St John Baptist, Clewer, was one of the fastest growing Anglican Communities and had many branch houses. The Community did not own all these buildings, though they owned some of them. Some of the buildings were leased by the Community for a short time, and others were owned by diocesan authorities or private individuals. In some cases the buildings were sold after the Sisters vacated them, and inevitably some were demolished at a time when Victorian architecture was the Cinderella of building styles. But towards the end of the twentieth century the mood changed and many of the former Community houses have been restored and new uses found for them. It has not been possible to trace every building—many of those that closed in the 1950s and 1960s have been lost forever, but some are still in use, often incorporating the words 'Clewer' or 'convent' in the new name. The later use of some of these buildings has already been mentioned in the main text but is also detailed below for the sake of comprehensiveness.

Clewer

'The Limes', situated on the corner of Clewer Court Road and adjacent to St Andrew's Clewer, has a Grade 2* listed status and is in private ownership, but now bears a blue plaque commemorating the pioneering work of Mariquita Tennant (see page 145).

The convent buildings, all of which are Grade 2 listed, were sold to a property developer, Westcombe Management, and have been transformed into sixty-four one, two and three bedroom luxury apartments, now known as Convent Court. Also, the grounds have been landscaped whilst retaining their former character. Externally the buildings are still recognisable as the convent, but internally they have been transformed, often out of all recognition, though still retaining distinguishing features such as window tracery and stone fireplaces. However, the Chapel of the Forerunner and the Chapel of St John Baptist (the latter is Grade 2*) stand empty and forlorn, and in increasing danger of dereliction and decay. In 2008 the developers successfully applied for local authority planning permission to change the use of the two chapels into venues for concerts and art exhibitions. But by early in 2012 it had still not been possible to implement this scheme. The two small chapels—the Oratory of St Mary Magdalene with its wall paintings and the Oratory of St Joseph—have both been retained in their former condition.

Before the convent was sold, the plaques listing the names of the departed Sisters were removed from the Chapel of St John Baptist and installed in the Lady Chapel at Clewer St Stephen (with the exception of the plaques for the CRJBS which are now at Southwark Cathedral). Also at St Stephen's is the wooden altar (now known as the Founder's altar), which was in the original chapel on the top storey of the House of Mercy before the Chapel of the Forerunner or the Chapel of St John Baptist had been built. It bears a small plaque with an engraved cross and the inscription:

Gloria in Excelsis

The first altar of the community of St John the Baptist

AD 1849

Deo Gratias

The date '1849' suggests that the altar may have been in use at 'The Limes' before the move to Hatch Lane and while Mariquita Tennant was in charge of the work. If so, then this is a real, tangible link with the rescue work before the foundation of the CSJB. The altar was certainly in use in the first chapel on the top storey of the new House of Mercy and it was later removed to St John's Home. In more recent years it became the nave altar in the Chapel of St John Baptist. When the Sisters moved to Begbroke Priory they took the Founder's altar with them and it served as the main altar while work was still being carried out to the main chapel. It fitted well into the chapel narthex and above it was a window depicting the Baptism of Christ by John the Baptist. As well as providing a focal point for the Sisters' prayer time it was also used as the Altar of Repose on Maundy Thursday. But it became clear that it would not be suitable for the new chapel at Cuddesdon and so it was brought back to Clewer where it now stands under the large wall painting of St Christopher on the west wall of Clewer St Stephen. The Sisters were present the first time it was used.

The large portrait of Mariquita Tennant that used to hang on the wall of the parlour at Clewer was taken by the Sisters to Begbroke Priory where it was placed on the wall of the main entrance hall. This, together with a portrait of Canon Carter, is to be restored and cleaned ready for the move to Cuddesdon where they will both find a new home. Also, the Sisters have commissioned a new portrait of Mother Harriet, to be painted by a local artist. This too will be housed at Cuddesdon.

A sanctuary lamp from St Mary Magdalen's Oratory is now in use at St Stephen's near the statue of the Blessed Virgin Mary. The silver-gilt chalice set with semi-precious stones, given by Sr Elizabeth at the time of her profession, was acquired by the Victoria & Albert Museum in 1962.

A statue of the Virgin and Child with rabbits is now in the care of St Saviour's Priory, Haggerston. This had been brought to Clewer in 1996 by the Community of the Companions of Jesus the Good Shepherd when the Sisters left their convent at West Ogwell to live alongside the Clewer Sisters, and was placed in the sanctuary of the Chapel of the Forerunner. The statue was made in 1925 by Sr (later Mother) Maribel of the Community of St Mary the Virgin, Wantage. Before joining the CSMV Sr Maribel had studied at the Slade School of Art under Professor Henry Tonks and after joining the Community she was permitted to continue with her artistic work. Soon she became renowned as an artist, sculptress and wood carver and her works of art were commissioned from all over the world. She often included animals such as rabbits and squirrels in her work, and the 'Virgin and Child with rabbits' shows the infant Jesus trying to reach down from his mother's knee to touch the rabbits at her feet.

Houses of Mercy
Highgate
The Highgate House of Mercy, formerly Park House on North Hill, finally closed in 1940. The building survived until the post-War Council estate called Hillcrest, comprising blocks of flats, was built. Work on Hillcrest began in 1947 and was completed by 1949. Park House, along with a number of other large buildings in the vicinity, was demolished to make way for the new development. The chapel of the House of Mercy, designed by Arthur Blomfield and opened in 1877, was demolished in 1946.

Great Maplestead

St Mary's Home, Great Maplestead, designed by Henry Woodyer (and from 1929 known as St Mary's House) became in 1944 an orphanage run by the Waifs and Strays Society, currently known as the Children's Society. The building was later demolished.

Stone House Refuge, Pimlico

The Sisters worked there from 1869 until 1919 but it has not been possible to trace the later history of the building. It may have been a victim of wartime bombing.

Bovey Tracey

The Devon House of Mercy, Bovey Tracey, was closed by the Sisters in 1940 shortly before it was damaged by a landmine. After army occupation it was converted into flats and is known as 'Devon House'. In July 1986 the property attained Grade 2 listed status but not before parts of it, in particular the chapel, had been unsympathetically altered. The description supplied by English Heritage at the time of listing gives the details: "… Much of the original glazing survives, with 2 or 3 panes per light and also much old glass. Chapel radically altered with C20 flat roof and fenestration. Buttresses survive and also the 3-sided east end; each of the 3 sides contains a triple lancet window (now blocked), although on the north-east side the lower part of the window has been replaced by a C20 one. Only a small part of interior [was] inspected; a few chamfered, 2-centred arched stone doorways survive …"

Salisbury

As noted in chapter 18, the Sisters withdrew from the former Diocesan House of Mercy at Salisbury in 1947, after which it became a retreat house. The Sisters returned to run the retreat house from 1959 until 1971. The buildings were not listed and after the Sisters finally left they became semi-derelict but have been taken over by Salisbury College (not to be confused with Sarum College in the Cathedral Close). Now restored and known as St Mary's House, the Victorian buildings have been extended to form ninety-four study bedrooms and a higher education complex.

Oxford

The Manor House, Holywell is a Grade 2 listed building and possibly the oldest building occupied by the Sisters, parts of it dating from 1516. It became the Oxford Diocesan House of Mercy and was run by the Sisters from 1860 until the work moved to Littlemore in 1929. In 1933 the house became a hostel for Balliol College students and now provides accommodation for most of Balliol's post-graduates. It has not been possible to trace what happened to the house at Littlemore after the Sisters left in 1949.

Hempsted, Gloucester

Newark House at Hempsted near Gloucester was built on the site of a manor house dating back to the early 1500s, said to be the summer residence of the Prior of Llanthony. The house had been considerably altered in the mid-17th century by Viscount Scudamore and was further altered in 1830, though retaining some of its 17th-century features in the stone mullioned windows. It was this later house that was occupied by the CSJB from 1883 until 1912. After the Sisters left, the house had a chequered history and during World War II accommodated injured RAF officers. In 1986 it was converted into luxury flats which are highly sought after. Unfortunately the house did not gain its Grade 2 listing until December 1998. The name 'Newark House' has been retained.

Leamington

St Michael's Home was a diocesan House of Mercy and the original home and laundry was in Charlotte Street, but later the work moved to a large house on Milverton Hill. After the Sisters gave up the work in Leamington in 1950 the house on Milverton Hill was demolished (along with several others) and was redeveloped for commercial and residential accommodation.

Orphanages & Rescue Homes
St John's Home, Clewer

The orphanage, opened in 1858, was the earliest of the Community branch houses. Designed by Henry Woodyer in the same style as the House of Mercy, it stood just a few hundred yards away. In 1932 the building ceased to be an orphanage and became a guest house for elderly ladies, and by 1946 it was known as St John's Retreat House until part of the former House of

Mercy was made into a retreat wing in 1955. In 1961 St John's House as it was then called, was renamed St Anne's House and continued to care for elderly ladies. In 1974 the residents of St Anne's House moved into part of the main convent buildings which in turn were being refurbished. The Sisters hoped to sell the old St Anne's House to help finance the refurbishing of the convent. But a heritage society intervened with a preservation order which effectively stopped any sale or development of St Anne's House. With the benefit of hindsight this may be looked at in a more positive way inasmuch as an important Victorian building was preserved from possible demolition. Even so, it was a difficult situation at the time because the building fell into disrepair and was subject to vandalism. In 1981 the Sisters were at last able to sell the building to developers who transformed it into business accommodation whilst conforming to the Grade 2 listing requirements.

St Barnabas Orphanage, Pimlico

The Sisters began this work in 1860 and the home closed in 1913. It has not been possible to find out what happened to the building, but it may not have survived the Wartime bombing.

Rose Street, Soho, and All Saints' Hawley, Surrey

The orphanage and Community mission house at 9 Rose Street, Soho, was removed to Leytonstone in 1899. The Rose Street premises were subsequently demolished when Foyle's Bookshop was extended and took up the whole of the north side of Rose Street.

All Saints' Home, Hawley, in Surrey had been built in 1881 as a convalescent home for the people of a poor parish in East London, but before it was put into use the founder (Mr Charles Randall) died. His widow, Mrs Eden Randall, decided to complete the work and offered it to the CSJB as a country outlet for the home in Rose Street, although independence from Rose Street soon followed. Through the generosity of Mrs Randall, All Saints' church was built adjoining the home to serve as a chapel. In 1937 the orphanage became a guest house for elderly ladies and the Sisters finally gave this up in 1954. The Community gave the chapel, All Saints' Cottage (formerly the chaplain's house), and a small fund, formerly for the chaplain, to the parish of Hawley for the benefit of the new housing estate nearby. The Royal United Kingdom Benevolent Association (known as RUKBA) took over the responsibility for the home in 1954. At the time of writing in 2011, the building is known as Randall House and continues to be a care home for the elderly.

All Saints' Church had always maintained close links with the parish of Hawley, and after the Sisters' withdrawal it was handed over to the Church Commissioners in March 1955 and consecrated by the Bishop of Guildford on May 8th 1955. The windows and furnishings reflected the Anglo-Catholic worship that had always been the tradition at All Saints'. However, by the mid-1970s the building needed major repairs and also the population had moved nearer to Farnborough—the church was now in the wrong place. It was deconsecrated in 1976 and a new All Saints' was built about half a mile away, near a large new housing estate. The old building still stands, though unused. At the time of its closure two important artefacts were removed and taken to St Andrew's Church, Clewer. A stained glass window depicts St John the Evangelist holding a Gospel book and chalice, but the face is that of Canon T T Carter who had attended the dedication of the chapel in 1882. The inscription reads:

D.G. In memoriam Thomas Thellusson Carter Priest R.I.P. 1901

Also taken to Clewer was the carved wooden reredos (altar piece) designed by Cecil Hare and erected in 1931 in memory of Sr Mary Cecilia. She had spent nearly all her life as a Sister at Hawley and was Sister-in-Charge from 1922 until 1930. An inscription reads:

Pray for the soul of Sister Mary Cecilia CSJB who died on the feast of St Phillip & St James 1930. This reredos was given by her relatives, friends and "Old Girls" as a Thank-offering for her life. LAUS DEO

Leytonstone & Burton Latimer Hall

In 1865 Miss Agnes Cotton had founded a 'Home for Friendless Girls' in Leytonstone, which was then in the Essex countryside. In the late 1870s she bought the estate of the late William Davis and renamed the house, which dated from the early 17th century, 'The Pastures'. In 1881 she built the Home of the Good Shepherd alongside 'The Pastures'. Agnes Cotton had made provision for the Clewer Sisters to take over the work in the event of her death, and in May 1899 she died suddenly aged 71. The Sisters closed down the home at Rose Street, Soho, and moved to Leytonstone.

During World War II the Home of the Good Shepherd was closed down and Sisters and residents were evacuated to Burton Latimer Hall in Northamptonshire. This was a manor house, parts of which dated from the 15th century, with later additions. By World War II it was in a poor state of repair and the Sisters closed this particular work in 1942: the children presumably were taken by other homes run by the Community. The Hall reverted to the owners, the Harpur family, who still reside there. 'The Pastures' at Leytonstone became derelict but the Home of the Good Shepherd was used for a time as the Civil Defence HQ for Leyton. In 1966 the London Borough of Waltham Forest acquired the site and demolished 'The Pastures' (and presumably the Home too), but in its place there now stands 'The Pastures Youth Centre'. A modern mosaic adorns an external wall bearing a dove of peace and the words 'forgive and forget'. Agnes Cotton would no doubt approve of the sentiment.

St Lucy's Home, Gloucester

The original home was at Kingsholm on the outskirts of the city, but in 1876 it moved to new premises consisting of a large house on the corner of Hare Lane and Pitt Street, close to the Cathedral. Nothing is left of St Lucy's Home except the name 'St Lucy's Garden' given to a footpath with planted borders near the Cathedral Close. Planned as a picnic area, it is more of a pedestrian thoroughfare. A plaque fixed to the wall of a neighbouring office was inaccessible to me in the summer of 2010 due to the overgrown state of the shrubbery. The office block is possibly built on the site of the home, hence the plaque. But a chalice, paten and ciborium (vessels used for Holy Communion) from the Chapel of the home may be seen on display in the Cathedral Treasury.

St John Baptist Home, Newport

The Sisters withdrew from Newport in 1939 and the home closed at the end of that year. Before the mid-1960s the home was converted into flats (which saved it from possible demolition) and the whole complex is now known as Clewer Court.

St Augustine's Home, Clewer

There had always been problems with this building and in 1921 it finally closed. The site was occupied by Maxwell's garage for some years with the home still visible in the background. Eventually the home was demolished and there is now no trace of it.

Rescue Homes and Hostels
The House of Charity, Greek Street, Soho

The building dates from 1746 and has a Grade 1 listing. The Sisters withdrew in 1939 but the work of the House continued. In 1961 the name was changed to the House of St Barnabas, and in 2006 it closed as a residential hostel and was relaunched as a conference venue and life-skills centre.

The Home for Working Girls, Nelson Square, Southwark

The phrase 'working girls' has a different connotation in the 21st century to that of the 19th, but this hostel for homeless girls who were in work as shop assistants or factory workers was important. The Sisters withdrew in 1923 and during the Blitz Nelson Square suffered badly. Those houses that were not demolished by the Luftwaffe were later razed to the ground by property developers.

Homes for the Elderly
St Basil's Home, Oxford

St Basil's building had been a problem for many years and an appeal had been launched in 1952. After the Sisters closed the home in 1966 it was demolished.

St Andrew's Lodge, Clewer, formerly known as St Andrew's Cottage, Clewer

In 1977 the Abbeyfield Society took over the running of St Andrew's Lodge.

St Andrew's Cottages, Clewer

These were almshouses and were demolished in 1984. Another residential home, Winton House, was built on the site.

See also above, St John's House, Clewer, St Anne's House, Clewer and All Saints' Home, Hawley.

Hospitals

St Andrew's Convalescent Hospital, Clewer

There is nothing left of Henry Woodyer's great building, constructed in the same style as the House of Mercy and opened in 1866. Situated on land opposite the House of Mercy, the only clue to its one-time existence is the street of thirty-eight houses dating from the mid-1950–60s era, called Carter Close. It had ceased to function as a hospital in 1939. During World War II it was requisitioned as a hostel for nurses, and when the Ministry of Health finally released it back to the Sisters in the early 1950s, it was in a dire condition. In 1954 it was sold to developers, who demolished it. Despite English Heritage listing having started in 1950, St Andrew's Hospital slipped through the net as did many Victorian buildings at the time. Nowadays no doubt it would be luxury apartments.

St Andrew's Convalescent Home, Folkestone

Founded in 1875, St Andrew's Home was a 'sister' home to that at Clewer, and the new buildings on the East Cliff were opened in 1884. The Home was closed in 1940 and the Sisters sold it in 1946, when it became clear that repairs would be too costly. In 1947 it became the St Andrew's Workers' Travel Association guest house and in 1976 it was purchased by the Galleon Hotel Group. In 1978 the name was changed to the Continental Hotel but by the mid-1980s it had closed. Since then the building has been converted into flats and now bears the name "St Andrew's". In April 2007 an earthquake measuring a magnitude of 4.2 hit Folkestone, causing considerable damage to neighbouring St Peter's Church, which just a few years previously in 1996 had suffered an arson attack.

St Lucy's Hospital, Gloucester

The hospital building was next to the original St Lucy's Home at Kingsholm on the outskirts of Gloucester. (In 1876 the home moved to Gloucester as noted above.) The hospital continued to function for some years after the Clewer Sisters finally gave up working there in 1939. In 1941 the accommodation was increased but the hospital was closed in 1947 and sold to the City Corporation, the proceeds of the sale being used to support a fund for the relief of sick children. The hospital buildings were used for a nurses' home for the Gloucestershire Royal Hospital until the mid-1970s and were demolished in 1979.

Torquay

St Raphael's Home (women) and St Luke's Home (men) were convalescent homes sharing the same grounds in Higher Lincombe Road. St Barnabas' Home was about ten minutes walk away and was for advanced cases of consumption. The Sisters withdrew from all three in 1959. Shortly afterwards, St Raphael's became a school for boys from difficult backgrounds and was known as Pitt House School. It closed in 1984 and the site was developed for housing. All that remains of St Raphael's is a lodge and a smaller house called Little St Raphael's. St Luke's and St Barnabas' Homes have also been demolished.

Schools
St Stephen's College

Part of the original College buildings survive as parish rooms next to the church of Clewer St Stephen, although those in Oxford Road, including the main entrance, were demolished to make way for housing (possibly in the late 1950s or early 1960s).

In 1919 the College moved to West Folkestone and remained there until 1940. There were several buildings at West Folkestone, one of which was known as Clewer House. After being used for a number of purposes it became the administration and reception block for the Folkestone School for Girls (formerly the Folkestone County School for Girls). By mid-2011 St Stephen's House on the same site was no longer in use and fast approaching dereliction, and Clewer House was under threat of demolition.

In 1940 St Stephen's College was evacuated to Taplow Court near Maidenhead. This Victorian mansion had been home to the Grenfell family. After the College left in 1946 Taplow Court was bought by British Telecommunications Research, a subsidiary of Plessey Electronics. Since 1988 it has been owned by a lay Buddhist community, who have restored the house and open it to the public from time to time in the summer months.

In 1946 St Stephen's College moved back to the south coast, to Broadstairs, where they occupied a building dating from c1830. Large extensions were added over the years. The College closed in 1991 and some of the buildings were given a Grade 2 listing in 1992. Most of the College site has been developed for housing; nothing has been left of the cloisters, chapel, form rooms and gym, but in 2011 the Grade 2 listed north wing was still intact. Now called the Mansion, the north wing has been developed into six apartments and a penthouse suite.

St Stephen's High School, Clewer

The High School grew out of the need for provision for day scholars, St Stephen's College being for boarders. Later boarders were taken at the High School too. After the College left Clewer, the High School took over some of the buildings to augment their own buildings opposite the College. After the closure of the High School the site was redeveloped and occupied by Windsor Grammar School (now Windsor Boys' School).

St John Baptist High School, Newport, Monmouthshire

I have been unable to trace what happened to the school buildings after its closure in 1939 but as these were near to the children's home they may have been redeveloped at the same time and may now be part of Clewer Court.

Pimlico & St John's Wood

St John's School, Bloomfield Place, Pimlico opened in 1860 and moved in 1877 to Hamilton Terrace in St John's Wood. In 1899 it moved to South Hampstead and closed in 1907. Owing to the constantly changing face of London, especially after the bombings in World War II, it has not been possible to trace the later history of these buildings.

St Anne's School, Baltonsborough

The Sisters ran this school near Glastonbury for a very short time—from 1882 until its closure in 1894. The building still exists and provides off-campus accommodation for Millfield School (7 km away). In 2001 a purpose-built annexe was added.

Churches where the Sisters worked
Clewer St Stephen

Designed by Henry Woodyer, Clewer St Stephen is still a parish church and, as mentioned above, has given a home to items from the Chapel of St

John Baptist. Also, on the wall of the south aisle there are two memorial plaques to Sr Emily, who started the St Stephen's Mission in 1863 while she was still a novice (see chapters 7 & 13). St Stephen's is now part of the Windsor team ministry.

St Mary & St Eanswythe Folkestone
This is still a parish church and open for worship.

St Saviour's Folkestone
St Saviour's is a thriving parish church now part of a newly created benefice with St Mary & St Eanswyth and St Augustine.

St John Baptist Newport
On July 24th 1955 St John's was destroyed by fire but was rebuilt from 1955–58. Fortunately many of the interior fittings were saved from fire damage. The church contains many stained glass windows by distinguished artists including C E Kempe and Sir Ninian Comper. In addition there is a stained glass window by Kempe and Tower in memory of Sr Selina CSJB. This bears an inscription:

> In mem. of Sister Selina CSJB Foundress and First Superior of the Mission House of St John the Baptist's Children's Home 1877–1915 and also the assistance of Sister Elise Jane CSJB. Dedicated on June 23rd 1916 by Canon Dawson of Chislehurst, a former Chaplain of the Sisters. The window was the gift of the congregation and friends.

St John's is still an active parish church.

St Frideswide Poplar
St Frideswide Poplar was an attractive Victorian building similar in style to Clewer St Stephen, though not one of Woodyer's designs. As noted in chapter 15, after the Sisters gave up the work at St Frideswide's in 1914 the clergy gave a large crucifix to the Sisters. This was placed over the rood screen in the Chapel of St John Baptist, Clewer. St Frideswide's was badly damaged by bombing in the Blitz and was completely demolished in 1947. The St Frideswide's Mission House in Lodore Street survived bombing in

both World Wars and is now known as Christ Church House. It has been converted into six apartments. A small statue of St Frideswide at the top of the stone entrance gives a clue to the origin of the building.

All Hallows' Southwark

This church by George Gilbert Scott had a very short life span, not having been completed until 1892 and was partially destroyed during the Blitz. A poorly designed replacement was built on the north side in 1957 and at the time of writing in 2011 there are plans to redevelop the site, retaining the original chancel and crypt, whilst demolishing the 1957 church building and adjacent hall. Also on the site there will be a Canon Pastor's House and some one, two and three bedroom dwellings. The Dean and Chapter of Southwark Cathedral own the site and in 2011 the redevelopment was still at the planning stage, having been fraught with difficulties and some controversy. The parish has been merged with that of St George the Martyr Southwark.

St Barnabas Pimlico

St Barnabas is still a parish church and open for worship.

St Mary of Eton Hackney Wick

The Clewer Sisters' work at St Mary of Eton was very brief. The church is still a parish church and open for worship.

St Alban's Holborn

St Alban's was badly damaged in the Blitz and only the Mackonochie Chapel escaped unharmed. However, the church was rebuilt after the War and is still a parish church and open for worship.

St John the Evangelist Smith Square, Westminster

The Sisters' work spanned only nine years (1885–94). St John's was designed by Thomas Archer in the English Baroque style and dates from 1728. It now carries a Grade 1 listing. During the Blitz it was destroyed by incendiary bombs leaving only the shell. In 1962 the Friends of St John's was formed and as a result of their efforts it was restored and reopened in 1969 as a concert hall.

St Mary Vincent Square, Westminster

The Sisters withdrew from St Mary's in 1910 and the church closed in 1923.

St Mary's Crown Street, Soho

This church closed in 1932 and was later demolished.

St Alphege Southwark

This church was closely associated with the Community of Reparation to Jesus in the Blessed Sacrament (CRJBS) whose last Sisters came to live at Clewer in 1980. The church of St Alphege was declared redundant in 1983 and various proposals for alternative use came to nothing. Demolition followed in 1991 and the site was leased to the Peabody Trust. Furnishings from the church were salvaged and are used for worship in the hall near the site of the old church where the former congregation meets for services.

INDEX